THE RURAL HOUSING QUESTION

Communities and planning in Britain's countrysides

Madhu Satsangi, Nick Gallent and Mark Bevan

First published in Great Britain in 2010 by

The Policy Press
University of Bristol
Fourth Floor
Beacon House
Queen's Road
Bristol BS8 1QU
UK

Tel +44 (0)117 331 4054
Fax +44 (0)117 331 4093
e-mail tpp-info@bristol.ac.uk
www.policypress.co.uk

North American office:
The Policy Press
c/o International Specialized Books Services (ISBS)
920 NE 58th Avenue, Suite 300
Portland, OR 97213-3786, USA
Tel +1 503 287 3093
Fax +1 503 280 8832
e-mail info@isbs.com

© The Policy Press 2010

British Library Cataloguing in Publication Data
A catalogue record for this book is available from the British Library.

Library of Congress Cataloging-in-Publication Data
A catalog record for this book has been requested.

ISBN 978 1 84742 384 9 paperback
ISBN 978 1 84742 385 6 hardcover

Cover design by The Policy Press
Front cover: image kindly supplied by Plain Picture
Printed and bound in Great Britain by TJ International, Padstow
The Policy Press uses environmentally responsible print partners

FSC
Mixed Sources
Product group from well-managed
forests and other controlled sources
Cert no. SGS-COC-2482
www.fsc.org
© 1996 Forest Stewardship Council

For Nirmal

Contents

List of figures, tables and images

Figure

Tables

Images

Foreword

There is a housing crisis in rural Britain that is threatening the future prospects for the 'living, working countryside' ostensibly championed by governments across Britain in the early 21st century. Unlike a century ago when it was housing quality that was seen as the main problem, the key issues today revolve around availability and cost and focus especially on the affordability of housing for those who work in the countryside and their families. Even so, this is not something that has taken us entirely by surprise, far from it. Thirty years ago Mark Shucksmith (1981: 11) already felt able to point out 'the essence of the housing problem in rural areas' as now being 'that those who work there tend to receive low incomes, and are thus unable to compete with more affluent "adventitious" purchasers from elsewhere in a market where supply is restricted'. Despite this recognition, the problem has not gone away and indeed would now seem to be significantly worse. Indeed, things in England have now reached such a pass that the Taylor Review (2008: 3) felt able to claim that 'The countryside is at a crossroads', echoing statements being made in the Celtic nations.

In this context, a new book that aims to get at the heart of the 'rural housing question' is extremely welcome and very timely. It documents the various facets of the challenge facing those who wish to live in the British countryside and how these have been changing. As well as detailing the problems facing traditional rural workers in accessing affordable housing nearby, the book covers the new pressures posed by international migrant labour after the expansion of the European Union in 2004. There are also chapters on the other three principal sectors of rural housing demand, namely, commuters with urban-based jobs, retirement migrants and second home buyers. These chapters are also valuable in revealing how the relative importance of these sectors varies geographically and thus how much diversity exists across rural Britain in the dynamics of its housing markets. The book also deals systematically with each component of the supply side, covering house-building for sale, the private and social renting sectors, the planning frameworks within which these have to operate, and the types of policy intervention that have been devised to address unmet needs. Finally, and perhaps most importantly, it goes on to compare the situation prevailing in England, Scotland and Wales with the rural housing picture observed in Ireland and other European countries. This demonstrates the unique character of the British scene and reinforces the authors' central argument about the origins and implications of a very distinctive 'rural housing question'.

Moreover, this central argument is a compelling one that digs beneath the headline issues in order to unearth the fundamental explanation as to how this housing problem developed and why, despite having been recognised at least 30 years ago, it has been getting progressively worse rather than being solved. The direct cause is the policy of urban containment that was ushered in after the Second World War, following the 1942 Scott Report on Land Utilisation and its recommendation for tight controls on urban development. As so carefully documented by Peter Hall and his colleagues in their 1973 book *Megalopolis Denied*, the main effect of restricting the lateral spreading of the major urban areas while trying to redevelop them at lower density was to prompt city-dwellers to 'leapfrog' the green belts and move into the smaller towns and villages beyond. In fact, as I spelt out in my 1998 CPRE (Campaign to Protect Rural England) report *Urban Exodus*, this accorded with strongly held residential preferences fashioned by William Blake's 'satanic mills' view of urban Britain and the 'rural idyll' notions of the Romantic era. Moreover, as urban containment policy bit ever harder in the last quarter of the 20th century and the cities became more costly and congested, out-migration increased in volume, geographical extent and social selectivity. This process was aided and abetted – and this is the nub of the 'rural housing question' – by the fact that development controls came to be imposed just as strictly on rural towns and the deep countryside as on the major cities. This was mainly due to central government applying a blanket policy across the whole of Britain – itself partly a response to a 'rural preservation' campaign dating back to the setting up of the CPRE in 1926 – but has been reinforced by the NIMBY effect of in-migrants wishing to retain what they have bought into. The result has been a galloping 'residential gentrification' of much of rural Britain and a virtual embargo on new business enterprise. The lack of new jobs as well as of affordable housing represents a double whammy as far as the continued presence of less well-off families in the countryside is concerned.

This overriding message is an extremely challenging one. In a nutshell, the book is asking what the countryside is really for and, more pointedly, who it is meant to be for. As such, it should be required reading for all those concerned with the rural arena and indeed all those whose decisions and activities have knock-on effects on the rural parts of Britain. This is irrespective of whether the aim in reading it is in order to try and prosecute an action programme designed to achieve real and lasting change or in order to develop a counter-case that the countryside is not a suitable place for the less well-off sections of society to even contemplate living in. We seem to be facing the stark choice of either the majority of the British countryside soon becoming a museum in which only a select few will live (with others merely visiting or passing through) or it being regenerated into a 'living, working' arena that contributes to national wealth and offers opportunities to a much broader section of society. As this book maintains from the outset in Chapter 1, it is high time that there was a real public debate on this so that, rather than sleepwalking further down the current track, a clear set of decisions are consciously made about the future role of the countryside. A book like this provides the best guarantee of a fully informed discussion. Or are governments' most recent reviews, and this book, wrong? Has the point of no return already been passed?

Tony Champion
Emeritus Professor of Population Geography, University of Newcastle upon Tyne
February 2010

Acknowledgements

This book draws on our own research and investigations with colleagues, past and present. Some of this research was funded by government and its agencies. All of it drew on the experiences of politicians, of public and voluntary sector professionals, of community groups and of people living in Britain's rural communities. The production team at The Policy Press, especially Emily Watt and Leila Ebrahimi, brought a huge amount of enthusiasm to this project and provided us with careful and insightful guidance. We owe a debt of gratitude also to the anonymous reviewers who offered their opinions on our original proposal to The Policy Press in the summer of 2008. Hopefully they will recognise some of their content and structural contributions to this finished text. Likewise, the independent reviewer also left his mark on the project, helping us condense and distil our arguments into something more coherent and polished. We are also grateful to the colleagues whose images can now be found in several chapters. In particular, we would like to thank Neil Stephen, Mark Scott, Sue Kidd, Mark Shucksmith and Richard Yarwood. However, as with all such projects, the responsibility for any omissions or inevitable shortcomings rests entirely with the authors.

Acknowledgements

Part 1
Introducing the rural housing question

ONE

The rural housing question

This book is about housing in rural Britain[1]: the countrysides of England, Scotland and Wales. As its title suggests, it focuses on what can broadly be described as the 'rural housing question'. But what is this question and why is it important? Is the question about the quantity or quality of housing being planned for and being supplied in rural areas? Is it about the price of housing and who is able to access it? Is it about the state of rural economies, rural employment and the capacity of people to find a deposit for a home and subsequently pay mortgages? Or is it about the cost of renting: or about the operation of the housing market generally, and who wins and who loses in terms of enjoying access to housing at a cost that is personally reasonable? Perhaps it is about pressures on this market, because of commuting, retirement migration or the purchasing of second and holiday homes? Does the rural housing question affect everyone, or create specific hardships for the young, for older people or for families? Is it about retirement and the trials and tribulations faced by older people in the countryside? Is it about rural development and constraints imposed by the planning system? Is it about national and local politics, the preservation of the countryside and attitudes towards development? Is it about the 'sustainability' of new homes and their impact on the environment? Is it about how local communities help themselves and try to meet their own needs? Or is it about how we, in the nations of Britain, think about rural areas and whether or not there should be less or more residential development outside of towns and cities?

In truth, there are many rural housing questions but, in this book, our aim is to think about what ties them all together: to arrive at a defining question that explains why, for decades, governments have grappled with but failed to provide adequate answers to the most basic question of who and what the countryside is for. During 2007 and 2008, Matthew Taylor, Member of Parliament for Truro and St Austell in Cornwall, undertook a review of rural housing and the rural economy for the British Prime Minister, Gordon Brown (Taylor, 2008). After a year's detailed research, painstaking analysis, countless meetings with local groups, consultations with national bodies and so on, he concluded that the countryside is 'at a crossroads' (Taylor, 2008: 5): that rural areas *could* be put on a path towards greater sustainability and that a new balance might, through different policy approaches, be struck between the needs of the rural environment and of rural communities and economies. Dozens of recommendations showed how this might be done.

Anyone reading Matthew Taylor's review from outside of England (the review focused specifically on the English situation) could have been forgiven for thinking that this was the first time government had directed someone to look at development tensions in the country's rural areas. They would probably think that new planning policies had created some inadvertent side effects: too few homes being built in smaller village locations, insufficient opportunities to diversify local economies, some social polarisation, too much emphasis on market towns and so on. But they would doubtless be shocked to discover that these policies had been around for more than 60 years and, moreover, that the tensions and inequities they had created had been observed on countless previous occasions. The distant observer might be shocked, but the old hacks know that Taylor's crossroads has been reached many times before and that the shock and dismay that accompany periodic reviews of the rural housing situation in Britain quickly recede, to be replaced by quiet acceptance of the status quo. This suggests that there must be some intractable problem that makes the British quite incapable of dealing with the issue of rural development. On the face of it, the rural housing question *is* merely about finding a bit more land for development (perhaps taking it from agriculture), easing planning restrictions, allowing a diversification of economic uses, investing in (or levering investment into) the provision of affordable homes and developing policies that support the development of local communities. But there is a more fundamental question – or fundamental block – that makes all these things seemingly impossible to achieve. The nature of this question is also the focus of this book.

Who and what is the countryside for?

If we – in whichever nation of Britain we happen to live – do not believe that the resources of the countryside – principally its land resources – should support the development of rural communities, then this belief will shape the future of these communities, in much the same way as it has shaped their past. Famously, Martin (1962) observed that the lowland English village changed little between the Peasants' Revolt of 1381 and the Second World War. But since the end of the war, these same villages have been transformed by the changing fortunes of agriculture and by the process of counter-urbanisation. Many lowland villages have today become islands of gentrification, enveloped by either intensive farming or unproductive land. In either case, development of this land, or a switch from farming, is rarely permitted – and only in exceptional cases – and so there is little room for villages to grow or to adapt to changing economic and social circumstances.

It is easy to lay the blame at the door of the planning system: to point to the development of 'rural resource' planning in the 1920s and 1930s and to link this thinking to the 1947 Town and Country Planning Acts[2] and the development intolerance that the planning system subsequently supported. But planning systems operate in a political context that expresses underlying fears and desires: our values are imprinted onto the landscape by the processes of parliamentary democracy. In England, Scotland and Wales, rural planning has become what we want it to be: a set of regulations that determine how land is used and by whom. The system has generated privilege. In 1947, this privilege was given to the farming sector because a significant objective at that time was to achieve food security. But somewhere down the line, this imperative faded. It would be easy to argue, therefore, that the system lost pace with reality, protecting farming for no good reason. But this would lead to the suggestion that the countryside was (but should no longer be) fundamentally for farmers and for agriculture. If this were the case, then surely this sector would have suffered the same fate as coal-mining, being cast aside when its output no longer seemed necessary.

The fact that farming avoided this fate suggests that it is not what farming produces that is seen as significant – valued by wider society – but rather some other output from the productive process. Under a previous Common Agricultural Policy (CAP) regime, farmers were rewarded for their stewardship of the countryside and taxpayers seemed relatively content to foot the bill. This provides some clue as to what the countryside is for. In a sense, it is for nothing: we should do nothing with the countryside other than ensure that it remains as it is, or rather as we understand it to be – timeless and tranquil – or we think it *should be*. Paradoxically, the countryside is for people but is not for communities. It is people who have constructed a particular view of the countryside, and seek its protection through the planning system, but it is often communities who have an immediate need to change the countryside in order to meet basic human wants. But can we realistically conceive of a conflict between people and communities? Surely they are one and the same?

A hundred years ago, this whole debate would have seemed nonsensical. Rural communities expanded in response to economic change. Landowners simply built additional workers' cottages in response to labour needs, without any reference to local authorities. Villages grew as need dictated. It would have been impossible to farm land without sacrificing a portion of that land to development given the link between the intensity of farming (the dominant economic activity) and the need to house farm workers. Community and economic needs were inexorably connected. The declining need for labour, as a result of mechanisation during the 20th century, weakened this connection and generated an expectation of reduced need for development in rural areas. But at the same time, the expansion of towns and cities placed new pressures on the countryside: the natural economic relationship between food production and rural development gave way to a perceived threat to the 'rural resource'. In the 1920s, this resource was still viewed by many as a productive reserve: urbanisation was a threat to farming. But another view was also taking root at this time: that the countryside offered a respite from the frenetic pace, and the griminess, of life in urban Britain. A hundred years earlier, William Blake had captured the educated classes' nostalgia for pastoral England in his preface to *Milton: A Poem*, subsequently put to music and renamed 'Jerusalem'. By the early years of the 20th century, this nostalgia for England's 'green and pleasant land' had been transformed into a political movement, first given shape by the creation of the Council for the Preservation of Rural England (the CPRE) in 1926.[3]

There have been several problems with the subsequent campaigns to preserve or protect rural England, Wales and Scotland from development pressure. First, they frequently fail to distinguish between urban encroachment and endogenous rural development, meaning that they oppose urban growth into rural areas and the development of villages with equal vigour. Second, the campaigns are indiscriminate, often preventing development that might help the rural working population and save a village's services. Taylor is clear on this point in his 2008 review, suggesting that different rules should be applied to smaller villages, giving them a chance to grow. But these problems are not fundamental. The campaigns run by environmental groups, conservation lobbies, friends of this, that or the other, are not actions within a rural vacuum, but further evidence of how we think about the countryside, and of diverging discourses, each with its own momentum and power. With the decline of agriculture (which has affected the sector's contribution to gross domestic product [GDP] and not its importance as a land use) it has become easier to dismiss the development needs of rural areas. The prevailing view, since the end of the Second World War, has been that the evaporation of agricultural activity has created a potential vacuum in the countryside: and the risk with any vacuum is that alternative activities will be sucked in to replace what has left. In this context, it has been easy to convince the wider public of the need to resist perceived threats to rural areas including miscellaneous forms of inappropriate development ranging from major infrastructure projects to ugly housing estates promoted by unsympathetic speculators. At the time of writing, sustainability appraisal has become the latest planning tool used to promote development intolerance, with the promotion of sustainability generally being seen as an objective militating against all forms of land-use change in the countryside.

Wittingly or unwittingly, many of us have already joined the conflict between people and communities. Assuming they are not part of the working rural population, the people of England in particular – though neither Scotland nor Wales are immune from their equivalent forms of rustic nostalgia – have probably bought into a bucolic rural idyll of rolling hills, picturing a patchwork of fields and lanes inset with villages of low-beamed cottages. With this image in mind, much of Britain is outraged when sections of the press spin the headlines that huge faceless corporations are plotting to 'concrete over the countryside', or spineless planners have made some seedy deal to sacrifice the nation's rural heritage to monstrous wind farms. The counterpoint story – of rural residents eager to embrace economic, service and housing development as a way of saving their fragile communities – merits few, if any, column inches.

In order to get to the heart of the rural housing question, it is necessary to begin by questioning our own understanding of the countryside. The image painted earlier bears little resemblance to the modern reality of lowland England, let alone the valley or upland communities of Wales or any of the landscapes of Scotland, and emphatically not its Highlands and Islands. From this starting point, it is possible to launch a more thorough investigation into the contested nature of rural development and then into the array of housing outcomes and tensions that together form the broader rural housing question with which this book is centrally concerned.

How the book is structured

This book addresses the underlying causes of rural housing tensions in Britain's countrysides, before examining how these are manifest in general outcomes and local experiences. Different tensions are highlighted in each chapter: critical housing demand, supply and affordability issues are quantified in Chapter 14. It also considers the planning policy response, support for different tenure arrangements and other forms of intervention, either strategic or community-led. By focusing on debates, especially over land use and planning, that are central to rural housing outcomes, the book attempts to move to a series of answers to the rural housing question. These are not intended to be detailed or definitive, but rather areas for further consideration in the years ahead as those charged with alleviating the pressures faced by some rural communities, and revitalising rural economies, continue to think about the most effective frameworks and interventions for creating more equitable and liveable countrysides. With this end in mind, this book is divided into five sections and 20 chapters. None of the chapters is particularly long and each deals with a specific issue set against a backdrop of broader concerns and thinking set out in the book's first section and against the aims detailed earlier.

This first section (comprising Chapters 1 to 5) develops the arguments introduced in this chapter. It begins by expanding our initial analysis of how society in England, Scotland and Wales thinks about the countryside, which itself determines what and who the countryside is for. It builds an argument from the skeleton established in the last few pages, but also tracks evolving debate on the nature of the countryside in different parts of Britain as well as engaging with the meaning and modern relevance of the adjective 'rural' and the nature of the rural economy. The second section focuses on demographic questions: on population movement in the countryside, retirement and the issues raised by second and holiday homes. The third section looks at broad supply questions – at planning, land and house-building – and at specific supply initiatives aimed at targeting affordable housing provision and at prioritising and meeting local needs. The fourth section broadens the discussion of intervention by considering housing policy and housing system responses, centred on supporting particular tenure arrangements. It also explores the structure of responses and the changing nature of the most obvious symptom of market and policy failure – rural homelessness. The final section addresses the means by which we might overcome the 'fundamental block' on rural development sitting at the heart of the rural housing question, first considering strategic and community-led responses to market and policy failures. It places Britain within a European context: many of the rural development problems experienced in England, Wales and Scotland remain an unfathomable mystery to our European neighbours, whose understanding and treatment of the countryside bears little or no resemblance to the experience across Britain. We conclude with reflections on the answers to the rural housing question that seem to emerge from our discussion, again offering broad conclusions that might be turned into more detailed policy.

Notes

[1] Throughout the book, we refer to Britain rather than Great Britain. The appendix discusses the definition of rurality.

[2] That is, the Town and Country Planning Act for England and Wales and the Town and Country Planning (Scotland) Act, which were enacted in July and August of 1947, respectively.

[3] Sister organisations were created in Scotland in 1927 and Wales in 1928 (see Chapter 4).

TWO

The British countryside: nostalgia, romanticism and intervention

Popular conceptions of rurality are not accidental, nor are they natural representations of fact. Rather they are evolving social constructs, based in part on received remembrance of a past, and in equal part on antipathy to the dual opposite of the urban set against idealisations of the rural. The media – literature, painting, film, TV, radio and newspapers – have all transmitted and reinforced these idealisations. Rural spaces and places have a number of associated visual images that have popular resonance amongst both residents and tourists. A recent book of photographs by Somerville (2001) is one of many to grace coffee tables and show 'myriad treasures: from the woodland villages of rural Surrey and the historic resonance of "Shakespeare Country", to the hidden valleys of Wales and the rugged grandeur of the Scottish Highlands'. Similarly, lids on boxes of chocolates celebrate the historic, the rustic and the quaint, regularly reproducing images such as Constable's *Hay Wain* (1821) that brush out the reality of rural impoverishment, whether in 19th-century or contemporary expression. As observed by Bryan MacGregor, such images are 'much nearer to the jolly village green on the pantomime stage than reality' (MacGregor, 1976: 524).

Image 2.1: The Hay Wain, John Constable, 1821

Such constructs are powerful because they shape views not only on what the countryside is actually like, but also on what it should be like. The move from observation to the normative is also a move that engages the political sphere and this chapter begins with an exploration of how different actors have shaped, and are empowered and constrained by, the rural idylls.

The romantic myth

A myth, in a sociological sense, refers to a set of ideas and images that have currency in a particular period, and which are commonly transmitted from one generation to the next. As they are transmitted, they are also transmuted: some elements are lost and there are progressive accretions. The core of the myth is, however, fixed and may be factual or may be imaginary – 'mythical', in the common figurative use. This section looks at the respective cores of Britain's rural myths – or rural idylls as they are commonly known – and critiques their constituents. In doing so, it aims to draw out important symbols that shape understandings of, and responses to, the rural housing question.

England

The most pervasive myth is best expressed in the final verse of William Blake's preface to *Milton: A Poem* (written and illustrated between 1804 and 1810):

> I will not cease from mental fight,
> Nor shall my sword sleep in my hand,
> Till we have built Jerusalem
> In England's green and pleasant land!

There are a number of important elements in this verse: first, the effective equation of 'green' and 'pleasant'; second, that of land being under threat and in need of mental and physical defence; and, third, Blake's explicit reference to his home country.

The first element, 'green and pleasant land', is probably the most important figure, giving symbolic virtue to agricultural and forested landscapes and, by the same token, denigrating anything that intrudes on those territories (Newby, 1979). Almost a century later, Ebenezer Howard used the same symbol to describe the magnet of the countryside (Figure 2.1). His (approximate) contemporary Tönnies (1887) invoked it in his opposition of community and anomie. The contrast was to become spatialised as an opposition of the rural, endowed with symbolic virtue, against the urban, bereft of such quality. Less familiar, but equally significant, is that Tönnies (1887) saw community not as a static outcome, but as a dynamic process, a conception that we explore further in Chapter 18.

Second, the fight and the sword: Blake's composition dates from an era of urban-based industrialisation and of disquiet at some of its blights – including the exploitation of child labour, the harsh lives of the working classes and pollution of the natural and built environments. Indeed an earlier verse of the poem refers to these in the figure of 'dark Satanic mills': the work of the Devil. The ills of 19th-century British capitalism were yet to be portrayed by Dickens and Disraeli and yet to be analysed so trenchantly by Engels and Marx, but they were visible threats that raised fear and a desire to escape them. They were blights that were also to lead to public health and town planning legislation – mental fight by the state.

Figure 2.1: The three magnets, Ebenezer Howard, 1898

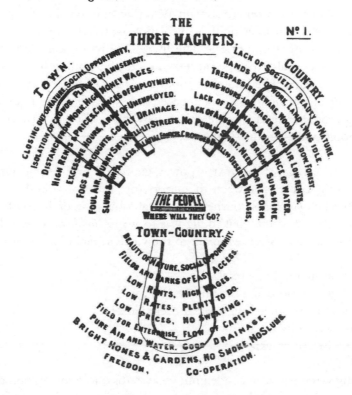

Third, Blake seeks to idealise lowland England. In an era where people generally travelled relatively short distances from their birthplace, this is understandable – he uses what he knows. But two centuries of myth-making raise some questions about the conception. The first tendency is of generalisation, so that Blake's representation of a particular context in rural England is seen as applying in any part of rural England. Furthermore, the internal, quasi-imperial nature of Great Britain means that lowland England's myths are transposed to, and imposed upon, the Celtic countries in representations of their countrysides. The witness to these tendencies is that reference is frequently made to 'a' or to 'the' (i.e. singular) British rural idyll.

Scotland

Rural Scotland has two distinct, yet related, historically derived and transmuted images. Both images are, fundamentally, reflections of power: one testifies overtly by contrasting the lives of the inhabitants of rural Scotland, the second celebrates natural grandeur and a countryside that elites do not allow to become spoiled. The first is reflected in the work of Walter Scott. At the start of the eighth chapter of the novel celebrating the hero *Waverley*, Scott writes:

> It was about noon when Captain Waverley entered the straggling village, or rather hamlet, of Tully–Veolan, close to which was situated the mansion of the proprietor. The houses seemed miserable in the extreme, especially to an eye accustomed to the smiling neatness of English cottages. They stood, without any respect for regularity, on each side of a straggling kind of unpaved street, where children, almost in a primitive state of nakedness, lay sprawling, as if to be crushed by the hoofs of the first passing horse. (Scott, 2008 [1832]: 32)

The central metaphor of this text is power, expressed in different dimensions. First, there is the contrast between 'the proprietor's mansion' and the 'miserable' houses of the labouring poor. Journeying through rural parts of the southern states of America 140 years later, Neil Young was to write *Southern Man*, a depiction of power imbalance as overt testament to the virulent racist legacy of slavery:

> I saw cotton and I saw black,
> tall white mansions and little shacks.
> Southern man, when will you pay them back?
> I heard screamin'
> And bullwhips crackin'[1]

While Young was vitriolic in condemning that status quo, Scott accepts the status quo he sees and tacitly seeks its continuance.[2] Second, the language of order: Scott is critical of the straggling village, although non-nucleate settlements are the vernacular for much of the country outside of (his native) Borders and some of the east coast counties including Fife, lowland Perthshire and Kincardineshire. He berates the people for their houses' lack of respect for order, admiring instead the 'smiling neatness' of English cottages. He juxtaposes the unpaved street and children's primitive state of nakedness. The message is clear: a condemnation of rural Scotland as backward.

The exercise of power looms large in what is probably the central theme of the Highland myth: the history of clearance and crofting, documented most notably by James Hunter (1976, 1994, 1999; see also McCrone, 2001). The title of Hunter's (1994) book is synonymous with a song from the group Runrig, *Dance called America*, which captures the pain of clearance:

The landlords came
The peasant trials
To sacrifice of men
Through the past and that quite darkly
The present once again
In the name of capital
Establishment
Improvers, it's a name
The hidden truths
The hidden lies
That once nailed you
To the pain[3]

The imagery of cruelty and the abuse of landowning power, of thousands of people forced to migrate from their homes to bare subsistence living on the seaboards or into emigration to the USA and Canada, is an imagery that is repeated in literature (for example by Sorley MacLean [1943], Iain Crichton Smith [1968] and John McGrath [1981]) and in two paintings, *Lochaber No More* by John Watson Nicol and *The Last of the Clan* by Thomas Faed.

Revisionist histories dispute the extent of forced migration and cruelty, attesting that without 'improvement', Highlanders' lives would have been shorter and considerably harsher, but the weight of evidence seems counter to their claims (see for example Richards, 2007). The political legacy of the clearances is important: first, crofting tenure evolved as a means of protecting the security of tenant farmers in seven counties in the Highlands and Islands (following the 1886 Crofters' Holdings [Scotland] Act). Second, the dynamics of the Highland economy and its consequences for migration had periodic hearings in Westminster after the First World War, eventually leading to the formation in 1966 of a regional economic and community development agency, the Highlands and Islands Development Board. Finally, over a century after the end of the clearances, the Scottish Parliament passed a series of pieces of land reform legislation (2003) that drew in spirit on national antipathy towards the abuses of monopoly land ownership. Whether that legislation really offered sufficient remedy continues to be debated and we take up this theme in Chapter 18.

Image 2.2: Lochaber No More, John Watson Nicol, 1883

Image 2.3: The Last of the Clan, Thomas Faed, 1865

It is clear that the Highlands and Islands do form a large chunk of the total Scottish land mass; however, in much discourse they have become the entirety of rural Scotland.

The second image is of natural grandeur. Particularly in much fiction and in music, rural Scotland is imbued with the characteristics of being an untamable wilderness. This largely tells the tale of the development of the heroic Highlander myth, with elements such as wild hordes of Gaels fighting against English imperialism, ship captains bravely struggling against fierce seas off the north and west coasts and heroic explorers battling near-Arctic conditions in the Cairngorms. Preserving the wilderness has also become one of the objects of power: a telling witness was provided by the last laird of Eigg stating his wish for the island to retain its unkempt Highland character (Satsangi, 2007). It should also be noted, however, that exercising power to maintain true 'wilderness' is often moderated today by an ostensible concern for stewardship of rural communities and a search to ensure that there is at least a minimal return on the land, usually from hunting, shooting or fishing (Wightman, 1996; Jarvie and Jackson, 1998). Nonetheless, the generality that Bryan MacGregor noted in the 1990s, that 'in many areas of rural Scotland, large landowners play a crucial role in local development: they are the local planners' (MacGregor, 1993, cited in Wightman, 1996: 15), remains the case despite land reform legislation and the intrusion of some community landowners (see Chapter 18).

Image 2.4: Typical crofting dispersed settlement, Shetland © Mark Shucksmith

Wales

Joining Scotland as a Celtic country, Wales also has some similarity with Scotland in some of its rural images. Cloke et al (1997: see esp pp 16–30) draw attention to regions of identity, identifying a rurality of the Welsh-speaking heartland (of the western part of mid-Wales and much of the county of Gwynedd) as being marked with strong use of the language, a distinctive identity and a greater degree of civic nationalism. In contrast, in 'British' Wales (the eastern border areas and Pembrokeshire) little Welsh is spoken, Welsh national identification is weaker and conservatism stronger. Its rurality is rather closer to that of lowland England. It seems likely that some of these characteristics have altered since the mid-1990s, since, post-devolution, deliberate policy to encourage the use of the Welsh language across the country has been enacted.[4] Language has been and continues to be an important identifier and is highly politicised (Carter and Williams, 1978; Bowie and Davies, 1992; Robertson and Satsangi, 2003).

Thus, at least some of rural Wales has a symbolic association between language and resistance to English imperialism. The metaphors invoked to describe Scotland's countryside: the images conjured by Walter Scott of power imbalance, the heroism of James Macpherson's *The Works of Ossian* (1765) and of the power of natural Scotland in Mendelssohn's *Hebrides Overture* (1830) are distinct markers of Scottish national status. Each of these metaphors possesses the feature of being markedly different from the metaphors of Blake's poem. The conclusion must be that it is therefore inappropriate to speak of a single British rural idyll.

Myth and class

A key theme in rural research in Britain has been the linking of the idea of rural idylls to class-based representations, or constructions, of the countryside. This link was drawn, in particular, by Burgess (1987), who saw many television documentaries as expressing middle-class notions of 'traditional rural' lifestyles. Other research has critiqued this argument – suggesting that it yields a 'static image' (Savage et al, 1992; Bell, 1997), that it neglects cultural content (Cloke et al, 1995; Halfacree, 1998) and that it ignores constructions that are not class-determined (Cloke and Little, 1997; Little, 2002). Phillips et al (2001) examined three English rural drama programmes, concluding that rather than just being visions of idylls, they are also performances of class identities. Whether class is a pervasive and general determinant of (mis)understandings of the countryside is unclear. However, the values that gentrifiers and incomers project onto rural areas and the way in which they can help perpetuate the popular myth of the countryside has been an important topic for research at least since Pahl (1975) and Newby (1979) charted the social changes in rural areas attendant on post-war counter-urbanisation.

Indeed, social class has been one of the most debated dimensions of the changing nature of rurality. Fundamental to the discussion is examination of the social class consequences of the changing economic base of the countryside: from productivism to consumerism. One of the consequences of this economic shift is selective migration, both to and from rural areas. As discussed in Chapter 7, the focus is on whether rural Britain, or particular parts of rural Britain, have been and are being gentrified, losing working-class populations (notably younger adult members) and gaining middle-class populations (particularly more elderly cohorts) (Newby et al, 1978; Spencer, 1997; Boyle and Halfacree, 1998; Stockdale et al, 2000; Phillips, 2005). Cloke and Goodwin (1992: 29) suggest that new rural residents tend to experience a '"sanitised and commodified" idyll that contrasts with longer-term residents' ... more "realistic and pragmatic" view'. Woods (2005b) argues that these same new residents frequently bring with them different expectations of the countryside. He suggests (2005b: 210) that the processes of social and economic restructuring affecting England's rural areas in the 20th century have created an *in situ* ideological division between the proponents of further development, advancing an economic rationale, and the defenders of the existing landscape, who argue a case for preserving the openness and character of rural England. In recent times, the idea that England's open countryside should 'remain a pleasant place to live, whose attraction rests on the absence of industry' (Woods, 2005b: 210) has been in the ascendancy, largely because of urban-to-rural migration by households whose interest is to seek peace and quiet and a degree of openness that had not been available to them elsewhere. Whilst this movement may alter the social configuration of rural areas, the extent to which it is class-specific is not entirely clear.

Respecting the idylls

Are rural idylls a peculiarity of the nations of Britain? Images of *la douce France* (literally, 'Sweet France': a rustic, agrarian countryside sprouting small villages – see Huebener [1940] and the song of the same title by Charles Trenet and Léo Chauliac [1943]) and Ansel Adams' photographs of 'wilderness America' suggest not. Similarly, Svendsen (2004) draws attention to modernist-agriculturalist and (post-1970s') non-agriculturalist discourses of rurality in Denmark, whilst Ehrentraut (1996) comments on the symbolic harmony between traditional farmhouses, sheltered valleys, brooks running with crystalline waters and soaring mountains of the Alpine regions of Europe and Japan. This book does not attempt to trace connections between discourses of rurality and those of development in a comparative way, fascinating as such a research agenda might be (see Bunce, 2003). What is important in the current context is the specific legacy of Britain's rural idylls for the diagnosis and treatment of the rural housing question.

The particularity of Eigg as a small Scottish island can, in a very important sense, be generalised across rural Britain. Conserving the past and preserving what are seen to be its virtues has been a powerful motif of rural development attitudes and policy (Woods, 2005b). The most powerful expression of these forces is the post-war treatment of the primary sector, notably agriculture and to a lesser extent forestry. Britain's experience of wartime blockades, food shortages and rationing generated a belief that agriculture should be a special priority, exempted from many of the controls of post-war planning. This meant that farming development could bypass a planning regime stringently applied to similar activity that did not have an agricultural objective. At one level, such policy was and remains common sense. As Lowe (1989: 124–5) points out, there was a post-war assumption that agricultural prosperity would yield rural community sustainability whilst being crucial to safeguarding rural landscapes. At the same time, as we see in Chapter 3, that assumption would also endow the farmer with increasing power.

Britain was of course not unique in this experience. The birth of the European Free Trade Area (EFTA), the adolescence of the European Economic Community (EEC) and maturity of the European Union (EU) saw and succoured the promotion of farming interests across Western Europe. For much of the post-war period, subsidy regimes favoured the growth of bigger farms intensifying production (see Chapter 3). Like many other industries, one of the most effective ways of doing this was to substitute capital – machines or chemicals – for labour. By the early 1970s, many commentators were arguing that unequivocal support for farming as a means of enhancing Britain's 'green and pleasant' heritage was in fact delivering something that could more accurately be described as brown and foul, as pesticides were pumped into the land, and hedgerows and woodland were ripped down to make way for factory-style production.

A belief in the 'trickle-down' benefits of agricultural expansion has also coloured understanding of rural development. Beyond living memory, farming has been seen as the motor of the rural economy. Modern policy still has entangled definitions of farm and rural diversification. The fact that the local, regional and national GDP contribution of tourism, not to mention non-agricultural production, far outweighs that of agriculture can be overlooked by eyes transfixed on the mythical past.

This productivist perspective is accompanied, sometimes in concert, sometimes in conflict, by notions of Britain's countrysides as sites of consumption. The result is that there are multiple and conflicting visions of rural spaces among the groups in society who have populated rural localities (Cloke, 2003; Burchardt, 2007). Crucial here is a reading not only of the dominating views of particular social groups, but also the absences and visions of rural spaces that have become subordinate or subsumed. Not only have the views and experiences of some groups in society been downplayed or ignored, but their very presence in rural localities has been airbrushed out of idyllic portrayals of rural localities.

More than this, it has been argued that the very mechanisms that have enabled the production of specific rural landscapes in parts of Britain, as an outlet for the profits derived from the slave trade and the fruits of Empire, have been written out of history (Neal, 2002). For the purposes of this book, it is the way that specific groups have projected their own idealised view onto the various countrysides that they have chosen to live in which has led to very particular outcomes in terms of housing provision. In this respect, NIMBYism[5] has been identified as a key barrier and challenge to housing provision at the local level (Best and Shucksmith, 2006), being grounded either in simple vested interest or in a dominant representation or expectation of what is and is not acceptable in 'the countryside' (Woods, 2005b). Such expectations are, as we suggested in the opening chapter, not only present in rural areas themselves, but shape common understanding of the world outside of towns and cities. Idyllic and partial representations of rural spaces have a profound impact on planning and housing policies at national and regional levels as well as on the local decisions that occasionally divide rural communities.

Notes

[1] Excerpt (1971).

[2] As an aside, it is worth noting the vernacular translation of Scott's written English: the proprietor's mansion becomes 'the (laird's) big hoose'.

[3] Excerpt (words by R. Macdonald, 1988). The *Dance called America*, furthermore, names the bright dance and tune performed by landowners and their acolytes on the quayside as their former tenants were herded on to boats for the transatlantic crossing.

[4] We are writing before the 2011 Census of Population that should yield data to update the characterisations.

[5] NIMBYism is derived from the phrase Not In My Back Yard, and denotes people who object to developments in their neighbourhoods.

THREE

Protecting and consuming the countryside

Historical tradition and popular myth concerning the British countrysides have had a powerful impact on policy discourse. The countrysides of England, Scotland and Wales have been shaped not only by economic forces, but also by the values of those who believe that rural areas should be used and enjoyed in a particular way. Understanding of the countryside, as we saw in the last chapter, is moulded by a degree of retrospection: a sense of nostalgia for rural life. In this chapter, we develop the themes introduced in Chapter 2 by considering how the planning system today – and the evolution of rural policy and planning since 1947 – often expresses a particular representation of the countryside, and certain beliefs regarding the proper use of rural land. In particular, the spotlight is trained on those policy regimes, emerging after the Second World War, which shaped policy towards development in the countryside and towards rural housing. It is argued that culturally specific attitudes have expanded their boundaries, surviving beyond their time, creating a raft of difficulties for particular communities and areas. Indeed, policies from the mid–1990s promoting 'sustainable communities' are seen to represent an evolution of the historic antipathy towards development in rural areas.

Rural planning – the legacy

Many commentators have recognised that Britain's spatial planning systems have grown within a culture of control and restraint rather than one of enabling or facilitating development (see, for example, Rydin, 2003; Cullingworth and Nadin, 2010). Rural planning in Britain illustrates this tendency particularly well (Gallent et al, 2008). Britain's regimes have three historical axes – 'containment', 'productivism' and 'environmental preservation' – that together form what has now become the traditional basis of rural planning. The destination to which the journey along these axes has brought us – sustainable development – is examined at the end of this chapter. Does this provide a fresh outlook for rural planning, brushing aside nostalgia, or is sustainability merely a gloss behind which business carries on as usual?

Containment

The risk of urban growth and associated urban problems spilling into the countryside in the 19th century galvanised support around the need for 'urban containment': a brake on the outward spread of towns and cities. There were two rationales for such containment: first, agriculture needed protection so that Britain could achieve greater food security (a German naval blockade during the First World War had demonstrated the case for protecting domestic farming); and, second, the English countryside (in particular) was increasingly viewed as a 'retreat' from grimy industrialisation, and as an 'idyll' that stood in contrast to the 'dark Satanic mills' (to quote William Blake) of the Industrial Revolution. Together these two rationales added up to one thing: that the countryside was a resource requiring protection; in this context, the word 'rural' became strongly associated with idyllic pastoralism, and strongly disassociated with the word 'development', which was the realm of the urban.

In this emerging context, the influential planner Patrick Abercrombie wrote *The Preservation of Rural England* (1926) and inspired the creation of the Council for the Preservation of Rural England (CPRE), also becoming its first chairman. The philosophy of the CPRE – and equivalents in Scotland and Wales – has undoubtedly been shaped by Abercrombie's belief in an 'obligation' to 'preserve and save' the countryside as a whole:

> we speak eloquently of the obligation that is on us to preserve and save from destruction the ancient monuments of this land ... but we are apt to forget that the greatest historical monument that we possess, the most essential thing that *is* England, is the countryside, the Market Town, the Village, the Hedgerow Trees, the Lanes, the Copses, the Streams and the Farmsteads (Abercrombie, 1926: 6, quoted in Winter, 1996: 181)

The need to 'protect' rural space from 'urban encroachment' became the critical mission of rural planning, initially finding expression in the 1935 Restriction of Ribbon Development Act and eventually through the evolution of statutory green belts.

The early vestiges of what came to be seen as planning for rural areas can in fact be traced to a specifically urban concern. Although their origins lay in 19th-century urban growth, it was not until the first part of the 20th century – and specifically during the interwar period – that public and political concern triggered a planning response. Between 1919 and 1939, London's population grew by around 2 million (from approximately 6 million to 8 million people). However, whilst the population increased by just over 30 per cent, the land area occupied by the English capital increased fivefold (Hall et al, 1973: 84) during the same period. Sprawl had been motored by population growth, increasing affluence (with a concomitant growth of home ownership) and the increasing use of public transport, both buses and then electric (rather than diesel) trains. The consequence of adverse reaction to the sight of the countryside being 'consumed' was the pursuit of containment policies for major urban centres across Britain.

This was expressed most directly in the 'green belts' of Abercrombie's 1946 plans for London and Glasgow. As noted by Frey (2000, cited by Bramley et al, 2004:19), Abercrombie made a distinction between London's belt, being a development-free ring to constrain sprawl, and Glasgow's, allowing pockets of development with open space between, that is, managing outward growth. However, planning practice north and south of the border from the 1950s adopted the London approach of the green belt as a strategic planning rather than a conservation tool: designating development-free bands round the major conurbations, regardless of whether they were really 'green' or whether any section of the population placed any particular scenic or recreational value on them (Hall, 1975:162). The same broad intention was to remain in place for the remainder of the century: an indication of the strength and rationale of the policy was set out, for England, in the 1980s' version of Planning Policy Guidance Note 2: 'The fundamental aim of Green Belt policy is to prevent urban sprawl by keeping land permanently open; the most important attribute of Green Belts is their openness' (DoE, 1985: para 1.4).

Containment policy appears to have had a sound empirical base in view of interwar London's geo-demography. But how sound was this base for application around northern English, Scottish or Welsh[1] cities? Population census figures for the interwar period for the major conurbations of the Celtic countries suggest much less of a problem with sprawl: Glasgow had a population of 784,000 in 1911, growing by 40 per cent to 1.1 million by 1939, but the city's land area increased by only around 12 per cent in the same period (see also Randall, 1980: 103) suggesting the city's considerable densification from 1871 to 1931. The population of Cardiff grew by around a fifth in the same period with no change in area.

Comparative data for six major cities from 1931 to 1951 are presented in Table 3.1. These data (with the exception of those for Cardiff) are for the standard metropolitan labour area (SMLA)[2] to obtain some degree of comparability from place to place and over time. The Welsh capital is the only city to see growth in land area in the period, with all of the English cities – capital, midlands and

Table 3.1: British cities: populations and densities, 1931–51

City (SMLA)*	1931		1951		% Change in population 1931–51	% Change in land area 1931–51
	Population (000s)	Population density (persons per acre)	Population (000s)	Population density (persons per acre)		
London	8,628	8.99	9,112	9.55	5.61	−0.58
Birmingham	2,148	3.72	2,488	4.66	15.83	−7.54
Manchester	1,989	6.82	2,012	7.01	1.16	−1.59
Newcastle	1,021	4.87	1,025	4.89	0.39	−0.02
Glasgow	1,088	25.00	1,079	25.05	−0.83	0.00
Cardiff*	649	3.48	658	3.48	1.39	1.39

Note: * See main text for definition of 'standard metropolitan labour area' and discussion of Cardiff data.
Sources: Hall et al (1973: 254–93); www.demographia.com/db-glasgow.htm (accessed 9 June 2009).

northern – seeing area reductions. The Scottish city cited – Glasgow – shows a static area. Glasgow is also the only one of the six cities to have witnessed a population decrease in the period: all of the others show increases, most notably Birmingham. So, prior to the formal adoption of containment policies across Britain, major cities were generally showing areal contraction and development densification rather than population and development sprawl.

Moving on from the 1950s, a wider evaluation of green belts in England recognised that they had prevented uncontrolled sprawl of the built environment (DoE, 1993), but that they had been powerless against the rapid de-concentration of economic and residential activity that characterised the period until the mid-1970s and beyond. McCallum (1980: 15) demonstrated that in 1951 seven conurbations (Central Clydeside, Greater London, Merseyside, South East Lancashire, Tyneside, West Midlands and West Yorkshire) were home to 18.7 million people: 38 per cent of Britain's entire population. By 1971, the conurbations had lost 1.5 million people, whilst total population had grown by 5 million. Thus, the conurbation proportion had fallen to a third of the population of Britain. Part of the change can be attributed to spatial variations in birth and death rates, but much more significant was out-migration, associated with sectoral shifts in British industry and the relocation choices of surviving and thriving industries (Massey and Meegan, 1982).

In the light of such patterns, a proponent of containment might be excused for concluding that the relative 'weakness' of existing policy had resulted in the 'decline' of cities and the parallel loss of green land. The logical response would be to further strengthen green belts and other tools, restricting employment and population growth to existing urban areas. But there are a multitude of reasons behind this de-concentration, creating patterns of movement and relocation that are difficult to resist. Larger towns and some smaller market towns, for example, have become new hubs of economic activity drawing population into parts of the wider 'countryside'. Attempts in Britain and in continental Europe to prevent or compensate for sectoral shifts in industry (away from forms suited to urban or near-urban locations to those that are more footloose) have generally proved to be expensive failures, and – by swimming against a tide of change – the damage caused to national or regional economies can be significant. That is not to deny the considerable value in protecting urban assets, and the scale economies that can accrue from population concentration. But it is also the case that the drivers of rural protection, built on a belief in the need to conserve open countryside for future generations, are also drivers of rural consumption. The de-concentration of industry has gone hand-in-hand with a process of counter-urbanisation grounded in a rediscovery of rural living in the 20th century: a rural consumerism that coexists with productivism, but favours the preservation of those characteristics of rural areas – including relative tranquillity – on which it places a premium.

Productivism

The second axis of rural planning is the protection of farmland and farming interests. Heeding the advice of the Scott Report[3] (Ministry of Works and Planning, 1942), the 1947 Town and Country Planning Acts, for England and Wales and for Scotland, established a hierarchy of restrictions on the uses of agricultural land. The strongest restraint applied to the most productive categories of arable land, decreasing in intensity with the reduction in potential productivity. For even the most marginal agricultural terrains, however, the fact that they had some productive potential meant that they were afforded a degree of protection. The net result of this was a vetoing of, or at least negative planning attitude towards, the use of agricultural land for non-agricultural purposes, be these for housing, economic development or community facilities. Having enjoyed this degree of protection, farmers were, for most of the post-war period, keen to hold on to it. And despite the disappearance of rationing in the mid-1950s and the steady decline in agriculture's contribution to GDP from the 1960s, the system of protection has remained essentially untouched for over 60 years.

The protections handed to farming after the Second World War were intended to deliver 'food security' and were born of the experience of insecurity during the war itself, when blockades on British shipping threatened the supply of basic foodstuffs entering Britain. But food security after the war was interpreted as market protection: through such protection it was, in theory, possible to support the viability of food production so that Britain would never again be vulnerable to the threat of foreign powers. But whilst the geopolitical situation evolved, the desire to be shielded from market forces took a firm hold on the farming sector. Coupled with the effects of the Town and Country Planning Acts, the 1947 Agriculture Act created a system of capital and revenue subsidy emphasising the expansion of food production. British farming entered its 'productivist' phase, which continued and accelerated on accession to the European Community in 1973.

Since the 1970s, guarantees on prices for certain agricultural products have clearly incentivised production and brought a level of food security never seen before in Western Europe. However, overproduction and the spectacle of 'grain mountains' and 'wine lakes' brought the entire subsidy regime into disrepute, with commentators arguing that the European Union had overshot its original target and that intensive farming was doing far more harm than good: harm felt by the environment and by European consumers.

It is an axiom of basic economics that subsidies tend to lead to a net loss in social welfare. There are two parts to the argument: first, the setting of a floor price prevents prices descending to market-clearing level. With prices set higher than equilibrium level, farmers have an incentive to produce more of that foodstuff than consumers demand at that price – so leading to overproduction. Second, given a choice between producing two foodstuffs, one of which has a floor price, the other of which does not, it is likely, *ceteris paribus*, that farmers will expect (and attain) higher profits from the subsidised product, resulting in lower production of non-subsidised foodstuffs. If that lower rate of production meets consumer preferences, there is no impact on welfare. But in the more common case where less of the foodstuff is produced than consumers wish at a price they consider reasonable, there will be shortages. Market-clearing prices rise and a smaller number of consumers buy the foodstuff at prices above free market levels.

Food production subsidies accounted for 70 per cent of the European Commission's budget in 1984 (Woods, 2005b: 135). They have since been trimmed back considerably and a new focus has been developed around broader structural development, creating new opportunities for peripheral areas and the delivery of community goods. But the privileged position occupied by farming in the post-war period remains an important legacy for policy development in rural areas. Although some funds previously spent on food production have been siphoned off for local community-based projects, there remains a pervasive belief in the critical importance of farming to rural economies, often to the detriment of other economic activities and other policy objectives. Support for farming is not, of course, inherently wrong. But like any general intervention – including green belts – it may have unforeseen and unfortunate consequences if it is not tied and tailored to specific circumstances. Subsidy-driven farming was responsible for the destruction of a great many sensitive habitats, and overemphasis on it has left many communities bereft of economic alternatives. Likewise, the green belt policy has played an important part in preventing urban coalescence and sprawl in some areas, but it has created economic and social 'dead zones' elsewhere, restricting economic diversity and denying many rural residents the opportunity of a home of their own.

Productivism, then, has some profound economic consequences. It also has socio-political impacts in the promotion and privileging of farming interests at different scales. At the highest level, the most visible evidence of this was the close involvement of the National Farmers' Union (NFU) in the agricultural policy process, immediately post-war and thereafter, joined later by the Farmers' Union of Wales and NFU (Scotland). Following Marsh and Rhodes (1992), Woods (2005b: 132) views this as a prime exemplar of the operation of a closed policy community with, *inter alia*, a limited number of participants, dominated by economic and professional interests, frequent high-quality interaction, consistency of membership and continuity of values. At the local level, farming interests were strongly reflected by councillors, who commonly stood as independents or on Conservative or Liberal tickets. Thus, rural councils and the rural wards of otherwise urban councils were negatively inclined towards non-agricultural development – including housing – save where farmers stood to gain from land sales for that purpose (Shucksmith, 1990b). For this reason, productivism has often shaped the local politics of rural areas, extending privilege through the planning system and amplifying the effects of containment. It propagates a view that the only legitimate use of rural land is farming use: containment (of non-farming activities) gives national weight to this local political perspective, which is itself rooted in British and national policies that continue to shape rural policy despite the geopolitical and economic changes that have reshaped the world. These rural politics are examined more closely in Chapter 10.

Preservation

The third axis is environmental preservation. This has long been given expression through three acronyms – AONBs, NNRs and SSSIs[4] – and through the National Parks. The framing legislation, the 1949 National Parks and Access to the Countryside Act, applied to England and Wales and indicated that national parks were to be chosen for their landscape and recreational value. Areas of Outstanding Natural Beauty (AONBs) were to be selected on landscape value alone. The National Nature Reserves (NNRs) and (smaller) Sites of Special Scientific Interest (SSSIs) were designated in areas of particular ecosystem or geological interest (Lowe, 1989: 125–6). These designations confer the strongest presumption against the development of land.

National Parks have existed in England and Wales since the 1950s. They are a newer concept in Scotland, where the enabling legislation did not arrive until 1999. As might be anticipated from the preceding statements, the prime aim of the English and Welsh Parks, according to statute, has always been environmental protection first, access to the countryside for recreation second, any other use – such as concern for the Parks populations' livelihood – a distant third. This objective was given a small boost in the mid-1990s, in the light of some concern for the social well-being of rural communities (Countryside Commission, 1991), but it has to contend with a half-century legacy of at least an implicit anti-development rationale permeating thinking on the purpose of National Parks. In Scotland, the framing legislation adopted the rhetoric of 'sustainable development', but placed maintenance of 'viable communities' in the Parks on an equal footing with natural environment and recreation concerns (Richards and Satsangi, 2004). Thus, at the formal opening of Scotland's second (and Britain's largest) National Park, the Cairngorms, its chair stated that:

> We must make sure that the natural and cultural heritage are cared for as they are unique assets that can never be replaced … we must promote sustainable economic and social development of the communities that are such a vital part of this Park. (Thin, 2003)

The designations created during the formative years of the planning system give voice to a seemingly pervasive desire to preserve the 'best' of Britain's natural and landscape assets, though the strategy of 'singling out' particular places came under some criticism in the early years of the 21st century. It is somewhat counter to the view that it is the countryside more broadly that is deserving of preservation (Abercrombie, 1926) and it also runs the risk of unintentionally focusing visitor pressure on 'special' areas, denuding over time those qualities that made them special in the first place. In other words, such strategies of preservation are self-defeating. The second way in which preservation is expressed is through the activities of national and local amenity and 'conservation' groups. We draw particular attention to the choice of the term 'conservation' as it implies acceptance of a degree of change, whereas the more accurate (but with perhaps narrower political appeal) nomenclature of 'preservation' suggests resistance to any change. Local groups, commonly dominated by middle-class incomers (Lowe, 1989; Woods, 2005a), usually begin life as a reaction *against* a development proposal, with housing and wind farms provoking particular ire. The national organisations' choice of titles – such as the Campaign to *Protect* Rural England and Association for the *Protection* of Rural Scotland, *Friends* of the Earth, National *Trust* and National *Trust* for Scotland – suggest a motive of concern and stewardship. What that motive translates as, as well as the rather more naked aim of local groups, is a campaign to stifle development rather than ensure that development proposals are appropriate to context (as the groups often share the belief that *no* development would be *appropriate* in *this* context).

All of the groups are political, in the sense that they aim to influence the political process. Part of their *raison d'être* is frustration with the mainstream political parties. Thus, they are better conceived as pressure groups, albeit with local groups frequently becoming bedfellows of the Conservative Party. Woods (2005a) observes the closed, tight nature of many local groups, satirised by Ray Davies in his song 'The Village Green Preservation Society' (1968):

> We are the Sherlock Holmes English-speaking Vernacular.
> God save Fu Manchu, Moriarty and Dracula.
> We are the Office Block Persecution Affinity.
> God save little shops, china cups, and virginity.
> We are the Skyscraper Condemnation Affiliates.
> God save Tudor houses, antique tables, and billiards.
> Preserving the old ways from being abused.
> Protecting the new ways, for me and for you.
> What more can we do?[5]

These three axes of rural policy – containment, productivism and preservation – have readily combined to produce the rural planning and politics that are common to much of rural Britain. However, apart from productivism – which is arguably far more generic, extending across Europe since 1945 – these axes are most strongly associated with southern England, and especially with the Home Counties. Green belt was designed to protect these counties from London's growth, though this was achieved through a general policy built on a belief that what was generally good and progressive for London should also be available to benefit other parts of Britain, irrespective of local conditions or evidence. Although preservation was not born in the Home Counties, it was a product of middle-class sensibilities, closely identified with the southern counties during the first half of the 20th century, and extending out from London with counter-urbanisation after the Second World War (Newby, 1979). Counter-urbanisation brought with it an expansion of urban, middle-class lifestyles and tastes. New arrivals to commuter towns and villages brought with them not only their extended social networks (Pahl, 1975), but also a preconception of what the countryside should be, given voice and momentum through local preservation groups that grew into broader lobbies and quickly assumed national and Britain-wide standing, extending the reach of the urban middle class well beyond the confines of southern England.

Taken together, these three axes support a rural policy that is highly resistant to forms of development seen as inappropriate: that might threaten the openness of the countryside, that do not contribute to the farming economy, or that scar the face of the 'greatest historical monument that we possess'. Yet, the view that the countryside must continue to live and change has arguably provided a counterpoint to the desire to conserve or preserve rural landscapes. Across Britain, there has been acceptance of the idea that thriving communities play a part in the life of the countryside. So has this focus on sustainable development brought a step-change in British and national policy and local politics and any willingness to countenance 'essential' development in rural areas?

Building a sustainable future?

In this chapter, we have focused attention on containing development and preserving the character of rural areas. Together, these trends suggest a strong tendency across the British countrysides towards protecting rural areas from the forces of change. But these forces are strong, sometimes irresistible. In later chapters – and especially Chapters 7 and 8 – we examine post-war population changes affecting rural areas and the lifestyle choices that lead people to move to the countryside, sometimes permanently and sometimes seasonally. As well as being protected, the countryside is regularly consumed by an increasingly large section of society that finds things to do and see in rural areas. The de-concentration of residence and economic activity, noted in this chapter, also continues to challenge the belief that the countryside can be immunised from change. Indeed, the force of this change has led to constant challenges to the wisdom of green belt policy in its current form, and the logic of economic policies that favour agriculture over other forms of economic development.

The search for strategies and policies able to cope with this difficult dynamic has been ongoing since the 1990s: the pursuit of 'sustainable development' – alongside the creation of 'sustainable communities' – has become the central goal of spatial planning. But this pursuit is hampered by the uncertain and contested nature of its end goal. Contemporary definitions of sustainable development continue to build on the Brundtland Commission's view that 'development that meets the needs of the present without compromising the ability of future generations to meet their own needs' is sustainable (WCED, 1987: 43). Practically, this means balancing economic, social and environmental needs. But where does the right balance lie, and is the point of equilibrium the same in all areas? This is the critical question for 'sustainable development' in the countryside. The search for sustainable development occurs along three axes, which appear inherently at odds with one another. The need, for example, to fuel a modern industrial economy using fossil or nuclear fuel presents significant environmental risks, threatening the well-being of all communities, and especially those that are vulnerable to change.

But herein lies the difficulty – sustainability is all too often presented as a balance between environmental threat, economic uncertainty, and social vulnerability: the threat is certain, the benefit is unclear and communities are vulnerable to change. If any action is to be taken, the most obvious course is to reduce the threat to the environment. There is clear logic here given the sheer scale of the environmental threats that the world now faces. Translated into residential development in England, Scotland and Wales, this often means concentrating development in existing built-up areas, limiting extension onto greenfield land and accepting path dependency: not venturing anything new.

This generic interpretation of sustainable development has a critical bearing on rural housing. Planning policy and practice couched in the rhetoric of sustainability has meant the freezing of development in smaller settlements. This is particularly the case in 'village England' (Gallent, 2009a), where the crude use of sustainability indicators has justified the continuation of the long-running resistance to development in the countryside (Shucksmith, 2007a). Available data show that villages consistently fail to attract a fair share of development in those instances where there is evidence of local need (Bramley and Watkins, 2009), often because the 'rules' of sustainability combine with the current mode of production of affordable housing (i.e. procured as a development gain through the planning system – see Chapter 14) to direct residential development to larger nearby settlements better able to 'absorb' change (given that villages have a lower capacity to do so without offending those interests that wish these settlements to remain characteristically 'rural').

So the journey to sustainable development – along the three axes of rural policy – does not appear to bring us anywhere new and exciting. If anything, sustainability reinforces the cornerstone policies of rural planning. The application of a 'generic' brand of sustainability, with the reduction of environmental threat at its core, has been criticised in government reviews of the first decade of the 21st century (Taylor, 2008; Scottish Parliament Rural Affairs and Environment Committee, 2009). Protection of the rural landscape comes at a price: in many parts of Britain, rural communities are whiter, more middle class, more affluent and contain more retired people than at any time in the past. Is this the sustainable future that Britain wants or its countrysides need?

Notes

[1] Cardiff has a 'green wedge' separating it from Newport rather than a 'green belt' (Tewdwr-Jones, 1997).

[2] The figures follow the definition of SMLA used by Hall et al (1973: 128): an urban core of a single administrative area or number of contiguous areas with a density of at least five workers per acre, or single area with at least 20,000 workers plus a ring of administrative areas sending at least 15 per cent of their resident employed population to the core. In the case of Cardiff, the wider metropolitan economic labour area (MELA) is used, defined as the SMLA plus a ring of administrative areas contiguous to the SMLA that sends more of its workers to the SMLA core than to the core of another (Hall et al, 1973: 129).

[3] On 'Land Utilisation in Rural Areas'.

[4] Areas of Outstanding Natural Beauty, National Nature Reserves and Sites of Special Scientific Interest.

[5] Excerpt available at: www.codehot.co.uk/lyrics/ijkl/kinks/villagegreen.htm (accessed 12 June 2009).

FOUR

Evolving agendas in rural housing

The last two chapters have explored how representations of the countryside have been translated into national and local planning approaches – informing the system of statutory landscape protection and shaping attitudes to 'preservation' – which lend support to protection in a context of increasing consumption of the countryside. However, interwoven throughout this chronology of policy frameworks have been various attempts to take stock of, and reflect upon, policy outcomes. These reviews have provided a series of snapshots of how problems have been defined and the assessments that have been made of the demand and supply pressures in rural localities, including the differential outcomes and consequences for various parts of the population.

Indeed, few topics have been so frequently reviewed, by government, by charities and by pressure groups, as 'the rural housing question'. For the past 100 years, governments in Westminster (and the devolved administrations after 1999) have been compelled, time and again, to return to the search for answers in the face of mounting pressure to address the housing and economic challenges posed by a restructuring countryside. A range of actions have invariably followed these inquiries into 'housing conditions', 'rural poverty', 'affordability', 'economic opportunity' and 'sustainability': but none have so far provided a convincing solution, or at least convincing enough to bring this succession of reviews to a halt.

As noted in the Foreword to this book, there seems to be something *intractable* in this question, which defies resolution, and is perhaps more fundamental than housing conditions or affordability, or rural wage levels. This chapter briefly reviews the reviews, charting the trajectory of concern over the last century. It pulls together a sample of key inquiries from different parts of Britain, examines their central concerns and considers the extent to which they addressed 'rural fundamentals' (of the type examined in the last chapter), as opposed to highlighting the rural versions of generic housing problems. Did they advance critical understanding of the rural housing question, or did they instead generate lists of actions that governments might take to placate sections of the rural population: sticking plasters for gaping wounds?

Early reviews are significant and reveal how concern for rural housing, rural economies and rural communities evolved over the last century. Arguably, this concern, traceable in a variety of inquiry reports, became more sophisticated, more focused on the link between communities and economies and less concerned with the superficial state of the housing stock or basic public health and hygiene (a hangover from the 19th century, with the countryside seen as the last refuge of really bad, unsanitary housing). But perhaps it failed to become sophisticated enough, missing the bigger picture and failing to spot that the housing shortages of the 20th century came after the nationalisation of development rights in 1947 and the creation of a comprehensive system of land-use planning, and that they are tied to the question of what rural land is for if it is not a resource for rural development. It is no accident that a concern for very poor housing conditions in the first half of the 20th century was gradually replaced with a concern for housing shortages and housing costs – associated with counter-urbanisation – in the latter half of the century (although the question of housing conditions itself has never been entirely resolved).

This discussion is structured around a chronology of concern beginning immediately after the First World War and continuing throughout the interwar period. This is followed by a look at the rural implications of the social housing revolution, post–World War Two, quickly followed by counter-urbanisation pressures and gradual recognition of the fundamental social and economic changes affecting the countryside. From the 1990s onwards, government attention has refocused on the state of rural economies (in an era of post-production) and planning's fitness for purpose in the light of general regulatory reform and an acknowledgement that rural areas are experiencing their biggest cultural shift for a generation.

The rural housing question – origins

In 1829, an etching by the artist George Cruikshank showed London literally 'going out of town', with development spewing onto the countryside and threatening the tranquillity of pastoral England (Cruikshank, 1832). Britain's Industrial Revolution had prompted unprecedented urban growth, triggering two areas of critical concern for future policy-makers: the well-being of urban centres and the relationship between these centres and their rural hinterlands. However, a concern for rural housing had essentially the same origins as concern over the state of the 19th-century city: public health and the risk to economic productivity. But in the hundred years that followed, this concern changed and was tempered – in large measure – by a strengthening discourse of rural preservation. In the brief sections that follow, we chart the evolving rural housing debate in England, Scotland and Wales, referring to the periodic reviews of shifting concern.

Housing rural labourers: 1900 onwards

Writing in 1914, Savage (1919: v) observed that the 'rural housing problem is both an acute and an urgent one' but that 'it is important to realize that we are really making no substantial advance towards its satisfactory solution'. Savage attributed this lack of advance to complexity and to the politicised nature of the problem, with posturing and party politics put ahead of progress towards resolution. The problem in Savage's eyes was one of supply and of quality, with government called upon to engage in new cottage construction and the repair of existing homes (1919: 1). The need for homes, and for a repair programme, was linked to the demand for agricultural labour and a new intensity in farming activity. Because of government's post–war concern for mass housing, the rural housing question was carried on the back of this wider agenda. It was acknowledged that private enterprise was unlikely to meet the total need for new construction, particularly where rural wages were low, and the profitability of building working-class housing was limited. Therefore, the case for state subsidy was clear, with government called upon to bear the bigger part of the total cost (Savage, 1919: 4).

The basic question posed by Savage was how enough homes could be provided to meet the needs of the 'rural labourer' (1919: 11). After the First World War, this was conceived as the essence of the rural housing question: bringing forward a programme of development and rehabilitation linked to the needs of the farming sector. Savage's focus was firmly on the housing shortage. His background as the Medical Officer of Health for the County of Somerset explains his emphasis on the well-being of the rural population. In his view, the state of many rural cottages were 'a disgrace to the country' (1919: 174). A comprehensive and unprecedented programme of development, utilising the latest construction techniques along with the highest building standards possible, was, in Savage's mind, the only plausible solution. This would be paid for from a mix of private investment and state subsidy.

The preservation of rural Britain: 1920s onwards

Eighteen years later, the government's Central Housing Advisory Committee (1937) produced a report on the state of English rural housing that was similarly developmental in tone. However, this was preceded – in 1932 – by a rather different kind of review from the Council for the Preservation of Rural England (CPRE). The CPRE, formed in 1926, saw the control of housing development as crucial to its goal of maintaining the essential character of the countryside. Its objective in publishing a 31-page pamphlet on 'rural housing' (Morris, 1932) was not to challenge the prevailing concern for housing conditions in rural England, but to make a case for tighter controls over the form of future development in the countryside. Its particular concern at this time was for ribbon development and for the form and content of the 1932 Town and Country Planning Act: although the Act gave rise to a new emphasis on rural resource planning, the CPRE was determined that this should be extended and strengthened in future legislation. The creation of the CPRE in 1926 was followed by the creation of the Association for the Protection of Rural Scotland (1927) and the Campaign for the Protection of Rural Wales (1928).

The report published by government in 1937 mixed a predominant concern for housing supply and renovation with a concern for good planning. A new phenomenon was emerging at this time, affecting the available supply of homes for farm workers. An exchange in the House of Commons in July 1937 highlighted the issue of seasonal occupancy. Colonel Leonard Roper, Member for Barkston Ash, asked the Minister for Health whether he was aware of the 'growing tendency for town dwellers to rent or buy rural workers' cottages for occasional occupation, and that this is leading to an acute shortage of houses in many rural areas near industrial centres?' (*Hansard*, 20 July 1937, Volume 326, col 1983w). The response was that 'supply of housing accommodation for the agricultural population' was the concern of an ongoing inquiry by the Central Housing Advisory Committee.

The Committee was divided into three sub-committees, including the rural housing sub-committee chaired by Sir Arthur Hobhouse. The predominant concern of government, in the period leading up to the Second World War, remained the housing of agricultural workers, and this was reflected in official reviews and unofficial commentaries. But the formation of the CPRE and its sister organisations created new impetus for an environmental agenda that fed on a more nostalgic and 'monumental' perspective of Britain's rural areas (see Chapter 3; also Winter, 1996: 181). However, recognition of the appalling conditions faced by farm labourers in England and Wales (Central Housing Advisory Committee, 1937) and in Scotland (Scottish Housing Advisory Committee, 1937) meant that the growing interest in rural preservation took a back seat to the investment in, and improvement of, rural housing during the interwar years. Generally, the emphasis at this time was placed firmly on supplying homes to meet the needs of the rural economy, and replacing those that were deemed unfit for human habitation. Despite some early evidence of second home occupation, and therefore a potential shift in certain local economies, the predominance of a land-based economy at that time arguably made it much easier to muster support around a developmental agenda. Indeed, there was little evidence of concern for the incremental growth of villages, with the emergent CPRE campaign (and equivalent national bodies in Scotland and Wales) focused on the encroachment of larger centres into open countryside, and particularly the threat posed by ribbon development.

The social housing revolution: 1940s

Savage's early review, published in the same year as the appearance of enabling legislation for Lloyd George's pledge to deliver 'homes fit for heroes', did, however, highlight the shape of things to come. The 1919 Housing, Town Planning, etc. Act reinforced a message – first aired in 1909 – that 'housing is a primary consideration in the planning process, [and extended] the powers and responsibilities of local authorities in the provision of council homes' (Gallent and Tewdwr-Jones, 2007: 51). Savage (1919) had cogently outlined the need for state intervention in matters of rural housing provision, but the programme of public house-building between 1919 and 1939 had enjoyed only intermittent support and investment. It was not until the end of the Second World War that a more radical social agenda gained more widespread acceptance. In rural England, for example, almost 900,000 new houses had been constructed (most adjacent to towns) between 1919 and 1943 (Armstrong, 1993: 144), but few agricultural workers were able to access these homes, and nine out of 10 remained in tied accommodation in conditions regarded as 'relics of a barbarous age' (Armstrong, 1993: 144). The Third Report of the Central Housing Advisory Committee (1944), whilst retaining its focus on housing conditions and the extension of basic services to homes in the countryside (including piped water), sought a broader response to the remaining shortage in housing supply and the low standards found in much of the existing stock. Parliamentary debate recorded in *Hansard* at the time captures something of the continued interest in rural housing and the demand for a strategic response:

> there is undoubtedly awareness in the countryside to-day as never before of the deficiencies of rural housing and amenities. The countryside looks to the Government to do something to ameliorate that position, and I would urge upon them to give a fair share of Government energy and attention to the problems of the countryside. The Cinderella of the countryside has waited a long time to go to the ball, and awaits anxiously the arrival of her Prince Charming in whatever unexpected and unfamiliar guise he may arrive. (Derek Walker-Smith (Hertford), *Hansard*, 17 August 1945, Volume 413, cols 192–272)

Substantial investment in public housing had been seen as key in 1919, and after the Beveridgean reforms of the 1940s, it seemed clear that rural areas were to share in this investment, subject to good planning. Housing supply linked to the needs of the agricultural economy remained an important concern, but in post-war Britain the emphasis was to be placed on urban overspill (into New Towns after 1946) and the restoration of bomb-damaged inner-urban areas. A programme of public service investment, called for in the 1944 Report of the Central Housing Advisory Committee, was extended to rural areas, but these areas now faced the added pressure of a strengthening framework of landscape and environmental protection. Together with the general presumption against development beyond rural settlement boundaries (which may not in themselves afford much scope for growth), such pressures helped reduce the importance of council house-building in the countryside, reinforcing the dominance of tied accommodation. Short (1982) points out that, in 1948, 33 per cent of farm workers lived in tied housing; by 1976, the figure had risen to 53 per cent (Short, 1982: 218). The social housing revolution in the countryside was considerably more muted than its urban counterpart. Short adds that post-war 'planning controls, with their bias towards urban containment and against housing development in rural areas, have been used to create privileged areas free from further developments, whilst shifting the pressure to key settlements' (Short, 1982: 219). In many rural areas, Prince Charming – in the form of council house-building – simply was not welcome; rather, he faced 'antipathy' (Short, 1982: 218). The status quo remained very much as it had been before the war, making the countryside extremely vulnerable to the social and economic pressures generated by counter-urbanisation.

Counter-urbanisation and social change: 1960s

The 1930s had seen some early interest in the purchasing of rural cottages for occasional use, marking the expansion – or 'social democratisation' – of a trend rooted in aristocratic landholding (Gallent et al, 2005: 18). But this practice had not appeared widespread, and post-war austerity (in the later 1940s and throughout the 1950s) tempered any emergent second home trend. During the 1960s, however, various strands of counter-urbanisation gained momentum, though no serious reviews of their impact were undertaken until the following decade or much later on. The government's position was that an adequate framework had been put in place to deal with decentralisation from the core cities. Its 1946 New Towns Act catered for large-scale inter- and intra-regional population flows, whilst the earmarking of key settlements, within Structure Plans, meant that larger villages and smaller towns could absorb lighter flows of intra-regional movement through suburban-style development, though not without some controversy (Cullingworth, 1962: 15). But its position with regards to smaller settlements and the open countryside seemed indifferent: or, rather, the post-war policy of restricting growth in rural areas – that is, in lower-tier settlements – seemed to presuppose that these areas would not attract growth, at least not at any significant rate.

Although counter-urbanisation (ex-urban population shifts) and social change (more specifically, a process of 'gentrification') appeared to be key features of rural shift in the 1960s (Parsons, 1980; Spencer, 1997) it is perhaps not surprising that they went largely unnoticed for much of that decade. The collective gaze of policy-makers, and of many commentators, was on Britain's post-war recovery and on the experience of the New Towns. The important ex-urban shifts noted by Pahl in Hertfordshire (1965, 1975) and then Newby (1979), were perhaps treated with some indifference in Whitehall because they appeared simply to be breaking down traditional cultural boundaries, between town and country, and the need for any policy response was not immediately obvious.

For this reason, the reviews that marked this important shift in the rural housing debate tended not to be officially sponsored, but to come from local and regional lobby groups. They were also published much later on, once the implications of the trends were more fully understood. The principal strand of counter-urbanisation during the 1960s was commuter-led, affecting near-urban areas, with households overspilling to commuter villages (Newby, 1979: 165). Migrants made use of vastly improving transport links, but it was not until the 1990s that the CPRE and its sister organisations began to decry the loss of rural tranquillity attendant on the road building and widening programme that had begun 30 years earlier. The social changes had been picked up on a little earlier. In Wales, the Welsh Language Society chose to focus on one aspect of counter-urbanisation – the purchasing of second homes – highlighting how seasonal residence threatened the viability of communities by reducing demand for services and school rolls (Cymdeithas Yr Iaith Gymraeg, 1971). Its work was an early foray into the field of social exclusion, closely linked to counter-urbanisation pressures, which became gradually more important throughout the 1980s. Seventeen years later, Action for Communities in Rural England (ACRE, 1988) linked such pressures to the affordability of housing in villages that Pahl (1964) had described as being 'two class' (Pahl, 1964). ACRE's review drew on analyses from a number of important commentators, whose work looked at the drivers of counter-urbanisation, the impacts on rural society and local economies, and the prospects of a planning response.

From the 1960s onwards, it was generally recognised that ex-urban migration was a powerful force for change in Britain's rural areas. It was not only commuters who were arriving in large numbers, but also lifestyle downshifters and retiring households. However, in local debate and in policy circles, it became politically astute to almost sweep this issue under the carpet. These new arrivals to more rural locations were, in the minds of many, leading a revival of rural communities. More importantly, they were becoming local voters with a strengthening voice in many areas. For much of their history, lowland English villages had been seen as almost timeless (Martin, 1962), but they were now experiencing revolutionary change. But observation of this change did not lead to any direct response. There was of course greater concern over affordability and over the expansion of key settlements, but the arrival of new populations cannot be resisted without the inevitable political backlash. On occasion, concerns were aired over the numbers of retired people moving to the countryside and the impacts this might have on rural economies, but real vitriol was reserved for one aspect of counter-urbanisation: seasonal movement and the purchasing of second homes.

Conspicuous consumption and equity: 1970s

Increased enthusiasm for second home ownership in the 1960s became an established trend in the following decades. During this time, some parts of the countryside were socially transformed by a combination of counter-urbanisation and the insistence that the landscape must be shielded from development wherever possible. During the beginning of this period, there were a number of early reviews of second home purchasing and social impact. These tended to be sponsored by local authorities at the instigation of particular communities and ward members. Hence, there were early studies for the Highlands and Islands (DART, 1977), Denbighshire (Jacobs, 1972) and Caernarvonshire (Pyne, 1973). The evidence they produced tended to be anecdotal, and increases in second home purchasing were not positioned within the wider picture of ex-urban movement. Hence, it was uncertain whether the arrival of seasonal residents was a crucial driver of housing affordability or an added problem in areas feeling the pinch of bigger pressures. We look further at second homes in Chapter 8.

Rural economies: 1990s

A new and strengthening thread in these reviews was the rural economy, or the multitude of rural economies across Britain that need in some way supporting and diversifying if rural communities are to step out of poverty and have a real chance of competing for homes, and paying for services, in a rural landscape transformed by the changes of the past half a century. By the early 1990s, it had been established that the economy of the past – largely built on farming – had been replaced by multiple local and regional economies within an increasingly 'differentiated countryside' (Marsden et al, 1993). The economic needs of rural areas were of central concern in the early reviews of rural housing conditions, not perhaps because these areas needed to stand on their feet, but because their contribution to the national economy and well-being (through food production and security) was viewed as critically important. Sixty years ago, the rural housing question was never asked in isolation from the economic question: homes were built to serve the needs of farming.

Since then, the transformation of rural communities has been resultant on a fundamental change in their economic base, often paraphrased as a transition from a productive economy to one of consumption (see Chapter 5). In the more distant past, economic analysis of rural areas tended to focus on exogenous economic drivers, ignoring indigenous activities (emergent forms of farming, small business start-ups, new crafts building on tourist interest, etc). It was assumed that the economic case for local housing was weak and that the demand for housing was driven by external interest. Therefore, areas needed investment and subsidy to operate, and the prospect of enterprise tended to be underestimated.

However, analyses of rural economies from the 1990s onwards reveal remarkable variety, and also make a strong link to the housing question. They point to a heterogeneous, enterprising countryside in which economic development can be retarded by a lack of local housing. They point to the need to support diversity, to engage flexibly with rural businesses and to ensure – whenever possible – that development planning is not a hindrance to enterprise (DEFRA, 2008). Much of what is being said today echoes the reviews of the 1930s and 1940s, underlining the need to provide homes to service what could be, in some instances, a flourishing rural economy. The language of these reviews – and constant reference to a 'living and working' countryside – sometimes comes across as an admission of past mistakes. Has past policy emphasis resulted in a 'dead and redundant countryside'? Certainly, there is a strong link today between housing and the economic needs of rural areas. This came across clearly in the Rural White Papers for each of the nations of Britain published in 2000, which sought to link the rejuvenation of economies to modern services and affordable homes. Since the 1990s, an understanding of the transitions in and transformations of rural economies has been thrown back into the melting pot, and has joined social exclusion as a key aspect of the rural housing question: perhaps going some way to rebalancing what had become increasingly a question of acceptable development within the preserved countryside.

Planning as an integrating force?

The pace of review activity centred on the question of rural housing accelerated from the mid-1990s, but have the different perspectives of the past coalesced into something more integrated? One view is that the latest reviews – in England, Scotland and Wales – looking across the social, environmental and economic dimensions are more comprehensive, step out of the quagmire of 'party politics' (Savage, 1919) and start to address fundamentals. But they may also be interpreted as a continuation of official lip-service to this seemingly most intractable of problems.

In 2006, an Affordable Rural Housing Commission (ARHC) in England launched a report containing a raft of recommendations for government departments, regional assemblies, local authorities and communities. Revision of planning policy was a key suggestion of the Commission – moving away from an approach based on 'muddling through' to a more 'plan-led approach in partnership with communities'. The idea that planning can deliver consistent solutions to rural housing challenges, presumably by dealing with fundamentals rather than innovating around the edges of otherwise intractable problems, is critical. At the very least, there is some admission that there is something wrong at the heart of existing rural policy frameworks.

'Muddling through' and 'incrementalism' are terms regularly used to characterise policy processes in Britain (see Prior, 1999).[1] 'Muddling through' – a phrase employed by Hoggart and Henderson (2005) to describe reliance on the rural exceptions approach in England – was first used by Lindblom (1959) to explain how decision-makers work in reality. Policy development tends often to be incremental, involving small steps rather than sudden fundamental change. Lindblom's analysis of the policy process was a comment on the emerging idea of 'rational comprehensive decision-making', which was rapidly gaining popularity at the time (Simon, 1947, 1960; see also Hogwood and Gunn, 1984; Satsangi, 2006). The ARHC report, in referencing the idea of 'muddling through', therefore invokes one of the most important divisions in planning thought: drawing a line between comprehensive policy-making and liberalism; and between normative strategy and local innovation.

Ultimately, the ARHC report failed to attract the support it had wanted. There are a number of reasons for this. First, it was stuck in the mindset of innovating solutions rather than taking big, bold steps. Government may have welcomed this, but other groups were disappointed. Second, its concerns were narrowly focused, and it failed to show what linkages needed to be made between housing and related development and economic agendas. Its focus on land supply offered some useful pointers as to who might be recruited (which landowners) to support housing supply, but its approach was far from radical. The same criticism could be levelled at the JRF review on *Rural Housing in Wales* (JRF Commission on Rural Housing in Wales and Milbourne, 2008) two years later: there was a sense that the fundamentals had slipped from the review's radar and that an opportunity had been missed.

Whilst dealing with undoubtedly important issues, these reviews came across as rather superficial wish lists. They did not address the fundamental politics of rural development and land use, nor did they explore the basic links between community need and the state of local economies. Rather, their focus was simply on how to deliver more homes and how to do more with the existing planning system in the light of reduced public spending on housing, and the prospect of further cuts in the future.

Perhaps acceptance of a disappointment with the ARHC report was signalled by Prime Minister Gordon Brown's commissioning of a further review by the MP Matthew Taylor in 2007. This was a far broader examination of planning, housing supply and rural economies and made recommendations that dealt, again, with innovating solutions within a difficult planning process, but also with making that process *less difficult* for rural communities. Indeed, planning was viewed both as a brake on economic development and as an impediment to housing supply: it was seen to generate an unholy trinity between unjustified restriction, housing shortages and a stifled economy. Was this, at last, the integrated understanding of the rural housing question that had been hitherto absent, and would government take it seriously?

Frameworks for tackling fundamentals?

Taylor was unequivocal about the fundamental failure of planning in the English countryside. Whilst it had served part of its purpose well, blessing the wider population with a resource for future generations, it was systematically denying many communities the growth that they desperately needed. The 'restrictive nature of many planning practices' (Taylor, 2008: 8) contributes to the pressures faced by many rural communities, with smaller villages and hamlets caught in a sustainability trap, and only more flexible planning with a 'real sense of vision that is based on recognising how our rural communities can be rather than writing them off as unsustainable' (Taylor, 2008: 8) will offer them any chance of escape.

Taylor's major finding was that many rural communities are written off by the planning system as inherently unsustainable. Reflecting national priorities, communities are denied the chance to grow because of the desire to limit car-based travel (Taylor, 2008: 45). Linking to the economy, this inflexibility fails to safeguard jobs or provide the homes that are needed by these communities (Taylor, 2008: 16) and, for this reason, Taylor's primary recommendation was that there should be a new accommodation between the different strands of sustainability in rural areas: essentially, that a rebalancing is needed between environmental and social agendas (see Chapter 3).

The first two recommendations of the review dealt with the planning system. This represented a departure from past reviews, which had regularly offered means of innovating solutions, accepting the framework as a *fait accompli*. The first called on government to provide greater coherency in planning policy, creating this balance and, by inference, placing greater weight on community need. The second suggested a new requirement that local authorities take into account 'all three strands of sustainability [again] in a balanced way' and achieve this through a long-term vision that splices together different objectives. Many of the review's recommendations touched on the need to reform planning practice. The central message was that planning practice (and policy) is getting it wrong, creating many of the problems that rural communities currently face.

For Taylor, the interpretation of sustainability in planning guidance was too generic and should be applied more sensitively and flexibly in rural areas: only then will it be possible to deliver 'inclusive patterns of development' (2008: 30). This inclusivity is what many rural communities now lack, stemming from an inadequate supply of affordability housing and insufficient support for new rural economies, and particularly diversification away from farming.

So does the Taylor Review mark a turning point – at least in England – bringing hope to villages? Early in 2009, there was a real buzz in the professional and popular media. Government was about to 'curb' rural planning restrictions and allow rural councils to earmark land for affordable homes and for community needs (Oakshott, 2009). Whilst the Taylor Review offers real insight into the forces of change affecting rural communities, in a far more integrated way than had been achieved in past reviews, it is guilty of pulling its punches. It left government with a number of critical 'get out of jail' cards. The balance of blame between planning policy and practice was left unclear, allowing government to laud the significance of the review (DCLG, 2009a) whilst attributing failures where they were seen to exist to local authorities. There is little evidence in its response that any bulldozing of planning restrictions – or indeed any rebalancing – is on the horizon. But even if government were to change the rules of the game, would local authorities play ball? Where does the resistance to rural change really lie – in the corridors of central government, or in rural communities themselves? Taking Taylor as as a point of reference, it is clear that thinking on this issue has gained a great deal of sophistication, with many important linkages now receiving critical recognition. Resolution, however, is far from certain given entrenched resistance to real change in many rural areas.

Both the AHRC and the Taylor reports had explicit foci on policy and practice in England. The JRF inquiry was Britain-wide and suggested that Scotland faced some similar problems to England and Wales. There were important differences too, however, notably in land tenure and in the greater proportion of the population living in relatively remote locations. National policy debate and review had been strong in the late 1980s and early 1990s – Scottish Homes, the national housing agency created by the 1988 Housing (Scotland) Act, was to make rural housing the subject of its first policy statement (Scottish Homes, 1990) and this was accompanied by a series of rural housing market analyses. These recognised some of the constraints faced in affordable rural housing provision and spawned some innovative mechanisms to attempt to get around them (such as the rural home ownership grant that we look at in Chapter 16). But neither it nor the modestly ambitioned 1998 revision suggested a need to fundamentally rebalance planning restraint (Shucksmith and Conway, 2003).

This was, however, the tenor of the next national review. Amongst the conclusions of the Scottish Government's inquiry into rural housing was that 'there is an over-cautious planning culture in much of rural Scotland that has effectively entrenched a presumption against development' (Scottish Parliament Rural Affairs and Environment Committee, 2009: 2). It looked forward to a change in this culture, encouraging planning authorities to zone more land for housing and de-zone undeveloped land, public bodies to sell land for housing, and the rural-proofing of housing standards and specifications. It argued for more widespread use of compulsory purchase powers, though stopping short of using them where landowners seemed to be unreasonably withholding zoned land. The conclusions of the inquiry were consistent with the Scottish Government's intentions at the time to boost the responsiveness of housing supply. They were also, however, published in a context of housing market depression, with low rates of house-building starts and general market activity. For the responsible minister, these short- to medium-term preoccupations seem, at the time of writing, to be more pressing than elaborating a longer-term response to the Rural Affairs and Environment Committee Inquiry.

Taking stock of the current challenges

The similarity in these overall prescriptions between the countries within Britain obscures the huge differences that exist in their housing contexts at national level. Wilcox et al (2010) highlighted very tight housing markets in terms of the crude balance of dwellings over households in Wales and England, with a suggested shortfall in London and the South-East of the latter. In contrast, Scotland has experienced a more favourable balance of dwellings over households. Even so, the varied rural contexts that exist in Scotland suffer the same outcomes that are experienced in England and Wales, with many, but not all, rural localities having an under-supply of housing that is available to, or can be afforded by, low-income households.

Throughout the long period of interest in rural housing, there has been an acknowledgement that different areas face particular challenges and specific outcomes, resulting from the broader forces of change (see Dunn et al, 1981; Shucksmith, 1981). That particular combinations of circumstances produce distinct challenges at the local level has been recognised in numerous studies of rural housing, and also in various approaches to the issues and classifications of rural areas.

For instance, Shucksmith et al (1995) identified that there are many different types of rural housing *market* in England, characterised by greater or less supply restraint, by stricter or more relaxed planning, and by stronger or weaker external demand pressures. Similarly, research in Scotland has highlighted a range of housing markets in the rural areas of this country (Satsangi et al, 2000; Satsangi et al, 2001), as well as a diverse range of social and economic characteristics that impact upon local housing systems (Williams et al, 1998). Such studies look behind the statistics and recognise that there is more than one rural housing question. Indeed, the challenges faced by different areas may contrast sharply: not only areas located in different regions, but also areas that are contiguous, but subject to different landscape designations, are overlain by green belt, or have attributes that make them more or less attractive to incomers.

Other studies have recognised that within these local contexts, competing representations of the countryside also affect the trajectory of change. Marsden et al (1993), for example, were pioneers in developing a geographical taxonomy of rural localities, attributing not only changes in rural localities, but also variations across rural localities, to the dominance of particular socio-economic groups, leading to the argument for a 'differentiated' countryside (see also Murdoch et al, 2003). The notion of a 'differentiated countryside' was further developed by Lowe and Ward (2007), whose classification of rural areas in England and Wales brings together ideas of structural and socio-economic change. In Scotland, the evidence suggests that feudal and neo-feudal land tenure arrangements are further crucial differentiating factors (Satsangi, 2007, 2009). All of the studies emphasise that it is the diverse crystallisations of interests and power that drive the different types of rural area that can be discerned in Britain in the 21st century.

It is the very diverse profiles of social groupings and economic activity across rural spaces that underpins the distinct combinations of pressures that exist in housing and labour markets. These pressures have produced winners and losers in the way that housing is consumed in rural communities and a whole raft of very particular difficulties that need to be overcome if perceived imbalances in local housing markets are to be addressed. Chapter 15 quantifies the nature of the affordability problem, and the level of affordable housing that needs to be produced to overcome the barriers that households face. Research has emphasised that the heart of the problem relates to an inadequate supply of affordable housing, and especially social rented accommodation (Bramley and Watkins, 2009).

A key theme running through this and previous chapters has been a disjuncture between the recognition of the 'problem' of achieving an adequate supply of affordable housing in rural areas, against the implementation of policies that have proscribed this supply in favour of other policy outcomes. That the need for affordable housing in rural areas is recognised is not in doubt, but policy instruments for achieving an accelerated supply of affordable housing have been subsumed within an overarching philosophy of 'protect and consume'.

This chapter began by examining changing interpretations of the 'rural housing question' in Britain over the 20th century before giving additional attention to recent analyses and the differentiated context delivering different housing outcomes in different areas. It is in the nature of an overview to deal in broad terms and general consequences rather than local detail. Reviews have emphasised the range of dynamics that have reconfigured rural areas, and which have led to the diverse outcomes in terms of power relations and tensions in different rural localities (Smith, 2007). An overarching pressure has resulted from counter-urbanisation, and the movement of particular social groups into the countryside, with a counter-veiling trend resulting from the movement of young people out of rural areas (Jamieson and Groves, 2008; Champion, 2009). As we explore more fully in the following two chapters, the balance between out-migration and in-migration varies significantly across Britain and there is great diversity in the potential contributions of rural economies to regional, national and British economic output.

Note

[1] Often used in conjunction with criticism of the liberalism that came to dominate planning in the 1980s (Tewdwr-Jones, 2002).

FIVE

Housing and the rural economy

Neither in Britain, nor in its sister states in the EU and OECD, nor indeed globally, is concern for the downward trajectories of many rural economies a new phenomenon. In the rapidly urbanising, developing world, rural depopulation has been seen as an almost inevitable correlate of national economic progress. For many of these countries, there is an at least tacit acceptance of rural areas as 'backward'. In the advanced economies, where counter-urbanisation has been much more the norm for at least four decades, low-wage rural populations are seen to experience two sorts of problem – differential capacity for economic growth with the decline of fragile areas; and dual economies, where locals' buying power is outstripped by that of commuters or in-migrants. In this chapter we look at the economic base of the rural housing question. A central argument of the chapter is that perspectives on current rural housing systems are bound up with the fate of rural economies and views on the purposes of Britain's countrysides.

'It's the economy, stupid!'

Stated in his successful 1992 US presidential campaign, Bill Clinton's aphorism is as self-evidently applicable in thinking about a society's material standards of living, including its housing systems, as it is in thinking about its members' political choices. For, since the 1920s, real income growth has fuelled the satisfaction of increasing housing aspirations both qualitatively (more private housing of higher space standards being the clearest indices[1]) and quantitatively (through building rates that have almost kept pace with increased rates of household growth[2]). In the same period, there has also been a series of profound sectoral shifts in the macro-economy.

The first of these is the continuous growth of private service industries, such as banking, tourism and recreation, and public service industries in the welfare areas of health care, education and the full gamut of local government functions. The second shift is that of manufacturing industries, with a rise in fortunes until the 1950s succeeded by a fall from the mid-1960s. This became particularly acute in the late 1970s' to mid-1990s' 'deindustrialisation', and is being compounded in the late 2000s by the effects of the deepest economic recession for 30 years. Although the term 'deindustrialisation' has been used in a general sense, in reality, it applied mainly to heavier industries. Finally, the period from the late 1980s witnessed a growth of 'new' technology-related industries.

A third shift – which rural policy commentators commonly see as the one of greatest significance – is the fate of primary industries, including arable and dairy farming as well as extractive industries. The general trend is of increasingly capital-intense production, particularly from the 1950s, with a concomitantly decreasing demand for labour (figures for agricultural workforce decline are given in Chapter 7). In the increasingly global food and drink market, UK agriculture has been hard-pressed, and has not always competed successfully, as evidenced in its market decline, the reduction in its contribution to GDP and the fall in full-time farm employment. In the early 1970s, farming contributed 3 per cent of total UK income (4 per cent in Scotland; University of Aberdeen et al, 2001); by 1999, the figure was just 1 per cent (Cabinet Office, 1999).

These figures for the nations inevitably mask a great deal of regional variation. In England, in 1998, approximately 5 per cent of East Anglia's GDP was agricultural, whilst in Scotland three regions (Orkney, the Borders, and Dumfries and Galloway) had agricultural sectors that contributed between 11 and 15 per cent of total income to their respective economies (University of Aberdeen et al, 2001). Farming thus remains a significant income generator in many rural areas, which some polemics on the fate of agriculture seem to ignore. We look more specifically at employment impacts in Chapter 7 but, at the end of the 1990s, 4 and 8 per cent of the workforce in the rural areas of England and Scotland, respectively were employed in agricultural occupations (Cabinet Office, 1999; University of Aberdeen et al, 2001). Even assuming fairly generous multiplier effects, it is therefore hard to argue that agriculture has had a significant economic impact in Britain for at least 30 years. Its local contribution has often been proportionately greater, making it a mainstay of some rural economies. However, it is the shifts away from farming that brought the biggest impacts on rural areas.

Spatial impacts of economic shifts

The dynamics summarised earlier have had important spatial causes and consequences. First, globalisation has reinforced the post-war dominance of the US economy, with the Maastricht Treaty of 1985 seeing the attempt by European states to form a rival trading bloc and latterly the rise of Asian superpowers. Looking more closely at the EU, discussion from the late 1980s tended to forecast growth being increasingly concentrated in a 'golden triangle' with London at its north-western point, Munich at the south-east, with Brussels the final angle. Buffered by an intermediate zone, much of the rest of the continent, and thus the majority of rural and urban England and all of Scotland and Wales, was predicted to be squashed under a peripheral 'brown banana' of low growth and inexorable (relative, if not absolute) population loss.

The reality of economic performance from the early 1990s to 2007/08 tended, however, to confound many of these predictions. Most notably, the performance of the Republic of Ireland's 'Celtic Tiger' came as a surprise to many pundits (though in the late 2000s, the tiger looked decidedly out of sorts, having been hit hard by the global recession). Further, growth rates in the 'arc of prosperity' countries – including Sweden, Denmark and Norway – have exceeded those in countries closer to the golden triangle, though these too saw decline after 2007.

These major global shifts were expected to have a negative effect on Britain's countrysides, combining with structural changes in the farming sector to bring new economic hardships to many rural communities, or at least to sections of the rural population. Indeed, the major writings on rural Britain link a fall in demand for farm labour with the out-migration of young families and single people, shifting the demographic profile of many parts of the countryside. However, drawing on evidence from England, Hodge and Monk (2004) suggest that this 'stylised fallacy' looks increasingly flawed from 1991 onwards, retaining relevance in only a handful of areas. They claim that a range of other assumptions regarding rural economies – depopulation, relatively low incomes, limited local labour opportunities, relatively high house prices and relatively poor service provision – are not substantiated by data for rural areas in England. The critical point here is that the rural economies of England (and of Scotland and Wales) are heterogeneous, shaped by different processes in a variety of ways. The notion that all rural economies were once farming-dependent and that this dependency has declined at a uniform rate is deeply flawed. And (as we began to explore in the last chapter) attendant on this 'differentiated' economy are a range of social challenges and housing difficulties. Indeed, the rural housing question is really a set of questions linking to varying experience of rural employment, sectoral shifts, service provision and so forth, specific to particular localities.

A key problem that rural areas share, however, is that rural policy has failed to keep up with the pace of change. It was noted in Chapter 3 that a belief in the productive role of rural areas has survived since the Second World War despite the reality of revolutionary change. Given the intransigence of this mindset, policy development has struggled to respond to the restructuring of rural economies. Planning policies ostensibly designed to support the rural economy, for example, have regularly emphasised support for farming activities over alternative uses despite evidence that a consolidation of non-farming activity would bring clear economic and social benefits. Continued support for farming is seen by many not as a sensible economic strategy, but simply as a means of resisting landscape change, revealing that attitudes to economic development are tied up with broader attitudes towards change and development in the countryside. Indeed, policies are often formulated and implemented by those who view the countryside as an inappropriate context for development of any type, and whose intolerance to change is grounded in a view that rural areas are a context for quiet enjoyment rather than economic diversity (Woods, 2005b). But part of the problem, underpinning local politics, is the emphasis on sectoral development. The focus on farming, in a world where farming's importance has declined, has created a development stalemate in many rural areas.

Many commentators – including Huigen et al (1992) and Bryden and Hart (2001) – contend that rural development strategies should be territory-focused rather than sector-based, with planning policies reformulated so as not to give explicit or implicit bias to particular activities. However, rural policy across Britain has tended to eschew such advice, prioritising diversification strategies that remain focused on farming and farms as the unit of economic activity. Such strategies have achieved sporadic success, and have arguably limited economic diversity to those activities seen as appropriate to rural areas: or, rather, appropriate to those whose general view is that only limited change is acceptable.

Product diversification has been viewed as a means of increasing the stability of farm income, with a movement from 'traditional' foodstuffs to those that were once seen as 'niche', but which have rapidly become commonplace on supermarket shelves. Organic produce has been particularly important, with its increased production driven by a number of market shocks, partly associated with consumers' responses to growing environmental concerns.[3] First, agricultural intensification in the 1970s became associated with radical changes in many rural landscapes, including the loss of wetlands and hedgerows in Britain (Shoard, 1980) and the expansion of chemical insecticide use worldwide. A view developed that such changes were linked not only to food production and security, but also to cost-cutting, and resulted in more food (the mountains and lakes noted in Chapter 3) of lower quality and taste. Second, a string of health scares associated with fertiliser use, growth stimulants and disease control products dented public trust in factory farming. And third, a rapidly expanding animal welfare movement began to affect consumption habits, with shoppers turning away from intensively produced meat products. Consequent product diversification – a new emphasis on free-range eggs, 'traditionally farmed' vegetables and meats, and the rise in organic produce – alongside attempts to 'reconnect' with consumers through box schemes, direct selling and also by marketing 'farm-assured' and fully traceable products through supermarkets, has had a number of effects on the industry. Some big farms have turned away from intensive production, partially if not completely. And a new generation of farmers has entered the 'profession', viewing organic agriculture as a means of expressing environmental values. These changes have been generally positive for rural communities, though their effects have tended to be felt locally, further differentiating economies by relative sectoral strength.

The second form of diversification involves an element of sectoral shift: the replacement of primary activity with secondary and tertiary; farming and farm buildings with offices and other business premises; and food production with theme parks and bed and breakfasts. By the end of the 1990s, approximately a quarter of all jobs in rural Britain were in 'distribution, hotels and restaurants' (the standard industrial class encompassing tourism) with a further quarter in the 'public services' (Cabinet Office, 1999). Together, these categories accounted for six times the share of agriculture. Though the growth in these sectors cannot be attributed solely to on-farm diversification, the primary to tertiary shift signifies for some the replacement of a productive countryside with a consumed countryside, reinforcing an outlook of consumption with protection of valued areas for the appropriate economic function of the countryside. What has shifted more obviously, however, is the sort of goods that are being produced: instead of directly working the soil and rearing and harvesting its flora and fauna, today the soil, flora and fauna and their landscapes are instead worked into products for indirect consumption. National landscape designations – protecting areas of the countryside – work in tandem with this new form of indirect consumption, giving an economic rationale to conservation, which increasingly services a strengthening tourism industry.

Product diversification and on-farm sectoral shift can be viewed as the first two pillars of economic restructuring in Britain's countrysides, affecting localities in different ways. For instance, whilst product diversification at an 'industrial scale' is not local market-dependent, it is dependent on natural resources permitting such a change. Some key grain-producing areas remain locked into that activity, but areas suited to chemical-free production have been transformed by new scales of activity and critical changes in the farm labour market. More localised organic farming businesses have thrived in areas where there is strong local market support – concentrations of consumers who wish to participate in box schemes or attend farmers' markets. Affluent parts of the countryside, especially in southern lowland England, have seen an explosion of organic farming activity, supported by ex-urban households who see this type of agriculture as synchronous with their view of appropriate forms of rural production. Hence, this form of product diversification may go hand-in-hand with wider social changes affecting parts of the countryside. Likewise, the success of on-farm sectoral shifts is also highly location-dependent.

Switches to offering tourist accommodation work best in areas that are already popular destinations with holidaymakers, usually meaning that there are places suited to a range of recreational pursuits, such as walking or boating, perhaps in uplands, in coastal locations or in valued locations such as the National Parks. Leisure events such as paintball, quad-biking – or other team-building or stag-weekend activities – tend to work best in areas easily accessible to big towns and cities, and may have more limited viability in more remote locations. One of the consequences for many parts of rural Scotland of the growth of these leisure activities has been the reinforcement of their idyllisation as visitors' playgrounds, with contemporary pursuits slotting in – sometimes somewhat uneasily – alongside the traditional 'sports' (of hunting, shooting and fishing). Overall, however, the main conclusion here is that the opportunities flowing from such diversification will be place-dependent.

Location is also important for the third pillar of economic restructuring: the urban to rural industrial shift felt in many areas over the last three decades. A move towards de-concentration of economic activity was introduced in Chapter 3 and has been manifest in a tendency of some new and relocating enterprises to favour accessible, and sometimes even remoter rural locations, over conurbation locations. Keeble and Tyler (1995) attempted to chart this tendency through the 1980s and into the early 1990s. Using a range of data sets, they were able to show that during this period, rural settlements attracted a relatively high proportion of actual or potential entrepreneurs. Furthermore, rural companies – particularly those in accessible areas – achieved greater business success than comparable companies in conurbation locations: they were, for example, better able to identify and exploit target markets; they were more frequent product and service innovators; and they exploited locational advantages to a greater extent than competitor companies in more urban locations. The authors argued that this success built on post-war demographic change and a process of counter-urbanisation, which brought entrepreneurs closer to labour markets and to their potential customers. A similar observation was made by Massey (1984), who connected spatial economic restructuring during the same period to changing social structures and to an ascendancy of class interests over pure economic logic.

The evidence suggests that the trends established by the 1980s have continued unabated, and that the relative successes observed by Keeble and Tyler, Massey and others have been consistent. For example, the Commission for Rural Communities (CRC, 2008a) notes that between 1998 and 2006, England's rural economies – in aggregate – matched and occasionally surpassed the urban economic growth rates achieved in the rest of the country (excluding London). Business formation rates, business growth and output growth were generally stronger in rural compared to urban areas.

Coupled with migration trends (including selective out-migration and in-migration), growth in rural businesses translated into higher employment rates, increased household and personal disposable income levels and lower rates of income and employment deprivation in many rural areas. Such patterns can certainly be observed in more accessible, and even some remoter, rural areas of Scotland (see Scottish Parliament, 2001; Scottish Government, 2008a); and the picture in England is generally positive for a great many rural areas (CRC, 2008a). But there are two critical caveats to this analysis.

First, there is some contradictory evidence. Data from the Scottish Government (2008a) show that many small- and medium-sized enterprises in rural areas reported no growth in 2005/06, in contrast with good performance reported elsewhere. In England, areas of 'sparse' rural settlement, together with more peripheral districts, have consistently underperformed in terms of levels of 'gross value added', job creation, productivity and new business formation (CRC, 2008a, 2008b). Such observations are often presented as evidence of a complex picture of rural economic growth, with areas suffering particular locational disadvantages despite the generally rosy picture for the economy as a whole. Some areas are more fragile and vulnerable than others.

Second, the benefits of growth experienced in many areas are not always evenly shared. The migration trends noted earlier combine with entrepreneurial activity to reduce unemployment because those able to take advantage of new job opportunities move in, whilst those unable to take advantage move out. Hence, there is often a return flow of older households balanced by a loss of younger, less-qualified households. Such households are often displaced up the urban hierarchy, moving to nearby market towns where there is either a greater abundance of unskilled jobs, or where levels of unemployment (no longer recorded as 'rural unemployment') rise. It is also the case that demographic ageing – the tendency for some older, economically inactive people to relocate to the countryside –

may have a 'positive effect' on employment data. Because the number of people below statutory retirement age falls, recorded levels of unemployment also drop. Therefore, all of these migration flows – inward and outward – may mask true levels of economic activity in the countryside, displacing some of it to urban areas, and reducing the apparent rate within a restructured rural population. Some of these processes were observed by Pahl in the 1970s (1975). They are seen by some as part of a wider gentrification process (Phillips, 2005), and also as part of a broader economic reality in modern Britain, with pockets of disadvantage hidden behind data that tell a partial story and underplay the importance of individual experience.

Such experiences are part of a wider economic reality in which sections of the rural population – in some areas more than others – are locked out of both jobs and homes. However, pressure to define the essential characteristics of 'rural economies' means that inconvenient narratives are sometimes overlooked. The label 'economy' tries to capture and organise a disparate set of processes, but in order to gain a more complete understanding, it is necessary to untangle these processes. Drawing on the results of an international study into the comparative dynamics of rural areas, Bryden and Hart (2001) argue that the rural economy aggregation needs unpicking. These authors suggest that the 'rural economy' in fact encompasses a number of meta-themes, which have interlinkages.

First, rural economies are differentiated by cultural tradition, by established pattern of organisation and by the social conditions that they support. In Britain, the organisation of farming communities supported a particular pattern of community and of rural residence for many centuries (Martin, 1962; Newby, 1979). The restructuring of these communities, and of rural residence, is evidence of a fundamental change in rural economies, and one that it is difficult to resist. It reveals something of the unbreakable bond, however, between society and economy.

Second, economies are underpinned by their infrastructure and by questions of location and peripherality. Hence, economic restructuring has delivered an increasingly differentiated countryside, as different areas have been better or worse placed to take advantage of different opportunities. Location has shaped economic fortunes, and in doing so reshaped communities in many different ways.

Third, governance, leadership, institutions and investment all play their part in shaping rural economies. Rural areas in Britain have differentially felt the hand of national, regional and local intervention. Some areas (such as the Highlands and Islands) have been subject to policies designed to counter their perceived 'peripherality', and particular institutional arrangements have been made to guide their economic development, with investments made in specific sectors based on evidence of expected benefit. Likewise, non-institutional actors have also played a role in effecting change in rural economies, protecting farming interests, promoting entrepreneurial enterprise or supporting development. Sometimes, their impact on economies has been indirect, with more conservative parish and district councils resisting the developments that would have nudged economies in a new direction, or supporting 'traditional' enterprises that were felt to sit more easily with the character of a local area.

Fourth, the importance of entrepreneurship for rural economies is difficult to gauge, though the strong association between migration and micro-business start-ups in England is widely acknowledged (Bosworth, 2006). Generally, entrepreneurial activity – set within an enterprising culture – is important to any area and its absence has been identified as a critical shortcoming in command economies. Its benefits in Britain's rural areas are only difficult to gauge because uncertainty surrounds the way these benefits are shared, and – depending on the success of skills development – whether rural populations are able to draw down these benefits.

Fifth, the general economic structure and organisation will determine the shape of an economy and the extent to which it will be differentiated, either because of coincidental locational attributes or because of planned specialisation. The former is obviously more important in rural Britain, and the extent to which some areas have been affected by past specialisation has diminished.

And finally, human resources and demography will influence how an economy develops over time. These influences are not fixed. Regional planning has an important role to play in shaping the human resource context, facilitating the provision of additional homes as a means of increasing potential labour supply and thereby servicing economic need. Levels of provision in particular areas have a profound impact on local economies and on travel-to-work patterns. In some rural areas, demographic change is viewed as a hindrance to economic development, starving businesses of younger workers, and replacing them with economically inactive households.

These meta-themes provide some clues as to the strength of relationship between rural housing and rural economic development. As well as being an expression of economic change, community development and interventions around housing have a significant potential to directly and indirectly impact on rural economies. Housing is part of the infrastructure underpinning economic development; and it provides a context for the development of the human resources that all economies rely on. It is little surprise that housing availability looms large in narratives of the fate of rural settlements. Nor is it unreasonable that economic regeneration strategies for fragile rural areas should embrace housing concerns. The tragedy is that silo mentalities limit the spread of good demonstrations of joined-up thinking.

Linking to rural housing

Britain's rural economies have been subject to an array of distinct forces, underpinning broad pillars of change that have produced different outcomes in different places, depending on the particular assemblage of characteristics catalogued in the last section. There have been broad sectoral shifts and also myriad geographical consequences, mapped in a number of studies including those by Murdoch et al (2003) and Lowe and Ward (2007). The fortunes of rural economies have also been strongly affected by changes within urban economies, by both de-concentration and the relationships that many rural hinterlands share with core cities (Hoggart, 2005) and the subsequent bonds in terms of labour, capital and goods (Gallent et al, 2008). Whilst some rural areas have faced radical restructuring, others have experienced a far slower pace of change. Some of the most peripheral and challenging areas (challenging by virtue of climate and topography) – including parts of the Scottish Highlands and the uplands of England (NHF, 2009) – continue to derive their livelihoods from traditional rural activities, including hunting, fishing and shooting, or from marginal hill farming. However, for most of the rest of rural Britain, economic life has been revolutionised by an emphasis on product diversification; by protection of the countryside (and the implications this has for new forms of economic activity); and by tourism and residential consumption, which have fuelled the growth of the rural service sector.

Critically, protection creates infrastructural scarcity (limiting housing supply), whilst consumption further depletes the remaining infrastructure: together these create the context for economic development, limiting it to particular forms judged acceptable by those who hold power in rural authorities. Likewise, the combined effects of protection and consumption create the human resource context for economic development, largely by limiting housing supply to those with an ability to pay higher market prices.

The rural housing outcomes documented in this book need to be understood in relation to the shifting economic context and in relation to the effect housing supply has, in turn, on future economic development. A familiar narrative in rural planning concerns the repopulation of rural areas that had previously felt the effects of depopulation. Commuting households, retiring in-migrants and seasonal residents have filled the empty homes left by farm workers and by those previously employed in forestry or extractive industries. The effects of this bloodless exchange are often benign: newcomers spend money in local shops and on local services. They have income and wealth to spend on their properties, and so they engage local contractors and improve the quality of the local housing stock. However, there are also more pernicious consequences. Consumption of the countryside has fuelled the growth of a new low-income economy in many rural areas. The new farm jobs are in hotels, guest houses, catering and the leisure industries, all characterised by low wages, and by seasonal and informal contracting.

The economic and social changes that have occurred since the Second World War have arguably created a more difficult economic situation for significant sections of rural society. Much of rural England (but not the other nations of Britain) has seen the demise of the paternalistic landlords of a hundred years ago, who provided tied cottages for their workers. The relative social situation has also worsened for many, with rural residents on low incomes confronted on a daily basis by the conspicuous consumption of many new and seasonal residents: an experience that seems to deepen the trauma of being homeless, or inadequately housed, in the communities where they grew up.

In locations where local economies are weaker, and where out-migration predominates, issues of lower demand for housing prevail, and new affordable housing has a role in facilitating the social and economic regeneration of these areas. In Scotland policies to alleviate these types of difficulties are targeted at fragile areas, using mechanisms such as Initiative at the Edge,[4] which focuses on community-led social and economic regeneration activity.

The net result of this changed economic situation was neatly summarised in the title of Shucksmith's (1981) book on the subject: *No Homes for Locals*. Despite the passage of 30 years since its publication, there is plenty of evidence in 2009 (see for example, Best and Shucksmith, 2006; Taylor, 2008; Scottish Parliament Rural Affairs and Environment Committee, 2009) that little has changed.

Notes

[1] Notwithstanding the space problems that have crept back in to some forms of private housing in recent years, including low standards in starter homes (Karn, 1995) and limited space in some urban flat developments, arguably impinging on the utility of some homes (RIBA, 2007; CABE, 2009). We pursue this theme further in Chapter 12.

[2] Though a debate remains as to whether set building rates adequately cater for need or in fact depress rates of household formation (Gallent, 2005).

[3] However, middle- and higher-income consumers have been more able to express choice than those on lower incomes.

[4] See www.hie.co.uk/iaao.html

Part II
People and movement in rural areas

SIX

New residents in rural areas

In the early decades of the 20th century, the majority of rural areas were losing population. This pattern of change in some parts of Britain had been established much earlier on. In Highland Scotland, for example, many clan chiefs who had come to see themselves as landlords forcibly cleared their former clanspeople from their homes seeking general 'improvement' through commercial farming and forestry. Gaelic-speaking communities were particularly severely affected with those displaced either emigrating or being moved to townships in areas of poorer quality land. Clearance and enclosure also became a feature of feudal Lowland Scotland. Something similar had happened in Wales, beginning in the 17th century (as part of the broader drive towards enclosure in England and Wales) with areas of 'Ffridd' (between upland and lowland habitats, usually rough grazing land) being closed to upland communities, preventing them from grazing sheep on what had previously been common land (Thomas, 1967). In lowland England, the process of enclosure happened in several phases in the centuries leading up to the Industrial Revolution. It began in the late 15th century and was complete by the end of the 19th century,[1] expedited by legislation in the late 18th century (culminating in the Inclosure Consolidation Act 1801). The objective of enclosure – in later periods – had been to increase the overall efficiency of agricultural activity, moving from a system of three-field crop rotation to one of 'enclosed' fields, necessary to increase food output and feed the growing population. The process removed traditional 'common rights' (restricting such rights to rough pasture) and extended private ownership, establishing exclusive rights to profit from land.

The impact of these processes on rural population levels had been dramatic: consolidation of land ownership in fewer hands together with the transition to more modern farming methods underpinned a fall in the number of people scraping a subsistence living from the land. Clearance and enclosure have been seen as part of the rise of modern capitalism, associated with the loss of individual rights and freedoms. But, in England at least, they have also been viewed as part of the transition away from medieval ignorance towards scientific enlightenment, fundamental to Britain's Industrial Revolution.[2]

By the beginning of the 20th century, Britain's upland areas had experienced greater levels of out-migration than the lowlands, though all rural areas had been steadily losing population relative to the rapid growth in towns and cities, but also in absolute terms, for several decades (since 1861 in England and Wales, and since 1841 in Scotland: see Table 6.1). The Industrial Revolution brought unprecedented change to the countryside. It not only resulted in depopulation, but – coupled with growth in international trade – also ended reliance on some traditional rural products. In the 1920s and 1930s, the slate mining industry in North Wales was brought to an abrupt halt as new cheaper roofing materials became available. Tin mining in Cornwall survived a little longer, but it too eventually succumbed to competition from cheap imports and alternatives. Such localised events were responsible for a differentiated geography of rural depopulation. Whilst some areas remained relatively stable in demographic terms, others haemorrhaged population at a considerable rate. But it was the intensification and mechanisation of farming that dramatically altered the relationship between people and land.

Table 6.1: Population change in Britain, 1801–1911

	England and Wales		Scotland	
	Rural	% of total population	Crofting counties	% of total population
1801	5,883,276	66.2	302,817	18.8
1811	6,442,231	63.4	318,266	17.6
1821	7,195,702	60.0	361,184	17.3
1831	7,743,567	55.7	388,876	16.4
1841	8,221,022	52.7	396,045	15.1
1851	8,239,682	46.0	395,540	13.1
1861	8,282,168	41.3	380,442	12.2
1871	7,910,166	34.8	371,356	10.8
1881	7,794,322	30.0	369,453	9.7
1891	7,401,513	25.5	360,367	8.7
1901	7,155,994	22.0	352,371	7.8
1911	7,603,097	21.0	341,535	7.2

Note: Law's figures are recalculations from census reports with the non-urban population attributed to smaller settlements and areas of dispersion, low density and low 'nucleation' (Law, 1967: 130). Law calculated the rural population as a 'residual' of the growing urban population. In the absence of historic 'rural' data for Scotland, figures for 'crofting counties' (Shetland, Orkney, Caithness, Sutherland, Ross-shire, Inverness-shire and Argyll, with Ross-shire including Lewis and Inverness-shire including the Western Isles, Skye and the Small Isles) have been used here. Data on their population were monitored following the Crofters' Holdings (Scotland) Act 1886. These figures have been attributed to the Earl of Dundee, who presented them in a memorandum to the Scottish Office in 1965. They are derived from Census Returns.

Source: For England and Wales (Law, 1967); for Scotland Census of Population (various dates)

Given the above synopsis of change, one might expect to observe a draining away of Britain's rural population after the Second World War. In relative terms, rural areas lost ground to the big towns and cities. The populations of London, Manchester, Cardiff and Glasgow all grew rapidly during the latter half of the 19th century (from 1851) and the early decades of the 20th (to 1931), by 201 per cent, 150 per cent, 828 per cent and 517 per cent, respectively.[3] However, in absolute terms, the majority of rural areas held their own after 1945. Some experienced an immediate post-war fall in population, but the majority recovered in the 1950s and 1960s. Here lies the apparent paradox: whilst the number of jobs in the countryside plummeted (Table 6.2), population levels were maintained and even began to grow in some areas (Table 6.3). The population of 'more remote rural districts' in England and Wales,[4] for example, grew by 1.3 million persons between 1961 and 1991 (Allanson and Whitby, 1996: 6). Near-urban areas also experienced an increase: 'the decline in the farming population was more than matched, particularly in the areas surrounding major cities, by the movement of middle-class commuters, retirees and owners of second homes into the countryside' (Allanson and Whitby, 1996: 5).

This pattern of change is frequently ascribed to a transition from production to consumption. Before the Second World War, the link between rural population levels and employment in land-based occupations was strong. Those living in the countryside derived their livelihoods from the land and can be adequately described as being part of a 'productive' population. After the war, mechanisation eroded the link between people and the land, but counter-urbanisation began to return the rural population to its pre-war level. These were not the same residents, however, who had lived in the countryside a decade or two earlier: rather, they derived their incomes from town- or city-based jobs and came to the countryside to retire or to buy second homes. Many new residents were 'consumers' in the sense that they were not part of the 'productive life' of the countryside – rather, the rural population was 'increasingly free of farming as a source of either income or employment' (Allanson and Whitby, 1996: 7) – and they consequently brought with them a new perception of what village life should be, new aspirations and different values (Newby, 1979).

An extension of social networks also became a feature of rural society: extension beyond the confines of individual settlements, with these networks partly responsible for opening up the countryside to urban middle-class households

Table 6.2: Agricultural workforce, 1951–2008

	National data from agricultural and horticultural censuses			Aggregate data from labour market statistics		
	England	Wales	Scotland	Total UK labour	UK farm labour	% of UK workforce
1951	921,000	–	–	–	–	–
1961	696,000		–	26,189,000	–	–
1971	521,000		–	26,285,000	–	–
1981/83	505,200	66,721	76,295	26,223,000	645,000	2.5
1991	445,000	64,589	69,030	28,301,000	659,000	2.3
2001	368,300	56,362	68,816	29,890,000	455,000	1.5
2004/08	360,100	57,465	67,152	31,661,000	499,000	1.6

Sources: England and Wales (1951–1971) from Allanson and Whitby (1996: 6) (based on full-time equivalents). Disaggregated data for England (1983–2007) from DEFRA Observatory Indicators (B9 Labour Profiles): 'total labour force' includes 'seasonal, casual or gang labour'. Disaggregated data for Wales (1981–2004) from StatsWales (002831: 'Persons engaged in work on agricultural holdings'. Data for Scotland (1982–2007) from Abstract of Scottish Agricultural Statistics, 1982–2007 (includes all full time, part time, casual and seasonal). UK aggregate data from ONS (UK Workforce Survey), employment in agriculture and fishing, based on 1992 standard classification (seasonally adjusted).

who were attracted to villages and small towns in increasing numbers. Writing in the 1970s, Howard Newby observed that:

> There are now few villages without their complement of newcomers who work in towns. These new 'immigrants' have brought with them an urban, middle-class life-style which is largely alien to the remaining local agricultural population. Unlike the agricultural workers in an occupational community, the newcomers do not make the village the focus of all their social activities. [They] maintain social contacts with friends elsewhere, and if necessary, make use of urban amenities while living in the countryside…. The newcomer, moreover, does not enter the village as a lone individual … newcomers arrived in such large numbers – perhaps due to the building of a new housing estate by a local speculative builder – that the individual 'immigrant' found himself [sic] one of many others whose values, behaviour and life-styles were similarly based upon urban, middle-class patterns of sociability. (Newby, 1979: 165)

Table 6.3: Population change in rural Britain, 1951–2008

	England and Wales		Scotland	
	Rural	% of total population	Rural	% of total population
1951	8,193,000	18.7	1,529,506	30
1961	8,954,000	19.4	1,528,723	29
1971	10,568,000	21.7	1,516,936	29
1981	11,320,000	23.1	715,342	14
1991	10,073,963	21.2	538,341	11
2001	10,460,900	20.1	880,268	17
2005/06	10,606,815	19.9	na	na
2008	na	na	954,009	18

Sources: England and Wales (1951–1981) from Allanson and Whitby (1996: 6); Scotland (1951–1971) landward population estimated from annual reports of the Registrar General for Scotland; (1981–2008) Census of Population and annual report of the Registrar General for Scotland. 1981 uses population in settlements of 2,000 residents or fewer (166,167) and those not considered to live in a distinct settlement; 1991 uses the latter plus those living in settlements of under 1,000 residents (93,259); 2001 and 2008 use the Scottish government's sixfold classification of settlements (see Appendix) using the classes 'remote rural' (319,043 in 2001; 336,056 in 2008), and 'accessible rural' (561,234; 617,953), therefore excluding 'remote small towns'. There is a major disjuncture in data from 1971 to 1981 that explains the apparent dramatic 'fall' in rural population. Similarly, data discontinuities militate against comparisons from 1981 to 2008, though 2001 to 2008 can be read as reliable. In Wales, the Welsh Assembly Government uses a broad unitary authority split to delimit 'rural' from 'urban' and 'valley' areas (Welsh Assembly Government, 2008a: 4). Thus the rural authorities (with population densities below the Welsh average of 140 persons per square km are Isle of Anglesey, Gwynedd, Conwy, Denbighshire, Powys, Ceredigion, Pembrokeshire, Carmarthenshire and Monmouthshire (Welsh Assembly Government, 2008a: 4). Figures for Wales for 2001 (960,900) and 2006 (986,114) are aggregates of the total populations of these unitary authorities. Figures for 1991 take 17 rural districts using a '*Tai Cymru*' (Housing for Wales) classification. Figures for England derive from State of the Countryside Reports. The 2004 version of the Report used 'rural districts', calculating the rural population to be 13.2 million in 1990 and 14.1 million in 2002. But these figures have since been revised, with towns with more than 10,000 population subtracted from the totals, and movement to a new classification of rural areas. Thus the 2001 figure is now 9.5 million. There is no figure for 1991, but this has been estimated as 9.25 million given the estimated increase between 2001 and 2005. The big change in classification after 2004 affects all data including and after 1991 (for England and Wales) and accounts for the apparent 'fall' in the rural population.

Concomitantly, service sector employment (see Chapter 5) has grown in many rural areas, serving the needs of both the new permanent population and of seasonal residents. Although population increases have not been shared evenly by all rural areas and socio-economic change has produced a diverse mosaic of local outcomes, in general terms, rural populations began to grow soon after the end of the Second World War, and the economies of rural areas have shifted towards a consumption base. Data contained in Table 6.3 show a slow absolute growth in the rural population of England and Wales after 1951. The fall between 1981 and 1991 is a result of a change in the way figures were collected and recorded. A more dramatic change of this type occurred in Scotland between 1971 and 1981. Overall, there were about 250,000 more people living in Britain's countrysides in 2010 compared to 2001.

Two questions emerge from this broad overview of changing population levels and resident characteristics in the British countryside: first, what put the countryside on this particular trajectory, and, second, what implications has it had for housing need, housing supply and, more generally, for the way in which we conceive and understand the rural housing question?

The drivers of counter-urbanisation

Counter-urbanisation is largely a post-war phenomenon and represents an inversion of the 'traditionally positive relationship between net migration and settlement size' (Buller et al, 2003: 8). Living in the countryside but working in the city has always been a feature of life in Britain, but before the 1960s this lifestyle was principally reserved for the aristocracy with their landed estates. The immediate economic situation after the war – Britain's austerity years – did not lend itself to any sudden change in the status quo. But by the late 1950s, Britain found itself in the midst of an economic boom: unemployment was low; disposable incomes were rising; new migrants were arriving from the former colonies; and population levels were surging. It was at this time that the Conservatives sought re-election under the campaign slogan 'You've never had it so good'. But how was this prosperity, and associated growth, to be managed?

The 1946 New Towns Act had already established a framework for decentralising population away from London, Birmingham and Glasgow. But private speculators began operating their own decentralisation programmes, bringing forward sites for development in hundreds of commuter towns up and down the country. Many near-urban villages were transformed, almost overnight, into dormitories for the growing population. This process was facilitated by road improvements and the development of motorways from the 1960s onwards. New infrastructure and cheap mass-produced housing made the 'ideal' of being close to the countryside, in well-proportioned new houses, a reality for many households.

At first, counter-urbanisation was primarily expressed in the growth of commuter towns and the selective expansion of villages (with selection guided by Key Settlement Policy, which directed development to specified centres: Cloke,

1979; Sillince, 1986), but this flight to the countryside soon broadened, with greater numbers of people buying second homes (see Chapter 8).

As well as seeing the aesthetic or lifestyle appeal of the countryside as a driver of counter-urbanisation, it is also necessary to relate disposable income or the growth in real wages that occurred in the 1960s with differentials in property prices. People flocked to commuter towns not only because the countryside was on their doorstep, but also because prices were lower than in overcrowded London, for example. These differentials drive the same patterns of movement today. And not only 'pull' factors are at play: there are negatives that prompt flight from cities (Champion, 2000) including a fear of crime (and the counter-perception that the countryside is safer, especially for children), a lack of space in or around urban housing, the cost of accommodation in some overheating urban markets, and other pressures including the quality of schools (again, perceived to be better in rural areas), pollution and the general belief that city living is in some way a constraint on family life. It is virtually impossible to recall the number of films or television serials aired since the late 1960s that have promoted rural over urban living, especially for families.

The army of researchers who have studied urban to rural population movements frequently point to 'lifestyle preferences' or 'way of life' as an important driver of these movements (Buller et al, 2003: 24), reinforced by generally positive portrayals of rural life. Fielding (1982) puts lifestyle preference among four key drivers of counter-urbanisation: the others are the 'changing geography of employment' (resulting from the de-concentration that has been attendant on emergent spatial divisions of labour [Massey, 1984], and improvements in transport infrastructure as a facilitating factor); 'production-led decentralisation' (which has various facets, from patterns of housing production in commuter towns observed by Newby in the 1970s to the promotion of new economic opportunities in larger rural centres from the mid- to late 1980s); and 'government policy' expressed in local planning, which may stem the flow of migration to some rural areas, and inadvertently channel it to others. Today, it is generally acknowledged that the significance of these big drivers varies from one area to the next: whilst they 'allow us to frame the principal causes of counter-urbanisation' (Buller et al, 2003: 24), patterns are nuanced and different places endure different pressures and have their own experience of change. Second home purchasing, for example, is not an endemic pressure on rural housing markets but tends to have its own peculiar geography.

At the root of the rural housing question?

There have been many analyses of the 'critical differences' between 'traditional' rural residents and 'newcomers'. Most of these were undertaken during the period of most rapid transition during the 1960s or immediately afterwards. Ray Pahl (1975) was an early observer of the changing social relationships within villages and commuter towns, providing insights into the many competing groups that came to occupy rural places. Howard Newby (1979) suggested that traditional community became 'encapsulated' within a transformed, mixed community eventually dominated by new residents. Parsons (1980), applying the London-based analysis of Ruth Glass (1964), pointed to the 'gentrification' of rural communities, accentuated by planning policies that aimed to restrict growth for the sake of maintaining rural character, irrespective of the impact on some households. In the early 1970s, Peter Hall and colleagues (Hall et al, 1973) linked social change in the countryside to containment policies, grounded in an 'unholy alliance' between new rural elites and urban development interests, whose desire to prevent development in the countryside, push up property prices and generally make rural areas more exclusive had become a powerful driver of rural social change. Similar themes have been explored by Phillips (2005), whose research into rural gentrification has become the seminal work on the subject.

Other analyses have focused on differences in market power between 'local' and 'newcomer' groups, often arguing that the eroded economic status of locals (because of weakening rural economies) prevented them from competing for a scarce housing resource (made scarce by planning restrictions) with economically more powerful newcomers (Shucksmith, 1981, 1990a). The argument is that counter-urbanisation combined with the environmental perspective of planning caused a market disjuncture to the detriment of the traditional rural population, and all other problems have flowed from this basic dynamic. Furthermore, the debate over what the countryside is for, explored earlier in this book, was coloured by this population shift. Newcomers were not part of the working rural population: rather, they were commuters, pensioners and holidaymakers. They had no interest in reviving the fortunes of farming, creating new jobs for former labourers or generally promoting economic alternatives. They brought with them a different view of the countryside (which had also been one of the reasons attracting them to move in the first place): not as a working, productive landscape, but as a place of peace and quiet; somewhere to rest and recuperate from the rigours of working life, or of a working lifetime, in the city. The last thing they wanted to see was 'development'. This could potentially have an 'urbanising' effect, destroying the very qualities of the countryside that they had bought into. So as well as the basic disjuncture arising from mismatched competition between those with urban and those with rural incomes, newcomers sought to change the rules of the game, to strengthen planning's presumption against development in the countryside, and to prevent what they viewed as unnecessary and unwarranted change – to use their new weight of numbers to minimise any chance that the countryside could fall prey to development.

This is one basic analysis of the root of the rural housing question, assuming that the question is predominantly concerned with a mismatched competition for homes, the supply of which was made scarcer by the prejudices and presumptions of a population that arrived in great numbers in the 1960s. There is some truth in this analysis, though it is not universally applicable and has more relevance in near-urban areas of England[5] where commuters arrived *en masse*. Elsewhere, such prejudices were in the minority: the handful of second home buyers arriving in

North Wales in the late 1960s, for example, had little hope of convincing their neighbours to end future development plans, or see the countryside as anything other than a working landscape. The view of rural areas that took root in England after the Second World War has not been so readily adopted in Wales and Scotland, where strong planning restraints are not always welcomed in situations where they prevent local people from developing local resources.

It is useful, therefore, to stand back from this analysis and look for a more basic dynamic emerging in the 20th century. The first thing we can say is that the tensions in rural housing supply today would surely have mystified rural society a century ago. There has been a complete turnaround in the basic dynamic in the space of a hundred years. The same is not true in cities, which were under almost as much pressure in 1910 as they are in 2010: space is limited; locations for development are hotly contested; and prices peak in central areas. This has been true throughout the modern period. But the rules of the game in the countryside have changed massively: in 1910, there was always room for growth, but little demand. At the time of writing a century later, it is argued that there is hardly ever room for growth, but demand has spiralled. The joker in the pack is the planning system: oriented, as we saw in Chapter 3, to ruralities of agricultural production, environmental conservation or recreational consumption. Planning has been able to neither track nor respond to population change. Its concern has been with the broad distribution of population, inter-regionally, and not the intra-regional movements that have been central to the rural housing problem. Arguably, it has not reflected any understanding of rural problems, let alone been able to formulate a response. Too often, it simply writes many rural communities off as unsustainable (Taylor, 2008; Scottish Parliament Rural Affairs and Environment Committee, 2009), ignoring the demographic pressures they face.

Demography, planning and rural housing

An understanding of demography and migration is central to the planning process. How many people there are in a country, a region or a locality – and how many there are likely to be in the future – provides planning with its starting point. In Britain, government has been projecting future population levels since the 1920s and household growth since the 1950s. Its method for doing so has been constantly refined, but the basic approach remains unchanged. Projections are made on the existing population base and these projections are 'spatial' in the sense that they are grounded in the current distribution of population and are generated for 'sub-national' areas. The Office for National Statistics (ONS)[6] takes each of Britain's countries and regions and projects what their population will be year-on-year until statistical confidence in the projection falls below an acceptable threshold. In practice, principal projections are made for the next 25 years so, for example, the 2006-based projections run until 2031. Projecting on the existing base means that centres of population grow, in absolute terms, faster than rural areas, so projections reinforce the existing distribution of population and, when translated into development rates for the regional planning bodies, they also reinforce the existing pattern of residential and associated development. For England, for example, Holmans and Whitehead (2008) suggest that the 2006-based mid-year population projections imply a national building rate of 245,000 homes per year taking into account the future demand for second homes. This is all very logical, and points to the need to concentrate development in larger centres. There are good reasons for doing so: concentrated populations are easier to serve; jobs and homes can be co-located; utilities can supply water, energy and sewage at reduced cost; land-take is minimised; as is the need to travel. Development concentration has several major advantages over dispersal and this is why regional planning tends to favour 'sharper' growth over housing provision in many smaller centres.

However, intra-regional movements do not always mimic this ideal and individual choices – driven by some of the factors highlighted earlier – may result in dispersion to these smaller centres. This has happened since at least the 1960s and is part of a continuing pattern of counter-urbanisation, which has transformed many smaller rural settlements. Because this trend is out of step with the planning ideal of concentration, it may reduce access to services or bring other tensions if planning policy cannot or will not respond to the choices of decentralising households, or these choices adversely impact on existing residents.

On the issue of housing numbers and movement, planning debate during the last decade has focused on how market preferences can be incorporated into the planning process so that some of these local, intra-regional movements can be tracked and responded to. Looking across Britain,[7] the first Barker Review (HM Treasury, 2004) suggested that price signals might provide a guiding light, with planning authorities called upon to supply more land for housing in response to price rises that revealed local market preferences. In fact, these might become a means of tracking local movements, creating a more flexible planning process. Initial fears that this would lead to a proliferation of development in areas attractive to new rural residents – commuters, pensioners and holidaymakers – proved unfounded, even before the market downturn of 2008/09. 'Housing market areas' – the spatial framework for the strategic market analysis required in planning policy guidance – invariably include market towns and where additional land release (from pre-designated buffers) is needed, it will always be directed to these 'key settlements'. Price signals are a crude means of directing land release and work better in theory than in practice: in the real world, the vested interests, politics and planning of rural areas mean that these signals are unlikely to present a green light to speculative development.

On the one hand, this is welcome news given the special context of rural areas and open countryside, but it also leaves a major dilemma unresolved, and the planning system open to the accusation that it is unresponsive to the rural housing question. Villages rarely share in the growth now occurring in the market towns. The price of housing, driven in part by a combination of planning constraint and population movement, continues to climb relative to local wages and available credit, and there appears to be no solution in sight. Should, therefore, a greater share of future growth be directed to smaller rural settlements in response to continuing demand for this type of rural living and the inevitable pressures (causing 'displacement') that the locally working population experiences as a result? We return to this question later in this book.

An imported problem

It is easy to view migration and counter-urbanisation, combined with a loss of land-based jobs, as the root of Britain's rural housing problems. Migration has quickened the pace of demographic ageing in rural areas; it has fundamentally changed attitudes towards rural development and it has been accompanied by a loss of younger people, seen as the economic lifeblood of many communities. But the countryside is not overflowing with people. Three quarters of all British residents live in built-up areas. Perhaps the most basic question, which we return to later in this book, is this: why is it proving so difficult to house a quarter of Britain's total population on something over 90 per cent of its land area? Are rural communities being treated unfairly, redlined as unsustainable places to live by local authorities who choose to ignore the obvious fact that many British households aspire to live in the country? This leads to one further, and equally basic, question: should authorities (continue to) discourage such aspirations or seek new ways to accommodate additional growth in towns and villages?

It is certainly true that the problems of lowland England are not always replicated elsewhere; Westminster politicians may mistake the acute affordability pressure in Berkshire, Suffolk or the South Downs – underpinned by migration from London – as a general problem shared across Britain. The challenges faced in southern England are as distinct as the region's rural landscape, and the same is true for other parts of the country. Equally, different regions of Scotland and Wales experience different sets of pressures. But in all these areas, demographic change has had a profound impact. Its pace may be variable, but all of the changes that have been experienced have been accompanied by new relationships between people and the land, by new attitudes towards private property and by new lifestyles and patterns of economic activity. Demography is a fundamental shaper of the rural housing question.

Notes

[1] Leaving England with its archetypal 'patchwork quilt' of fields, which is a less familiar sight in Scotland and Wales.

[2] This analysis is less common outside England, where clearance and enclosure are rarely viewed as a staging post on any path to enlightenment.

[3] 1851 to 1931 (last census before the war): London (2,651,939 to 8,110,358); Manchester (303,382 to 766,311); Cardiff (26,630 to 247,270); and Glasgow (176,523 to 1,089,513).

[4] This pattern is more complex in rural Scotland, though this complexity can be attributed to the changing delimitation of rural areas. Generally, these have seen an increase in the population since 1991.

[5] This is also an analysis applied, albeit in a diluted form, to the Scottish Lothians.

[6] Before 2006, this task was performed by the Government Actuary's Department (GAD).

[7] The core focus of the Barker Review, however, was very much on southern England.

SEVEN

Retirement and ageing

An ageing society represents a particular set of challenges and opportunities for Britain's countrysides. The population of rural areas is ageing more rapidly than in towns and cities. Although urban centres are likely to eventually catch up, there is pressure to respond more rapidly in the countryside in terms of how services may be configured in the future to meet this trend. As highlighted in the previous chapter, migration is a key driver of change in the social composition of rural areas. However, the development of an ageing population in these locations is not just down to migration decisions made at the point of retirement, but also those made earlier in people's lives. Much discussion defines older people as anyone aged 50 and over. Lowe and Speakman (2006: 13) have noted that although this figure is an arbitrary one, it captures the period when people make most of the key decisions, choices and transitions that shape their later life. Furthermore, the implications for demographic changes in rural localities are also affected by the decisions of younger age groups. In focusing upon the rural dimension of an ageing society, therefore, it is necessary to consider the migration decisions that people make across the life course in terms of shaping the specific demographic profiles that are emerging in rural localities across Britain, and which are predicted to develop in the future. This chapter highlights the nature of migration decisions of older people as part of the overall demand for housing in rural areas, before moving on to assess the wider implications of an ageing society for rural localities in the context of housing and planning policy.

Older people and the demand for housing in rural localities

One of the consequences of global economic shifts has been significant blurring in the way that people in later life disengage or re-engage with economic activity. Stockdale (2006) has applied the notion of 'retirement transitions' to an analysis of the migration of pre-retirement households (aged between 50 and 64) into rural areas. This notion refers to the way in which the prospect of retirement acts as a catalyst for changes in people's lives including employment, health, lifestyles and marital relations. The same author found that migration behaviour associated with moves into rural areas amongst the pre-retired age group in England largely mirrored the migration patterns of post-retirement groups not only in terms of their characteristics, but also destinations in terms of rural localities popular amongst retirees.

Research has identified the extent to which retirement itself provides an important trigger for migration. Pressure on rural housing markets tends to be concentrated on particular areas, especially rural and coastal settlements in the

South West and East of England (Warnes and Law, 1984). Specifically, Warnes and McInerney (2004) highlighted the strong demand on housing from people of late working age and retirees in the areas of the 'South West peninsula', Dorset and Somerset, Sussex and Surrey, Cambridgeshire, Suffolk and Norfolk. Warnes (1992) noted the strong counter-urbanisation trend in this regard, with the movement of people at the age of retirement out of London, conurbations and other industrial areas into environmentally attractive areas, such as the National Parks and coastal areas. Similarly, Lowe and Ward (2007) identify 'retirement retreat' areas in their typology of rural localities in England, comprising mainly coastal areas. However, within the broad areas identified within such typologies, micro-patterns of in-migration by different groups are apparent. Shucksmith et al (1995) provided a classification of rural housing markets at ward level in England, identifying localities characterised by demand from migration associated with retirement (which were also closely associated with demand for second homes). At the level of individual case studies, Phillips (2005) identified differences between villages in relatively close geographical proximity in terms of popularity amongst younger in-migrants as opposed to retirement migrants. One of the reasons for these differentiated patterns of destination between migrants is the degree of congruence between individual biographies and the nature of the location where migrants move to (Phillipson, 2007). In relation to varying patterns of consumption, subtle variations in conceptualisations of the rural idyll lead people to seek out particular localities that match their perceptions (Stockdale, 2006).

For Lowe and Speakman (2006), all of these patterns of movement have implications for the rapidity of the development of an ageing society in rural localities. In this respect, the typologies that have been developed reflecting diverse patterns of socio-economic differentiation within rural localities will increasingly be overlain by the demographic imperative of an ageing rural population. However, Warnes and McInerney (2004) point out that the South West of England had been a traditional destination for retirement migrants over 50 years, a fact that has impacted profoundly on the local economies and services in many parts of this region.[1]

Nevertheless, whilst retirement migration certainly comprises one facet of pressure on rural housing markets, it is important not to overstate its significance. As Hardill (2006: 66) has argued, 'the popular myth that most people who move to rural areas are retirees needs to be dispelled'. Findlay et al (1999) highlighted that about 9 per cent of rural in-migrants in England were of pensionable age. A similar picture was apparent in parts of Scotland, where the profile of in-migrants into the Highlands and Islands was shown to be close to the population at large, rather than comprising retirees (Hope et al, 2004). Robertson and Satsangi (2003) have also noted that migration in Scotland has tended *not* to be associated with retirement.

Far less migration is apparent amongst people in their 70s or older, as might be expected given the aspiration of many people of this age to remain in their current accommodation (Clough et al, 2004; Burholt, 2006). Nevertheless, a distinctive trend amongst people aged 75 and over in rural localities in England is a movement out of the smallest settlements and into nearby towns (Champion and Shepherd, 2006). It seems that these migrants tend to make relatively short-distance moves, and remain living in local authorities defined as rural. Wenger (2001) also noted that older people in rural localities across Britain tend not to live in remote, sparsely populated areas, with a pattern of migration from these locations into larger settlements to be closer to shops, services and other amenities. Thus, market towns perform a crucial role for older people in rural housing systems (Gilroy et al, 2007). It also suggests a particular response to older people's 'option recognition' linked with living in remote rural locations. The notion of 'option recognition' was advanced by Peace et al (2006) in relation to the way in which older people respond to their ability to cope with changes in their lives within the context-specific circumstances of their immediate environment. A feature of smaller settlements in many rural localities is the dearth of viable housing and support options for older people, necessitating a move to larger settlements, not only where there is readier access to services, but also where a wider variety of housing choices exist.

The development of an ageing society in rural localities

Champion and Shepherd (2006) examined trends in demographic ageing in rural localities in England. In the 10 years prior to 2003, the number of people aged 75 and over living in the 178 local authorities in England classified as rural rose by 20 per cent, compared with 9 per cent in urban areas. Higher proportions of rural populations in Wales also comprise households of pensionable age (Peace et al, 2006). However, whilst the development of an ageing society is well established in Wales, it has not been a uniform progression in terms of its impact on different rural localities so far, as Milbourne et al (2006) highlighted a decline in the proportion of people aged 65 and over in rural authorities in Wales between 1991 and 2001. Nevertheless, Gallent et al (2003) highlighted the overall projected growth of older people in rural areas of Wales. They identified specific areas where ageing was estimated to have especially strong growth, with the population of Ceredigion and Powys of retirement age projected to grow by 26 per cent between 1998 and 2021, in the context of overall population growth of 8.9 per cent in these two authorities.

Projections at the time of writing suggest a substantial growth in the population of people aged over 50 in the coming decades. Significantly, in England, the fastest growth is projected to take place in rural compared with urban areas (see Table 7.1). Further, these projections anticipate that it is the most rural local authority areas in England, the rural-80 category (that is, local authorities with at least 80 per cent of their population in rural settlements), which will see the highest rate of population increase in the oldest age bands. For example, the population of people aged 85 and over in these rural authorities is projected to increase by 131 per cent. By 2028, almost half of all residents in the rural-80 authorities will be aged 50 and over (Linneker and Shepherd, 2005). Part of this trend also relates to the ageing of the post-war baby boomers.

In Scotland, projections have focused upon people of retirement age. In 2004, 16.3 per cent of the population were aged 65 and over. Even under the most conservative projections this figure is expected to be 23.3 per cent by 2031. Such a trend is a result of the existing age structure of Scotland's population and the long-term decline in fertility levels. Regional differences in ageing across Scotland point towards greater proportions of older people in a number of rural local authorities (Wood and Bain, 2001). By 2016, Perth and Kinross, South Ayrshire, Argyll and Bute, Western Isles, Orkneys, Highland and Angus will have particularly high proportions of their populations comprising older people; similarly Dumfries and Galloway is projected to have a significant increase in the proportion of older people (Scottish Executive, 2006).

Table 7.1: Population change in over 50s, 2003–28, by urban and rural local authorities in England

Local authority type	2003 Persons 000s	2028 Persons 000s	Percentage change
Major urban large	5,198.9	6,680.9	28.5
Large urban	2,458.1	3,127.9	27.2
Other urban	2,194.1	2,953.4	34.6
Significant rural	2,314.7	3,180.5	37.4
Rural 50	2,227.2	3,150.1	41.4
Rural 80	2,302.0	3,392.3	47.7
England	16,695.0	22,485.1	34.7

Source: Adapted from Linneker and Shepherd (2005)

A number of factors are influencing the growth of the ageing population outside of towns and cities and demographic change is a product of differing processes that are taking place in diverse rural areas. A key aspect of ageing in rural localities is that it is primarily the result of adults ageing *in situ*, as well as a consequence of the movement of people in later life into rural areas to retire (Lowe and Speakman, 2006). The movement of people aged in their 30s and 40s into the countryside is particularly significant in this regard and commentators have noted that the latter trend will make the largest contribution to ageing in rural areas.

The growth in the proportion of the population in rural localities that is older has also been caused by significant migration flows of younger age groups moving out of rural areas. Drawing on the 2001 Census, Champion (2007) identified a particularly high rate of net loss amongst young adults aged between 16 and 24 in the villages and hamlets in the sparse areas of England, with an almost 10 per cent loss amongst this age group over the 12-month period under study. A significant proportion of this out-migration is thought to be due to people taking up opportunities in higher education. Nevertheless, as highlighted elsewhere in this book, the exodus of younger people is not only driven by positive aspirations for moving into urban areas, but also reflects constrained housing and employment opportunities (Ford et al, 1997; Rugg and Jones, 1999).

To a certain extent, such constraints are driven by the displacement effect of in-migrants upon the social structure in rural localities, and the impact upon house prices and the range of housing options that are available to lower-income groups. The term 'greentrification' was coined to describe processes of gentrification in rural areas, reflecting the consumption of amenity and environment by migrants (Smith and Philips, 2001). However, Phillips (2005) stresses not only the importance of the movement of people in generating such constraints, but also the movement of capital within processes of gentrification in rural localities. This point captures not only the class dimensions of demand-side influences of population movements, but also supply-side impacts of gentrification. One outcome of the efforts by households to improve property in rural localities is the stripping away of properties at the lower end of the price range, in addition to the conversion of formerly non-residential buildings into homes.

The movement of people in and out of rural localities reflects a clear intergenerational pattern, but the impacts of these movements on access to housing also reflects the heterogeneity of circumstances in which older people live in rural areas. In terms of counter-urbanisation, Phillipson (2007) has discussed the dichotomy between older people who have the resources to exercise choice in terms of where they live, citing the migration of older people to retirement

Image 7.1: The 'chocolate box' cottage, Mickleton, Cotswolds. Such cottages are highly sought after by retirement migrants. © Betty Stocker

hotspots in rural areas such as the Cotswolds (Image 7.1) or the Welsh Borders, compared with older people who have little option but to remain in areas of significant urban deprivation. However, there is also significant population ageing in rural localities as a consequence of economic decline and lower demand for accommodation. As Phillips (2005) has noted, gentrification requires the potential for lower-priced property to be bought up by incoming gentrifiers, taking advantage of the potential exchange value of buying into lower-priced areas. However, in some rural localities, heavy in-migration is not (yet) occurring on an appreciable scale. Instead, the legacy of closures in manufacturing and primary industrial sectors in the countryside has still produced a significant out-migration of younger age groups, leaving behind a growing older population who, as Scharf and Bartlam (2008) have highlighted, may experience a high degree of social exclusion. This trend is most marked in areas such as former coalfield villages in County Durham, the Dearne Valley, South Yorkshire or parts of Fife in Scotland.

Responding to an ageing population

In planning for the future needs of older people it is necessary to understand how the various potential transitions of ageing are shaped by the experience of living in different rural environments (see, for example, the range of work undertaken on the experiences of older people in rural localities in Wales; Burholt, 2006). Certainly the level of debate needs to move beyond ageist assumptions about older people, or of descriptions of rural areas simply becoming 'ghettos of the elderly'. Contributions from both academics and policy-makers mean that such views increasingly look anachronistic, given that trends within the rural areas of Britain are a reflection of demographic changes across the globe.

The specific issues that exist in many rural areas around transport and access to services and facilities suggest that housing solutions for many older people might be advanced by focusing attention on the wider environment. For example, being able to sustain the ability to drive was found to be an important determinant of older people's housing decisions (Bevan et al, 2006). Planning for the housing needs and aspirations of older people embraces not only a focus upon housing per se, but also much wider linkages with the provision of services in people's homes such as social care and health services, or formal and informal low-level support that enables people to sustain their everyday lives in their current homes (ODPM, DoH and the Housing Corporation, 2003).

A highly relevant policy aspiration is for the development of 'lifetime neighbourhoods' (DCLG, 2008b). The rationale for lifetime neighbourhoods is not to exclude people on the basis of age, frailty or disability, but instead to provide a built environment, infrastructure, housing, services and shared social space that allow people of any age to pursue their own ambitions for a high quality of life (Harding, 2007). A consideration of what lifetime neighbourhoods might look like in rural areas is important for shaping future service delivery in the countryside. Such issues go beyond the physical environment and embrace community cohesion. Rural areas are characterised as having strong informal support networks and a culture of self-help. Le Mesurier (2003) has emphasised how informal support and help is underpinned by volunteering amongst older people within rural communities. These activities go to the heart of meeting the gaps in statutory provision with regard to preventative, low-level support. However, questions have been raised about the patchy nature of volunteering activity across rural localities (Bevan et al, 2006). Indeed, Oldman (2002) went so far as to argue that the belief that rural communities 'look after their own' is largely a myth.

There is an issue here about not confusing communities of geography with communities of identity (see also Chapter 19). Any settlement will have a range of networks and communities, with some groups of people highly connected socially, whilst others in the same community can be isolated, either through choice or adverse circumstances. Thus, whilst rural communities are traditionally associated with strong supportive networks, this perception can hinder the development of new self-help schemes, as there may be a view that needs are already catered for. Certainly the Rural Community Council in Suffolk has not made any assumptions in this regard, and has developed a project to use evidence from village appraisals to encourage the development of 'good neighbour schemes' where informal support may be lacking. Cloke et al (2001a) have highlighted the crucial role of local authorities in supporting voluntary sector activity. The way that informal support and self-help can be enabled, and itself supported by statutory agencies in rural localities, will be increasingly tested in the future in response to changes in household formation within the context of an ageing society. For the second and third decades of the 21st century, a significant element of informal support and self-help is predicted to be enacted *within* households, given the propensity for older people to live in couples. Yet this facet of households itself is likely to alter, with an increasing proportion of households living alone by the 2020s and 2030s (Evandrou and Falkingham, 2000). Far greater help in the future will have to be drawn from support *across* households, from the wider family, from the state or the voluntary sector, or not at all.

Specifically, in relation to housing and support for older people, it will be necessary to broaden the range of options available, including achieving a balance between specialist, age-specific provision and designing general needs housing to meet the aspirations of as wide a cross-section of society as possible. A further challenge is how the nature of rural areas themselves will affect the way such services can be delivered and how services might be configured to respond to these factors. Accent Scotland and Mauthner (2006), for example, made a distinction between remote and accessible rural areas in Scotland in terms of the way that services might be delivered in the future. They suggested that remote communities may need the provision of services on the ground, while in more accessible areas providing transport to services in towns may be more cost-effective. Locating housing with care provision in rural localities encapsulates this dilemma. As an example, one provider in Suffolk found that a very high-quality service could be provided to older people by locating housing with care in a village, but that the revenue costs were so prohibitive that such a scheme was frequently unreplicable in other villages across this district. Instead, market towns and larger settlements can play an important role as hubs for age-specific accommodation, and the development of extra care, within such rural areas. In these instances, services can also be provided on an outreach basis to smaller villages from hub facilities.

Two different approaches have been tried in very remote rural parts of Scotland. The island of Jura suffers from 'double isolation' in that access to mainland Scotland necessitates two journeys by boat via Islay. The development of a progressive care centre on the island has offered the opportunity for older people who need residential and nursing care to remain in their own community, rather than having to relocate to the mainland. In contrast, intensive home care has been developed on the Western Isles to enable older people to remain living in their homes, with further spin-offs in terms of the creation of jobs (Hall Aitken, 2007). The latter approach echoes the conclusions of Philip et al (2003), who suggested that taking services out to people's homes in the form of intensive home care in rural areas may be a more cost-effective approach than trying to locate specialist housing and support provision in smaller communities. However, the term 'cost-effective' is a relative concept, and repeated studies have highlighted the premia attached to providing services in rural areas in England (Milne et al, 2007), although this difficulty is less apparent in rural areas of Wales and Scotland, where explicit recognition is given to this issue by policy-makers within the health context (Asthana et al, 2003). Given the rapidity of demographic ageing in rural areas, a worrying statistic is that fewer households in rural localities receive home-care services than older people in urban areas (Buller et al, 2003). Quite apart from these factors, there is also a recruitment and retention problem in terms of attracting health and care staff to rural localities. In part this relates to issues such as career prospects, rates of pay and professional isolation, but also embraces the wider constraints imposed by local housing markets.

A significant development in policy has been a focus on driving up design standards to make housing more inclusive of the population at large. In England, the strategy *Lifetime Homes, Lifetime Neighbourhoods* spells out the intention to encourage the private sector to adopt lifetime homes standards (DCLG, 2008b). Crucially, the strategy set out an option to review the situation in 2013, with the potential to legislate to compel the private sector to build to these standards. Publicly funded new-build housing schemes will be required to adopt lifetime homes standards from 2011. Whilst the lifetime homes standard remains contested in terms of the extent to which it remains too narrowly focused on physical access (Milner and Madigan, 2004), the intention to integrate the standard into nearly all mainstream housing design represented a positive step forward. A difficulty in rural areas is likely to be the slow rate of accretion of new housing built to lifetime homes standards: an increase in the housing options and choices facilitating decisions to move or stay put in rural communities as a result of mainstreaming lifetime homes standards will thus be a welcome, but very slow, process. This suggests,[2] with regard to smaller rural communities, a need for a more short-term focus on addressing the extent to which the existing housing stock can best meet the needs of an ageing population in these areas. However, it is the very services that address the existing housing stock, such as care and repair services, which have a very patchy coverage in rural compared with urban areas (Molineux and Appleton, 2005).

Furthermore, the requirement to build new social rented accommodation to lifetime homes standards, as opposed to an aspiration for the private sector to engage with this design standard, means that it is the former sector that may have an increasingly important role in widening housing options in later life. The 2001 Census highlighted the increasing role that social rented accommodation plays for older people as they age, especially for people in their 80s and over (see Table 7.2 for the situation in England). However, the significance of social renting for older people is somewhat less in rural areas than in urban areas. Table 7.2 shows that about 31 per cent of people aged 85 and over in England lived in social rented accommodation in urban areas, compared with 19 per cent in rural areas. There are a variety of reasons why this may be the case. One reason is that social renting in rural areas has low supply. Another factor, highlighted earlier, is the number of people in late life making moves away from smaller settlements, and into market towns.

Table 7.2: Tenure of older people aged 55 and over in England, by rural and urban area

Tenure	Rural/ urban	55–59 (%)	60–64 (%)	65–74 (%)	75–84 (%)	85+ (%)	All 55+ (%)
Owner-occupied	Rural	85.6	84.4	81.3	74.1	68.6	80.8
	Urban	78.8	77.2	73.9	65.2	58.1	72.9
	All	81.7	80.3	77.1	69.0	62.6	76.3
Social rented	Rural	6.7	8.4	11.9	16.6	18.6	11.3
	Urban	15.5	17.4	21.0	27.4	30.8	21.0
	All	11.7	13.5	17.1	22.7	25.5	16.8
Private rented	Rural	7.7	7.2	6.8	9.3	12.8	7.9
	Urban	5.8	5.4	5.1	7.4	11.1	6.1
	All	6.6	6.1	5.8	8.2	11.8	6.9
Totals %		100	100	100	100	100	100
Totals n		2,769,675	2,378,132	4,059,956	2,632,067	763,935	12,603,765

Notes: [1] Owner-occupied includes owners with and without a mortgage or loan, and shared ownership.
[2] Social rented includes people renting from their council or other types of social landlord.
[3] Private rented includes people renting from a private landlord or letting agency, and those living rent-free.

Source: 2001 Census

An overarching issue is the extent to which the housing on offer in the social rented sector, particularly sheltered accommodation, increasingly seems anachronistic and stigmatised amongst an ageing population where owner-occupation is so dominant. One of the themes developed later in the book (Chapter 15) is the potential of extending the notion of 'flexibility in use' of dwellings not only in relation to design features, but also to the variety of ways in which a household may own or rent their home. Affordable housing built on a tenure-neutral basis means that occupants will have more choice over whether they rent or buy their homes (as long as a covenant on resale ensures that accommodation remains affordable for future occupiers). It remains to be seen how far the potential of tenure-neutral developments may erode some of the stigma associated with social renting. If affordable housing were built on a tenure-neutral basis, then support for its development in rural areas may grow, increasing the proportion of housing suited to an ageing population.

The migration of older people is a significant part of the pressure on housing markets in rural areas. However, the demographic profile of rural localities, both in terms of current trends and projected increases, is a consequence of a much broader phenomenon. As Champion and Shepherd (2006) have noted, the ageing population of the future, for the most part, *already* live in rural areas, and are households in middle age, growing older *in situ*. Projections suggest that rural localities will more rapidly be shaped by the consequences of an ageing society than urban areas, and housing policy forms part of an integrated response to address these future challenges, as well as enabling the opportunities that an ageing society presents. The latter part of the chapter has focused largely upon the needs of frail older people, as it is this section of the population that will grow most rapidly in rural localities over the next few decades. Nevertheless, the challenges of broadening the range of housing and support options available, incorporating improved design principles into new-build (at least in the social rented sector), whilst retrofitting the current housing stock, will enhance the potential for housing to play a central role in meeting the aspirations of households of all ages.

Notes

[1] The potential for learning from the experience in this region in terms of how other rural localities might respond to an ageing society was grasped with a research programme to examine these issues. See www.newdynamics.group.shef.ac.uk/projects/34 (accessed 3 February 2010).

[2] At least at the time of writing.

EIGHT

Buying second homes

Second homes have almost invariably been painted as the wreckers of rural communities in Britain. One of the most trenchant critics of second home purchasing, the journalist George Monbiot, argued that owners of second homes were 'amongst the most selfish people' in the country (Monbiot, 2006). In earlier analyses of the topic, he had drawn a direct relationship between the number of second homes across England, Scotland and Wales and the number of people accepted as homeless, arguing that a similarity in the numbers 'is no coincidence' (Monbiot, 1999). Whether or not there is any direct relationship, or whether second homes on Welsh hillsides would – in a different life – have been occupied by people now sleeping rough in Cardiff or Swansea, is perhaps not the most pertinent question to ask. Of greater relevance to understanding the wider rural housing question is the extent to which second homes are important and the degree to which they contribute to housing pressures in the countryside.

In England, the Taylor Review found no clear evidence that second homes greatly affected affordability for local people 'given other market pressures and socio-economic drivers' (DCLG, 2009a: 35). This had been the general view of second homes for a number of years, but local focus on this visible target had arguably kept the issue 'rumbling away in the background, sucking momentum from a much needed supply-side response' (Gallent, 2008a: 125). Second homes have, during brief and sporadic periods, occupied the minds of national and local politicians. Whilst the former have tended to dismiss the issue as a distraction, the latter – perhaps for political reasons – have emphasised the inherent inequity of second home ownership in countries and in communities where not all households are decently housed.

Despite a long history of interest in second homes, rather little of the literature has looked at national situations or moved from local observation and conjecture to more solid and broader evidence. Two levels of debate have accompanied the growth of the second home phenomenon in England, Scotland and Wales. The first has a local focus, is concerned with the plight of particular areas or villages, and tends to conclude that second homes are a big problem for rural communities. The second has a broader national focus, is concerned with the 'placing' of second homes within a larger array of housing market pressures, and suggests that the movement of temporary residents to the countryside has a slight impact relative to housing supply constraints and more general population movements, which bring permanent migrants to rural areas (see DCLG, 2009a: 35). In fact, the debate often pits the local view against national priorities and although many areas have pressed for a policy response (i.e. some sort of curb or ban on second homes), such efforts have invariably been frustrated by the lack of enthusiasm for bringing national policy to bear on what is still seen as a local problem. A search of media references to second homes in Britain reveals this local–national split: whilst the local press and regional websites (especially in hotspot areas such as Skye, Snowdonia, Cornwall, the Lake District or the Cotswolds) make regular reference to the impact that second homes are seen to have on local housing access, the issue rarely makes newspapers that cover any of Britain's nations, and then only when given impetus from the weight of local feeling and the 'sheer injustice' of people having two or more homes when others have none.

The evolving debate

Concern for second homes has emerged from the 'bottom up': years of lobbying by local authorities and pressure groups prompted a number of broader studies. It is difficult to pinpoint the origins of concern for second homes: they have always existed, but it was not until more people started buying them in the 1960s that they became seen as a problem. The evidence that exists suggests that growth in real wages after the war caused a widening rift in the relative prosperity of urban and rural areas, fuelling a search for new things for people to spend their money on. Property – long seen as a safe investment – became a popular choice. And it was only logical that this choice would be exercised in rural areas, for several reasons. First, rural economies were not growing at the same pace as their urban counterparts, meaning that property prices were not rising at anything like the same rate; second, the countryside was seen to offer recreational opportunities for the working population, and was being opened up by roads and better railways at this time; and, third, post-war nostalgia for the countryside was burgeoning, sometimes built on wartime experiences, attracting back former evacuees. A home in the country or 'an escape' from the pace of urban living: these became new aspirations in 1960s' Britain.

At first, second home buying caused few tensions. Those looking for property tended to concentrate their search at the bottom of the market, buying old farm cottages – sometimes in isolated locations – that had failed to attract local buyers. The initial wave of second home interest focused on what was seen as the 'surplus' rural stock, with buyers looking for 'projects' that they could work on during their free time. This pattern of buying was repeated in France and elsewhere in the 1990s (Buller and Hoggart, 1994) and because the continent has a vastly bigger stock of derelict rural buildings, it was never seen as a major problem. But in Britain, this surplus stock was quickly depleted and very soon a growing army of second home seekers were turning their attention to village housing in a number of specific locations: locations in which villages were perceived to be quintessentially English (e.g. the Cotswolds) or where there was good access to the sea or to mountains for recreation (e.g. Snowdonia, the Lake District and much of the Highlands of Scotland). Very soon, the local backlash began.

Wales became an early flashpoint, probably because westward migration (into Mid-Wales, along the North Wales coast, and into Pembrokeshire and the Preseli

Hills) was seen as a direct threat to the resurgence of the Welsh language in these areas, and second homes were considered a particularly scurrilous component of this movement. In 1971, the Welsh Language Society published *Tai Haf* (*Summer Houses*: see *Cymdeithas Yr Iaith Cymraeg*, 1971), in which it outlined what it saw as the second home threat to Welsh rural communities and the language. Indeed, second homes quickly became a rallying point for nationalists. In 1973, coverage of the National Eisteddfod in Ruthin was dominated by a speech by Emyr Llewelyn in which he lamented the 'sale' of Wales to 'foreigners', and urged his followers to 'buy back every inch and part of her' (Llewelyn, 1986: 246). A less peaceful strategy was advocated by Meibion Glyndwr (the 'sons of Glyndwr', the leader of an early 15th-century revolt against English rule), who began an arson campaign in 1979 that lasted until 1990 and resulted in the destruction of 179 second homes, mainly in North and Mid-Wales.

The weight of local feeling – particularly in the Welsh heartlands – resulted in several attempts to legislate for change. In 1981, the leader of Plaid Cymru tabled a private member's bill seeking a change to planning law that would effectively mean that a person intending to buy a cottage and use it as a second home would require planning consent. An almost identical bill was tabled again in 1998, and the issue of using the 'use classes order'[1] as a means of controlling second home numbers rumbles on today. Matthew Taylor (2008: 15) suggested that some English authorities should be given leave to trial this measure. But like previous governments (under Thatcher in 1981 and Blair in 1998), the post-2005 administration was not 'persuaded that the problem, such as it is, could be tackled effectively through the planning system' (DCLG, 2009a: 35) and that the 'implied requirement for the individuals concerned to submit details about their living arrangements would engage Article 8 of the European Convention on Human Rights, with its right of respect for private and family life'. The Scottish Government studied the feasibility of the same measure: on the specific issue of creating a second home use class, research it commissioned concluded simply: 'definition difficult, implementation problematic' (Satsangi and Crawford, 2009: iii).

Yet the idea that second homes (and other unwanted forms of consumption) can be 'planned out' of rural environments retains its appeal in some areas. During the course of his (2008) review, Taylor met various representatives of the Lake District National Park Authority, which had been a vocal supporter of a strong planning response to second home pressure. The authority was no stranger to this issue and had had its own backlash against second homes in the late 1970s.

The Lake District Special Planning Board (the predecessor to the National Park Authority) sought to use Section 52 of the 1971 Town and Country Planning Act to control the occupancy of all new housing built in the Lake District, restricting 'all new development to that which can be shown to satisfy a local need' (LDSPB, 1977). Its aim was to combat the rise in house prices attributed to in-migration and second home buying by requiring all new housing to be built for 'local need'. However, the policy was in fact counterproductive: the amount of speculative building declined and second home buyers continued to compete for existing property in much the same way as they had done prior to the 'locals only' policy. Research by Mark Shucksmith was instrumental in showing that the concentration of competition in the market for existing homes combined with the reduction in house-building pushed up house prices, further disadvantaging local buyers. The reaction of government to this case was particularly significant. It believed that the Lake District Special Planning Board (LDSPB) had tried to use a sledgehammer to crack a nut and in 1981 required the deletion of the policy from the joint Structure Plan, asserting that:

> planning is concerned with the manner of the use of land, not the identity or merits of the occupiers. Planning permission for a particular use of land otherwise suitable for that use cannot appropriately be refused simply because the planning authority wishes to restrict the user. (DoE, 1981: 10–11)

What government said at the time and what it continues to say at the time of writing, despite several changes in administration in England and devolution to Scotland and Wales, is that 'distortions' in local housing markets rarely warrant a general response that stretches across an entire county or region, let alone the country as a whole.

But absolute second home numbers have continued to grow[2] (see Table 8.1) and the issue seems unlikely to abate. Despite the experience in the Lake District, authorities are queuing up for new powers. Their local difficulties – often experienced by a minority of households drawn from the working population who are having trouble accessing housing at a price they can afford – are viewed primarily as being externally driven. Even where second homes are not considered the primary driver of housing shortages, they are held up as a pressure making a difficult situation worse. And this is probably a fair assessment of their impact in many local markets.

National figures on second home ownership in England, Scotland and Wales are fairly easy to come by (via the Census), but nobody really seems to have much faith in them. A principal source of information used to be the local Council Tax Returns in England, Scotland and Wales. The returns for Scotland form the basis of the 'rural' figure (for 2007) shown in Table 8.1. These returns give running totals, derived for local authorities, on the number of homeowners applying for a discount against their property based on its use as a second home (and the implication that the owner consumed fewer local services). The discount was scrapped in Wales in 1998 and dropped to 10 per cent (from 50 per cent of the full rate) in England in 2004 (the reasoning being that second homes undermined the delivery of local services by reducing the customer base) at the discretion of charging authorities, reducing the likelihood of all households applying for the reduction. The same discretion – within the same 10 to 50 per cent band – exists in Scotland, so creating the same difficulty.

Table 8.1: Second and holiday homes: national figures

	1981[a]		1991		2001[b]		2001–07
	N	%	N	%	N	%	% in rural areas[c]
Scotland	20,589	1.03	21,094	0.97	29,299	1.26	7.0
Total Stock	1,987,987		2,160,186		2,308,939		
Wales	22,615	2.06	19,032	1.58	15,516	1.22	3.1
Total Stock	1,096,398		1,199,883		1,275,816		
England	120,859	0.66	127,544	0.64	135,202	0.64	1.6
Total Stock	18,237,509		19,938,302		21,262,825		
Total	164,063	0.85	167,670	0.72	180,017	0.72	–
Total Stock	19,333,907		23,298,371		24,847,580		

Notes: [a] Census only enumerated dwellings 'unoccupied at Census'. [b] Census aggregated second residences and holiday accommodation (1981 and 1991 had these as separate categories, but all are counted in the table totals). [c] For Scotland, this is the figure for 'remote rural areas' (2007) provided by the General Register Office (GRO) for Scotland. It includes holiday lets. For England, figure (for 2005: 94,000) taken as estimate from CRC (2008a: 158) and calculated as percentage of households (derived from rural–urban population split in 2009). Figure for rural Wales (for 2001: 13,422) uses the Welsh Assembly Government's delimitation of rural authorities (see Welsh Assembly Government, 2008a: 4). It is not possible to arrive at a figure for the three countries together as the national 'rural' figures are derived for different dates.

Sources: 1981, 1991 and 2001 Censuses

The main standardised source across all three countries remains the Population Census. In 2001, the figures for England, Scotland and Wales, respectively, stood at 135,202 (Table KS016), 22,299 (Table KS016 Scotland) and 15,516 (Table KS016). These were the total number of dwellings enumerated as 'second and holiday homes' on census night, 2001, and represent 0.64 per cent (of all housing stock in 2001, including vacant dwellings), 1.26 per cent and 1.22 per cent of the countries' total housing stocks. There are two reasons why these figures are disputed or people have little faith in them. First, national figures are thought to obscure the true problem: that of local concentration – so why bother talking about national figures in the first place? And second, other properties, not listed as second homes by the Census, were enumerated as being 'empty'. Whilst some of these properties may have been empty awaiting sale or were vacant for other reasons (we are not talking here about the long-term empties listed by the Empty Homes Agency), perhaps being 'between tenants', there is a good chance that some were second homes. There is certainly evidence of under-enumeration for England, derived from the Survey of English Housing (SEH).[3]

Evidence from 2006 suggested that 242,000 households residing within England also had a second home in England (DCLG, 2006c: Table S366). Fifty-five per cent of households gave their reason for owning a second home as 'holiday home/retirement/weekend cottage' (DCLG, 2006c: Table S355). In earlier versions of the SEH it had been possible to discount 'retirement homes' from the second home total, but this was not the case in 2006. However, the data show that 13 per cent of all second homes in 2006 were located within London (DCLG, 2006c: Table S356). If we were to discount 'second homes' used by students, by partners in a marital breakdown, or by those working away from their primary residence (including the very topical case of Members of Parliament residing in London second homes and claiming housing expenses), then 45 per cent of the grand total needs to be subtracted. A further 13 per cent needs to be taken away if London second homes are to be excluded (though the total number of 'urban' second homes might be significantly greater than this figure). With these subtractions, the number of rural 'recreational' second homes falls to just under 116,000: 0.6 per cent of England's total housing stock outside London. However, the figure excludes the urban second homes counted in the Census suggesting that the Census does indeed underestimate the national total.

Local perspectives

Inevitably, statistics fail to tell the local stories, but inform national perspectives on the issue: which have tended to be rather dismissive of local tensions. It is important to understand both perspectives to gain a balanced view of the second home debate: although second homes may not be a big part of the national picture, they are a key component of the rural housing question in many areas.

Like parts of Wales and the Lake District, Cornwall has been at the forefront of local debate over second homes. Some parts of the county have had particularly high concentrations of temporary residents, including Restormel District with its two coastlines and the key tourist towns of Newquay (on the north coast) and Mevagissey (on the south). This part of Cornwall has excellent transport connections: there are daily flights from Stansted and Gatwick airports; a combination of the M4 and M5 motorways afford easy access from Bristol, London and the Midlands; upgrading of the A30 in 2007 now means that road travel through Cornwall is much quicker; and there are also reasonably fast rail links entering the county from the east. Combined, these infrastructures have enhanced the attractiveness of Restormel as a second home location.

The interior of the district is dominated by large-scale excavations, which are a legacy of the china clay industry. The Eden Project – comprising a cluster of 'biomes' (pod-like greenhouses) – occupies an exhausted clay pit and says much about local and regional aspiration to consolidate the area's attractiveness as an important tourist destination. A dilemma arises, however, when those drawn to an area because of its accessibility, natural beauty and local interest decide to stay. For generations, Cornwall has been a honeypot for second home investors and attempts to 'put Cornwall on the map', through initiatives such as the Eden Project, seem only to consolidate this status. Some jobs may be created in the local economy, and there is certainly a beneficial knock-on effect, but the basic differential between local wages and the economic power of incomers remains and is reflected in housing affordability ratios and other measures of local housing stress.

Successive 'State of the Countryside' reports between 1999 and 2008 revealed Cornwall to be one of five rural counties with the lowest average level of weekly take-home pay (CRC, 2008a: 79) derived from local jobs. However, the 2008 report added that such income poverty is often masked by statistics that suggest 'higher gross incomes' in rural areas, which are in fact the incomes of commuting households. In addition, 'parts of Cornwall and Devon' have the highest rates of second home ownership in England (CRC, 2008a: 46). In 2008, the Government Office for the South West reported that the ratio between house prices and annual workplace-based earnings for the whole of Cornwall (with the Isles of Scilly) was 9.7, compared to an all-England average of 6.9 (GOSW, 2009: 5). House prices in the county appear to have moved well out of the reach of local buyers.

The second homes that exist in Restormel (and which comprise 2.7 per cent of the district's housing stock) are concentrated in the coastal areas. In 2001, the key concentrations (as a percentage of housing stock) were found in the wards of Fowey and Tywardreath on the south coast (249 dwellings or 8.5 per cent of stock), Mevagissey (177 or 8.8 per cent) and St Columb (106 or 5.2 per cent). The local housing authority attributed three major negative impacts to second homes: first, an escalation of house prices in some villages (though the evidence to support this was not clear-cut, as the same villages were also popular with retiring households); second, a selective reduction in service viability, especially public transport, villages schools and shops; and, third, a disproportionate effect on young local households trying to buy their first homes. The benefits of second home purchasing seemed less obvious, with the authority suggesting that this form of consumption brings few economic gains, although the process of gentrification leads to the renovation of homes and can be 'visually pleasant'. The political response across Cornwall has been to propose new powers: to limit second home numbers and prevent the loss of 'local homes' to outside buyers.

The views of officials are rather more restrained. In Restormel, the housing authority preferred to create new opportunities for local people rather than restrict market access for incoming buyers. Controlling occupancy was not a favoured response and, instead, the authority wished to consider a wider array of mechanisms for increasing the supply of affordable housing: through the use of planning; through the promotion of self-build and shared ownership; and through a strategy of working with local businesses and landowners to deliver discounted starter homes. Although it might be wrong to discriminate against different 'users' (echoing the view of the Department of the Environment in 1981), there is no reason to incentivise second home purchasing. It is only fair, for example, that a standard rate of council tax is levied on all homes, irrespective of user characteristics. The authority was clear that no further 'fiscal penalties' should be imposed on second homes. However, the view that 100 per cent council tax should be levied on homes that might be occupied for only a few weeks each year implies a belief that temporary residence impacts on services and should be costed.

A study for the National Assembly for Wales in 2001 looked at five local areas: at Gwynedd in North West Wales; at Ceredigion in Mid-Wales; at Pembrokeshire in the southwest; Radnor in the east; and the area around the town of Brecon. The biggest concentrations of second homes in Wales were in the northwest (in the Snowdonia National Park and extending along the Lleyn Peninsular) and in the horseshoe of the Pembrokeshire coast National Park. These areas share many of the amenity characteristics – proximity to the sea, access to relatively wild and picturesque countryside, and the advantage of added planning constraint that is likely to limit future change – which second home buyers look for. Gwynedd (where 7.8 per cent of total housing stock comprised second homes in 2001) is an interesting case study as second home purchasing has been seen as a threat to the future vitality of the Welsh language. Indeed, some communities – including Morfa Nefyn (18.8 per cent second homes), Porthmadog (22.5 per cent), Aberdaron (19.6 per cent) and Abersoch (44.9 per cent) – saw a decline in the numbers of Welsh speakers, which seems directly proportional to the increase in second home ownership. Whilst the numbers of second homes had doubled, the numbers of Welsh speakers had halved. A link seems obvious, though these communities are also associated with weakening rural economies and other housing pressures, especially from retiring households who enjoy easy access to this area along the A55 expressway (extended and upgraded west of Conway in the late 1980s).

Second homes in Gwynedd are concentrated in the coastal communities (the coastal town of Aberdove, for example, having the greatest concentration at nearly 46 per cent in 2001), although there was some inland extension to the market. The local authority identified a shortage of 'family housing' in these villages as being associated with the pattern of second home buying, but added also that 'any change' or market interest in the smallest communities could have a big impact because the capacity of these communities to adapt to change was inherently limited. In contrast with Restormel, the prevailing view in Gwynedd has been that it is impossible to rely on a supply solution to demand problems. There had, in the past, been ample provision of council homes in larger centres, but this had not addressed the issue of community cohesion in the county's smallest villages. Similarly, the expressed preference was for home ownership, not social renting and there was a strong political consensus in favour of supporting this preference. This might involve placing restrictions on second homes, but it could equally mean promoting low-cost home ownership, centred on the existing stock. Perhaps the most powerful view expressed in Gwynedd, by officers of the planning authority, was that local people should have the right to own their own home, and that the planning process should support this clear aspiration. This would involve finding the means to curtail the amount of buy-to-let purchasing, identified as a particular issue around Blaenau Ffestiniog. In addition, it would also require restricting the conversion of village housing to holiday lets, which is a process being led by more affluent local investors, as well as recognising that second homes 'undermine village vibrancy', and so should be reined in for the sake of maintaining sustainable communities.

The contrast between Gwynedd and Restormel is interesting. These areas have shared concerns, but the favoured responses are very different: Restormel is focusing on housing supply whilst Gwynedd's concern is to house its local population in its existing stock. There are critical contextual differences between the two areas: the central area of Gwynedd is dominated by the Snowdonia National Park and therefore by strict limits on further house-building. But perhaps more importantly, the Welsh language has shaped opinion towards second homes and the appropriate response in Wales. Because it is not possible to restrict the occupancy of all new housing, and because the in-migration that development is seen to attract may be viewed as a threat to the language, the preference has been for mechanisms that could potentially reduce demand for second homes or ensure that existing homes go to local people. Hence there is an enthusiasm for the 'HomeBuy' scheme, where local families are helped, by housing associations, to purchase part shares in existing homes. It is also notable that the private members' bills, put before parliament in 1981 and 1998, aiming to bring 'change of use' of first homes into second homes, both came from Gwynedd MPs.

For some reason, the situation in Scotland has tended to attract less media attention, yet there are many areas that have been affected by second homes and some areas that share similar concerns over the erosion of local culture and the potential loss of the Scots Gaelic language. In part, this situation may reflect the fact that a proportion of second home owners in remoter areas of Scotland have migrated to mainland Scotland to live and work, whilst retaining their (often inherited) family home on various islands as a 'second' home (Jedrej and Nuttall, 1996; Bevan and Rhodes, 2005).

Indeed, remoter rural areas tend to have the 'greatest concentrations of second homes' (Communities Scotland, 2005: 1). One such area is the Sleat Peninsula on the south of the Isle of Skye. Despite its location (peripheral to the central belt), in the late 1990s and early 2000s the area experienced population growth, increased interest in the housing market and significant infrastructure improvements – including tourism developments – that have opened the area up to outsiders. Perhaps the most significant development – which made the island and its communities more accessible – was the opening of the Skye Bridge in 1995. The additional development brought by easier access to the island has been cautiously welcomed, though some see this greater integration into a wider economy as a cultural threat, potentially weakening the island's Gaelic traditions.

There were fewer than 70 enumerated second and holiday homes in Sleat in 2001, but this number represented more than 10 per cent of the peninsula's housing stock and was seen as a cause of house price inflation (Sleat Community Trust, 2005: 2), a phenomenon that had affected the Highlands more generally (2005: 5). But equally important was the arrival of an increasing number of retirement migrants to the peninsula, as well as younger people seeking an alternative lifestyle. The housing market was unable to absorb these pressures, and despite the relative strength of the economy (compared to other relatively remote Scottish areas), many local households were forced into temporary accommodation (particularly caravans) or into extended stays with friends and relatives. Some rented second homes during the off-season, 'but then have a major problem when owners want the houses back for themselves, sometimes just for a fortnight, or for summer holiday lets which command much higher rents. This creates a lot of animosity in Skye where incomers can buy into the housing stock and locals find they have to move out in the spring'.[4]

There was – and remains – insufficient building land on the peninsula, even if planning was to allow a surge in development. It is this combination of external pressure and physical and political constraint in the land market that generates difficulties for those households seeking homes at a reasonable price. In Sleat, and elsewhere in Scotland, second homes bear the brunt of blame for this situation, not always because they are the most significant component of the housing problem, but because they symbolise the unfairness that locals appear to suffer at the hands of newcomers and an apparently unsympathetic planning system.

The broader impacts of second homes have been examined in all three countries, post-devolution. Pressure to take a serious look at the issue in Wales had grown since the 1970s (see earlier). In England, the plan to do away with the Council Tax discount in the early 2000s provided the catalyst for a national study. And in Scotland, the early years of the 21st century saw growing awareness of housing shortages in many rural areas and a commensurate growth in the desire to place new limits and restrictions on second home purchasing, especially in more remote rural areas (Bevan and Rhodes, 2005). In each country, second homes have been framed in a wider housing supply debate. Respective national governments seem to share the view that the overall market impacts of second homes are uncertain, suggesting that generic policy responses – through the respective planning systems – are unwarranted or unworkable. This is despite an almost constant lobbying from some local groups who maintain that an answer to second home pressures will go some considerable way towards answering the bigger rural housing question, removing a major source of local tension.

Yet, viewed nationally – across all housing markets and all rural areas – the impact of second homes appears slight. Their importance seems to be inflated by political posturing: there has been constant referral to second homes and to 'change of use' powers for three decades, perhaps because local politics precludes anything radical on the supply side, or because the possibility of limiting physical change in the countryside has broad appeal. Second homes occupy a precarious position between two powerful currents. On the one hand, the sanctity of personal choice and freedoms lends weight to the argument that second home ownership is untouchable; but, on the other hand, the desire to limit development in the countryside creates a pressure to make best use of the existing housing stock and in some areas, at least, this means that second homes are a visible target. They are also sandwiched between national and local politics: the former sees them as being of limited significance, whilst the latter presents them as a critical pressure.

In England, proponents of the local view have found some 'comfort' in a 'rapid evidence assessment' of existing literature published by the National Housing and Planning Advice Unit (NHPAU) (Oxley et al, 2008). Glen Bramley's foreword to the assessment gives weight to the view that second home purchasing is an issue of national significance. His headline – and the Advice Unit's rationale for focusing on the second home issue – was a simple one: that the release of land for housing, and target building rates set by Regional Planning Bodies, should take account of the growth in second home demand:

> in the absence of policy action to constrain demand, for the sake of local communities and future generations, this is an issue that Regional Planning Authorities need to grip by ensuring that their housing supply plans take second homes into account. (Foreword, in Oxley et al, 2008: 8)

This message was read by some as an acknowledgement that second homes impact on house prices. The view of the NHPAU was that they *could* impact on prices and housing supply, but that they should not be allowed to do so. Rather, the planning system should be releasing sufficient land for housing so as to meet the need for development implied by demography, plus this form of 'additional requirement'. This view was echoed, in the same year, by Holmans and Whitehead (2008), who argued that the then latest projections of demographic growth implied a need for 230,000 homes per year in England, and that the demand for second homes – plus vacancy rates – added another 15,000 to this annual total.

Second homes will only be a problem if planning authorities fail to allocate sufficient land for *all forms* of housing demand. This is a hugely controversial assertion, particularly as the new homes being planned are unlikely to become second homes, but are more likely to be occupied by rural households 'displaced' from villages. In other words, the additional 15,000 homes to be built (probably in larger towns and cities) will 'replace' those rural properties in villages that are predicted, in the future, to be second homes. The Advice Unit's assertion that the solution lies in supplying additional housing to meet demand has once again been read as a call to arms: to protect the 'interests' of villages (though in light of the huge social changes that have affected villages, it is not always clear where these interests lie). Is opposition to second homes really a resistance to the additional development demands that they might generate? Or is it triggered by concerns over community viability and cohesion? Opposition is probably built on a coalescence of interests that transcend the division between 'environmental' and 'developmental' rationales noted in previous chapters. Working households, possibly on lower incomes, have joined with commuters and retired households in a new and perhaps surprising alliance against an inequity *and* a potential environmental threat.

Where we are, where we might go and the likely response

If second homes are not the principal cause of apparent housing under-supply in some rural areas (although they are a component of the migration driver), they often compound the difficulties faced by households who have a need to live in a particular location but are unable to do so at a reasonable cost. There is a case for allocating more land for housing through the planning system in locations where second home demand is high (see also Gallent, 2009a). There is also a case for providing more affordable housing, and this is already being done in some locations. However, where existing homes have been 'taken out' of the 'local market' (or, rather, brought into a wider market that extends beyond local boundaries) there has been an inevitable degree of displacement. The argument that land should be released for community need is a powerful one, particularly if it supports broader rural development objectives. However, a regional perspective on this issue (advocated by the NHPAU in England) will not steer development to communities directly affected by second home pressures. Rather it will create 'outlets' for displacement in nearby market towns and larger centres.

Holmans and Whitehead's (2008) assertion that regions should collectively plan for 15,000 second homes per year is paradoxically encouraging and worrying at the same time: encouraging because it offers an answer, with strategic planning authorities needing to take account of broader pressures on housing supply; worrying because it tells us exactly how many properties that are permanently occupied now may be only temporarily occupied in the future. And this could have significant implications for those rural communities already struggling to maintain service levels, and for rural authorities that will need to identify more 'innovative ways of providing the affordable homes rural communities need without interfering with the rights of second home owners' (DCLG, 2009a: 35).

Notes

[1] The categorisation of development types in the UK. A switch between uses is a 'material change' and will usually require the granting of planning permission.

[2] The apparent fall in Wales between the Censuses is generally attributed to misclassification (and hence, under-enumeration) with vacant properties not correctly listed as second homes. However, it is not clear why this seems to have affected the Welsh figures but not the figures for Scotland and England in the same way. Generally, it is believed that misclassification may have had an effect on all these figures.

[3] Under-enumeration is an issue of methodology, and methodologies are consistent across Britain. It is therefore reasonable to expect that similar issues apply to Scotland and Wales.

[4] Previously sourced from: www.bambi.demon.co.uk/Skyedata/housing.html.

NINE

International migrants

Until the early 21st century, the movement of international migrants into rural areas of Britain had been a limited feature of any population gains. However, the arrival of migrant workers subsequent, in particular, to the enlargement of the European Union in 2004 significantly reshaped the patterns of international migration flows. A key dimension of these movements was their scale. For the first time, many rural localities in Britain hosted significant migrant populations (Robinson and Reeve, 2006). Similarly, the Commission on Integration and Cohesion (2007) highlighted that the particular challenges facing rural localities were due to the 'newness of diversity' in these areas, which had previously seen very little in the way of ethnically diverse populations.

Reviews of the impact of migrant workers have identified a range of factors affecting the workers themselves, and also the broader impacts on the communities where they live and work (see for example, Rolfe and Metcalf, 2009). Whilst such issues include services, employment, social activities and community cohesion, the focus of this chapter is upon the housing implications of flows of Accession Eight (A8) migrant workers both for rural localities and for the migrants themselves. Whilst the largest number of international migrants in rural areas was drawn from the 15 countries that comprised the European Union prior to 2004, the fastest growth was amongst migrants from the new A8 countries, who, in proportional terms, focused as much on rural localities as urban areas (Chappell et al, 2009).

A8 migrant workers in rural localities of Britain

The A8 countries, comprising Poland, Lithuania, Latvia, Estonia, Hungary, the Czech Republic, Slovenia and Slovakia, joined the European Union in 2004. Traditionally, migrant workers tended to concentrate in London and the South East of England. The precise number of A8 migrant workers in rural localities, as with other groups of international migrants, is difficult to pin down precisely because of shortcomings with the various data sets that are available. All A8 migrant workers are supposed to sign up with the Workers' Registration Scheme (WRS), and it is this source of data that has primarily been used to map their destinations in the secondary analyses that have been undertaken.

A review by the Commission for Rural Communities (CRC, 2007b), for example, noted that A8 migrant workers in rural areas of England had tended to focus on particular localities, the data pointing to clusters in the counties of Herefordshire, Lincolnshire, Cambridgeshire, Yorkshire, Somerset and Devon. Further, the number of migrant workers in proportion to the local labour force is highly concentrated in some specific rural areas, such as Boston, Lincolnshire

(CRC, 2007b). In Scotland, there are concentrations in the (Council) areas of Highland, Perth and Kinross, Angus and Aberdeenshire. The movement of migrant workers into Wales followed a different pattern to those experienced in England or Scotland. For one thing, the number of migrant workers moving into Wales has been at a lower level than the other two countries. Between 2004 and 2006, Wales had fewer migrant workers registered under the WRS than Scotland or any region in England. Further, the type of work undertaken by migrant workers in Wales was different from other areas of Britain. Land-based activities have featured heavily in the employment of migrant workers in Scotland and England. In Wales, however, relatively few migrant workers have been engaged in primary industries. Only 3.7 per cent of migrants worked in farming, comprising the paltry figure of 270 individuals across Wales. This trend reflected key differences in farming in Wales compared with the rest of Britain, with far less dependence on seasonal and temporary workers than elsewhere. Instead, migrant workers in rural areas of Wales have tended to focus on administration, business and management, as well as the manufacturing sector (Wales Rural Observatory, 2006). Woods and Watkin (2008) found that about one third of all A8 migrants were living in rural areas of Wales, although there were distinct geographical concentrations within particular rural areas of this country. Four in every 10 WRS registrations up to 2007 were in Carmarthenshire, with other significant concentrations in Pembrokeshire and Powys (Woods and Watkin, 2008).

Multicultural experiences of rural localities

The presence of A8 migrant workers sits within a wider context of the experiences of black and minority ethnic populations in the rural localities of Britain. Indeed, the arrival of A8 workers belies two long-standing trends within rural localities with respect to race and ethnicity. The first is the way that the landscape itself has become imbued with a racialised dimension as part of dominant social constructions of rural spaces. Various commentators have emphasised how rural landscapes in England serve as core symbols of English identity. In particular, 'whiteness' is strongly linked with rurality in defining what it means to be English (Garland and Chakraborti, 2006).

The second trend has been the long-standing presence of a small number of black and minority ethnic groups in rural localities in Britain as distinct from very new arrivals from overseas. Specific rural localities, such as Boston, Lincolnshire have hosted waves of migration from a variety of countries (Robinson and Reeve, 2006). Other localities have been the focus of migration for particular ethnic groups (Chappell et al, 2009). Although the numbers may have been relatively small in the past, a critical issue has been the extent to which the needs of such groups are acknowledged in rural localities, leading to de Lima's seminal work in this area emphasising 'needs not numbers' (de Lima, 2001). Here again, social constructions of rural spaces are highly significant. Cloke (2004) highlights the pervasive theme of social constructions of rural space to create idealised or idyllic versions that deny the existence of facets of the countryside that run counter to the dominant discourse. Cloke (2004) argues that in the same way that poverty and homelessness are downplayed (see Chapter 17), so too are racialised 'others' denied a legitimate place in rural localities.

Dominant social constructions of rural spaces in Wales and Scotland may derive strength by a distancing from the deeply racialised notions of rural England. However, in spite of perceptions of a greater degree of tolerance towards black and minority ethnic residents in rural areas of Wales and Scotland compared with England, research has pointed towards culturally specific dimensions of racism and intolerance that pervade both these countries (de Lima, 2006; Robinson and Gardner, 2006). Rolfe and Metcalf (2009) found evidence that residents of Scotland tended to be more welcoming of migrants than those of other parts of Britain, excepting London, although they noted that migrants tended to be poorly integrated into rural communities in this country. This latter point raises the extent to which particular types of locality within countries may be viewed as more racialised than others: Robinson and Reeve (2006) reviewed evidence that black and minority ethnic groups perceived rural areas, suburbs and estates dominated by social rented housing as more likely to be unwelcoming places than other types of neighbourhood.

In charting rural dimensions of intolerance and bigotry, Cloke (2004: 23) draws attention to the distinction between 'race', which marks out difference based on skin colour, and 'ethnicity', which defines groups linked by birth and which expresses their cultures and lifestyles. Although it is recognised that this definition is not without its critics (de Lima, 2004), it does nevertheless allow a distinction to be drawn between majority ethnic populations across the countries within Britain and the diverse international migrants from the European Union. A8 migrant workers thus form part of a wider constituency of black and minority ethnic residents in rural areas who have moved directly from overseas into rural areas, as well as British-born black and minority ethnic groups who have moved into and between rural localities. In spite of the heterogeneity of black and minority ethnic residents, one point of commonality and shared risk remains the potential for experiencing racism (Garland and Chakraborti, 2006).

It has been argued that one way in which social constructions of rural spaces have found practical expression has been in the historical denial of negative experiences of black and minority ethnic groups by policy-makers and agencies operating in rural areas. Local studies have formed part of the impetus to highlight specific rural dimensions to the experience of racism and intolerance that can be distinguished from metropolitan areas of Britain. Nevertheless, Neal (2002) noted some shift in the responses of agencies, with increasing attention given to the development of strategies to combat racism in rural localities. Further, the arrival of A8 migrants in rural localities provided the catalyst for more considered responses by agencies (such as the Commission for Rural Communities), not only in relation to tackling intolerance, but also providing advice and information to try and ease the process of assimilation for migrant workers, as well as trying to diffuse tensions between migrants and host communities.

Such local developments sit within the broader context of the recognition of the role that migrant workers can play in rural localities. There are a range of demographic and economic imperatives that have been recognised by national governments, at least, in attracting international migrant workers. In Scotland, in particular, policy-making at national level has sought to mitigate the twin impacts of long-term depopulation and demographic ageing through the encouragement of international migrants into Scotland. Rolfe and Metcalf (2009) draw attention to the anticipated key role that migrants will play in achieving the Scottish government's targets for growth not only in terms of its population, but also the nation's GDP. Tensions within rural communities may not necessarily only arise along racial lines, therefore, and may also have a demographic aspect. Areas that have witnessed the gradual ageing of their constituent populations have seen a sudden sharp rise in much younger age groups, as migrant workers move in to meet the needs of local businesses for labour, which may lead to the potential for intergenerational conflict.

Migrant workers and housing

Differential patterns of access to housing in rural areas has been characterised as low-income groups being outbid for increasingly expensive housing by relatively wealthy migrants, mostly comprising commuters and/or retirees and second home owners (see Chapters 6, 7 and 8). However, the arrival of migrant workers has had distinct and very different impacts on rural communities, adding to the complexity of demand for rural housing. For one thing, unlike other housing consumption classes, migrant workers may well be competing directly with other low-income groups in the housing market for limited supplies of accommodation, especially in the privately rented sector.

The issue here for local housing markets is the loss of accommodation suited to families as such properties are converted for multiple occupation. From the perspective of migrant workers themselves, a further question mark hanging over the supply of rural housing in the private sector for low-income groups has been the quality of accommodation that is available. As is highlighted in Chapter 15, a theme running through historical descriptions of housing provision for working people in the rural private rented sector, and the tied sub-sector specifically, has been for offering poor quality housing linked with insecure tenancy arrangements and insecure employment. The proliferation of A8 migrant workers in some rural areas has added a fresh impetus to this long-standing trend, with an intensification of a supply of housing with poor conditions in response to the housing requirements of these working households.

Whilst it is necessary to recognise the diverse housing experiences of A8 migrant workers, a significant issue is the extent to which they have created a new housing demand group in rural localities. In this regard, the arrival of A8 migrants has greatly enlarged a housing consumption class at the very bottom of the housing market. It is possible to put forward a housing consumption class made up of a range of diverse groups, characterised by their weak position in the housing market, and also their presence in rural areas for employment purposes. Spedding (2007) identified the following range of groups as making up migrant labour in Britain: people from local towns and villages; Travellers and Gypsies; EU nationals; students; and, finally, illegal workers. The housing needs and experiences of these groups will vary according to the diversity of their particular circumstances. Furthermore, overlaying some of these groups is the potential experience of racism based on their minority ethnic status, in particular with relation to their housing options. For example, there is a very rich literature detailing the experiences of Gypsy Travellers, especially the poor fit between the nomadic lifestyles of some Gypsy Travellers and the 'sedentarist' perspectives of planning authorities and housing providers (Niner, 2004). It is the potentially vulnerable situation of these diverse groups with respect to local housing markets that has enabled unscrupulous operators in both the housing and employment markets to take advantage of the situation.

The seasonal and temporary nature of the work undertaken by migrant workers is also reflected in the impact on the more insecure parts of the housing market, and there is a disproportionate impact on the private rented sector. Some areas have seen a sharp rise in the number of houses in multiple occupation (HMOs) resultant on the influx of migrant workers. One potential problem for migrant workers is that not only may the standard of accommodation be poor, but they may be expected to live in overcrowded conditions. Case studies from various parts of the country have identified the existence of overcrowding. However, not all overcrowding is a result of deliberate exploitation by landlords and/or employers. In some instances, landlords are unaware of tenants subletting to friends or relatives. In part, subletting like this may enable new arrivals to the UK to settle in amongst friends, or provide a way of reducing the rent (Integration Lincolnshire, 2007). In addition, within the privately rented sector, the provision of tied accommodation for migrant workers can be a significant feature in rural areas, and research has highlighted the vulnerable position of many migrant workers in this sub-sector.

Marginal forms of housing

Commentators have highlighted how labour market and housing market circumstances combine in different rural localities to produce very diverse outcomes for migrant workers. The Audit Commission (2007) noted that in some rural areas, such as the Fens in East Anglia, pressure on housing for migrant workers tends to be focused upon neighbouring urban areas, with workers being bussed into the surrounding rural areas to work. In contrast, the Audit Commission (2007) also highlighted that the very seasonal nature of agricultural employment in Cornwall and Herefordshire, linked with the limited supply of low-cost housing in these counties, has led to the proliferation of caravan sites for migrant workers.

Another local study around Evesham in Worcestershire found that the potential impact on the local housing market was limited partly because of the greater use of marginal accommodation outside of the permanent housing stock, such as caravans (Fox and Gullen, 2006).

Thus, although there is the perception that migrant workers are putting pressure on the existing rural housing stock, and taking housing away from local indigenous inhabitants, a feature of migrant worker accommodation in some rural areas is the number housed in forms of non-permanent housing that are in addition to the residential dwelling stock. Research in Scotland has also identified the use of non-permanent accommodation such as caravans and portacabins as well as farm buildings for migrant workers (de Lima et al, 2005).

The use of non-permanent accommodation in this way presents difficulties for local authorities in terms of monitoring the conditions in which people are living because of the amount of accommodation that is dotted about the landscape and that remains hidden from official view. The danger in this situation is that migrant workers are put at an unacceptable level of risk by some landlords and employers, who remain unchallenged by agencies with the powers to enforce minimum standards, as a result of the hidden nature of such accommodation. The result is a small, but steady, stream of fatalities and injuries. A fire in a caravan is nine times more likely to lead to death or injury than in a house (Wiltshire Fire Service, 2009). As a result of a fire in 2007, which caused fatalities on an unlicensed caravan site in Arbroath, Scotland, Angus Council acted to bring together legislation that would enable it to monitor and challenge poor housing conditions amongst migrant workers. A key element of this approach was a successful application to the Scottish Government to have an exemption from licensing for caravan or portacabin accommodation on agricultural land (originating in the 1960 Caravan Sites and Control of Development Act) lifted. This enabled the local authority to provide better protection for migrant workers by ensuring that a minimum standard of health and safety could be applied to all caravan sites across the district, no matter where or who was accommodated. Since the 2007 fire, inspections on 21 sites accommodating 1,800 migrant workers led to most farmers in the district taking significant steps to improve the accommodation offered to their workers. Leaving aside the abysmal level of protection afforded to *any* residents of mobile homes by the current legislative frameworks in Britain, it is still surprising that the closure of this gap in the 1960 Act has not been mainstreamed by national governments or more widely taken up by other authorities.

In England, other potential ways that local authorities can enforce standards for migrant workers in both bricks and mortar and mobile homes have been reviewed by Diacon et al (2008), and the agency that oversees enforcement activity for local authorities, the Local Authorities Coordinators of Regulatory Services (LACORS), has set out the activities that local authorities can undertake with respect to the housing of migrant workers. Joint working between housing agencies and the Gangmaster Licensing Authority has been highlighted. The Gangmaster Licensing Authority was established in 2005 to prevent the exploitation of workers in a range of primary industries after the deaths of migrant workers in Morecambe Bay. A significant part of its remit covered the accommodation of workers, and 30 out of 87 refusal and revocation cases with respect to licences were a result of the failure of gangmasters to provide an adequate standard of accommodation (Pati, 2008). However, in spite of the advances that have been made, it remains the case that some of the most vulnerable members of society, including migrant workers, have been left exposed to poor housing conditions, because the work that local authorities can undertake has been hamstrung by inadequate resourcing, as well as cuts and staff shortages amongst environmental health officers (Chappell et al, 2009).

Rural economies and low-cost housing

The debate over the impacts of the migration of workers from other countries into Britain's rural areas provides an illustration of the wider tensions over the role of the countryside. The presence of large numbers of migrant workers is a very visible marker of the role of rural localities as spaces of production, rather than just consumption. However, the issue of recruitment and retention of employees on relatively low wages in rural areas goes beyond the posts that migrant workers have tended to fill in agriculture, food processing and the hotel and catering sectors. Care agencies, including health and social care departments, also experience difficulties in filling posts and holding on to staff in rural areas. That has not stopped some commentators – such as those of the *Daily Telegraph* – from conflating cause and effect, and accusing migrant workers of causing young people to leave the countryside (Tibbetts, 2007). This type of accusation has resonances with the problems ascribed to second home owners in spite of evidence to the contrary, which shows that it is much wider societal processes that are driving changes in rural housing markets.

Such views conveniently ignore research that has sought the opinions of businesses in rural areas: these emphasise the extent to which migrant workers have enabled rural businesses to sustain themselves in the face of labour shortages. Research in both England and Wales has detailed the use of migrant workers engaged in land-based work in rural areas. These studies reported that businesses were relying on migrant workers because land-based activities were perceived as unattractive by the local workforce. However, some businesses went further, and rated demeanour, enthusiasm and team-working as necessary to do the job above technical skills or experience, which they are often willing to provide for suitable candidates. Overseas workers were often viewed as more likely to have these skills than UK nationals available to do similar work. Similarly, employers felt there was an 'attitude gap' rather than a skills gap, especially in younger UK workers, who were seen as unmotivated and unwilling to take low-skilled or seasonal jobs (Lantra, 2007: 5). On the other hand, it is not clear how far such descriptions about 'attitude' are a euphemism for not wanting employees who have a greater awareness of, and readiness to articulate, their housing and employment rights. A review of British evidence showed that all studies involving employer interviews found that available local labour compared poorly with migrants, but that there was also evidence of poor employment practice in relation to migrant workers, including the use of temporary contracts, exploitation by agencies, breach of regulations on working hours and sex discrimination (Rolfe and Metcalf, 2009).

Furthermore, predictions suggest that employers in the rural localities of Britain will have to compete more aggressively for migrant workers in the future if they want to sustain this supply of labour for their sectors of the economy. Pollard et al (2008) highlighted a combination of factors that have led to the conclusion that the number of new arrivals is likely to fall. These factors run deeper than the current recession. They include the improving economic conditions of sending countries; the diversion of workers to alternative destinations, as other EU states relax their restrictions on A8 and A2 nationals; the devaluation of the pound, and lastly, changing demographies of sending countries, with fewer young people (Pollard et al, 2008: 6). Not only that, but the migrant workers who remain in Britain will increasingly resemble the socio-economic profile of the ethnic majority, as they move away from low-income work and into employment in other parts of the economy. As Jentsch et al (2007) have argued with respect to Scotland, migrant workers may well take a cue from indigenous young people in rural localities, in that to get on you have to get out of the countryside. One of the principal barriers in many rural localities for migrant workers has been noted as the high cost of accommodation (de Lima et al, 2005; Chappell et al, 2009). Nevertheless, as patterns of movement between countries develop, and word spreads of migrants' experiences within sending countries, it is the quality, as well as the supply, of rented housing that has a role to play in encouraging migrants to continue to travel to the rural parts of Britain to take up work.

The rapid increase in the number of A8 migrant workers has represented a new challenge for many rural localities. In particular, the shortages of available, and suitable, accommodation for workers on low incomes in rural areas have been thrown into sharp relief by the arrival of international migrants, and by the use of insecure and substandard accommodation to meet the gaps. Key recommendations from reviews acknowledge that the housing requirements of migrant workers are part of a bigger picture with regard to the relative dearth of accommodation in rural localities that is available for any low-income households (Pollard et al, 2008). It is traditional at this point in any treatise about housing in rural areas to call for an increase in the supply of affordable housing. Increasing the supply of affordable housing through social rented accommodation is entirely laudable for many reasons, but is only indirectly relevant for most migrant workers. Kofman et al (2009) noted that migrant workers are under-represented in social rented accommodation, largely as a result of the stricter eligibility rules they have been required to meet for such housing. Indeed, in spite of the guidance from national governments in England and Scotland, Kofman et al (2009) suggested that there are widespread anecdotal reports of discrimination taking place at local authority level, with migrants being turned down for help. In terms of diffusing tensions between host communities and incoming migrants, part of the role that agencies can perform in rural areas is getting this message across: migrant workers have thus far had limited access to social rented housing, and a relatively low rate of acceptance as homeless compared with applications.

Instead, the needs of migrant workers require alternative, more specific, policy responses. The high proportion of migrant workers in the private rented sector suggests that it is this tenure where greater attention needs to be focused. The issue here is not only about encouraging supply. It is also about ensuring that the regulatory and enforcement functions of local authorities with regard to private sector housing receive a sufficiently high priority (Chappell et al, 2009). It is unfortunate to be talking about the necessity for re-prioritising a previously under-resourced area of local government at a time when the country is entering a period of public spending restraint. Nevertheless, the issue goes beyond migrant workers, and embraces how some of the most vulnerable members of society are protected, or not.

Part III
Planning, housing supply and local need

TEN

Planning and land for housing

In the mid-1990s, as Chancellor of the Exchequer, Gordon Brown commissioned a report on planning, housing supply and the economy. The Barker Review (HM Treasury, 2004) was prompted by concern that Britain's economic performance was being held back by planning constraints affecting particularly the allocation of land for housing. The Review, and a number of commentaries alongside it, suggested that there was indeed evidence to support such a correlation and that compared to its counterparts elsewhere in Europe, or the OECD, Britain has endured persistently low housing supply elasticity. That is, that UK housing plc tends not to bring new supply on to the market fast enough when prices increase. Land is, of course, a key ingredient in housing development and so fingers of blame were pointed at the volume of land available for housing and the speed at which that land is released.

Whilst Barker devoted most of her attention to regional planning and to the big cities (and especially to London), for many rural housing commentators this debate seemed like a tour around all-too-familiar territory. Similar evidence pointing to a slow and ineffective planning process, unable to keep pace with housing need or demand, had been presented intermittently over the previous 30 years. In this chapter we look at policy and outcomes at the end of the 2000s, tracing the persistence of the debate and its links with representations of the countryside since the 1970s. We also consider the latest developments, especially the call for a market perspective and more responsive land release (serving 'affordability'). We argue that one of the implications of strategic market assessment and the drawing of 'housing market areas' (noted in Chapter 6) – that is, that rural areas have no urgent affordability problem because rural residents are able to buy homes in nearby market towns or comparable centres – is an illusion that serves to perpetuate the social reconfiguration of Britain's countrysides.

A shortage of land?

The claim made by some commentators, and especially those linked to environmental lobbies, that Britain has an acute shortage of land appears highly questionable. Scotland, for example, has approximately 3 per cent of its land mass under 'urban use', that is, with any form of building on it (quoted by Towers et al, 2006). Wales has a similar proportion. The proportion in England is higher, but still less than 10 per cent (see Gallent, 2009b). Taking the most developed of the three countries, data show that England's developed area grew by less than 0.5 per cent between 1991 and 2001 (DCLG, 2007a). Even allowing for mountains and glens, Areas of Natural Beauty (AONBs) and Sites of Special Scientific Interest

(SSSIs), and taking the most productive arable land out of the equation, there seems virtually no basis for claiming that Britain will run out of developable land either in the short or very long term. If big changes in land availability do occur this is more likely to be a result of climate change, sea-level rises and exposure to flooding, any of which could render large swathes of land, especially in southern England, undevelopable at a reasonable cost.

Any claim of a land shortage needs to be qualified: some land is undevelopable, either because of its location or because of primary constraint, be that physical or political constraint. The key issue is how we choose to use the land we have around us. Trying to make that choice a sensible one in a shifting economic and socio-demographic context, and rational in terms of according with society's expressed economic, social and environmental objectives, is a shorthand description of what spatial planning systems are supposed to achieve. The reality, however, is of a housing land allocation process in rural Britain that does not always fit the rational model of decision-making or a world of perfect implementation (Hogwood and Gunn, 1984), as we shall see later in the chapter.

Indeed, as Evans (1991) pointed out, post-war planning in Britain has served to exacerbate land supply inelasticity in the context of persistently increasing housing demand, with inevitable consequences for land and house prices, 'town cramming' and the preservation of rural environments for an elite group. Evans' paper – 'Rabbit hutches on postage stamps' – alongside complementary work by Cheshire and Sheppard (1995), provoked considerable debate on land use and land policy in Britain.[1] The main areas of discussion were the way in which land restrictions worked in practice and their price consequences; distinctions between planning processes and observable outcomes; and the reliability of different means of estimating supply elasticity. Commentators were quick to emphasise that planning decisions affecting housing supply have both a short- and a long-term consequence. Over the short term, the planning system in Britain impacts on prices in a comparable way to planning systems elsewhere. Housing takes time to build, in part because of the planning tests that elongate the development process, and so there is a delayed effect of new supply on prices. Over the longer term, it is not always clear what effect planning, at its different levels, is having on prices and modelling this relationship is a complex business. However, there is certainly a discernible effect on density and layout, which influences viability and the cost of housing. This is true of all planning systems. In the aftermath of the Barker Review, Evans returned to this issue, highlighting Britain's poor performance in terms of housing affordability, density and quality compared to its neighbours in continental Europe (Evans and Hartwich, 2005, 2006, 2007). Planning can indeed have a detrimental effect on these outcomes anywhere, but Britain's brands of planning seem to accentuate market distortion and undermine quality, or at least fail to enhance quality in instances where the private sector delivers substandard homes.

It became a recurrent theme of policy debate from the mid-1990s that the planning systems of the different countries of Britain were failing to deliver an adequate quantity of housing of an acceptable standard, the 'adequate quantity' being estimated from models of demand that are demographic or economic. Whilst rural areas endure their own difficulties, they also share in this general problem. In the following discussion we look at why this should be the case: our argument being that there are gaps between *models* that embody the perfect identification of policy objectives, perfect specification of policy and the absence of conflict in objectives and perfect policy implementation, and the *reality* of how affordable housing supply is realised in the different parts of rural Britain.

Policy-making

A gap exists between the demand for homes and output through the planning system, first, because there are uncertainties surrounding governments' objectives. Prompted in part by the post-1997 UK Labour government's attempt to inject greater clarity into policy objectives and policy-making (Woods, 2008), the governments of each of the nations of Britain have sought to articulate economic, social and environmental objectives within contrasting visions of their respective countrysides.

In England, 'the government's aim is that everyone should be able to live in a vibrant and *sustainable community* ... where people want to live and work, now and in the future' (DEFRA, 2009, emphasis added). In Scotland, it has been suggested that 'rural Scotland ... is an integral part of the country's economy, environment and culture. The Scottish Government's aim is to *promote development* in rural areas and empower communities' (Scottish Government, 2009a, emphasis added). And in Wales, 'the Welsh Assembly Government seeks to support *thriving rural communities* where people live and work and enjoy a high quality of life' (WAG, 2009, emphasis added).

The statements show some differences in emphasis: for example, England talks about sustainability whilst Scotland seeks to promote development on the path to community empowerment. In Wales, the accent is placed on thriving communities, which may perhaps differ from the English conception of sustainable communities. However, they have an important similarity in the recognition of living rural communities. Yet the ambitions for vibrant or thriving communities and for promoting development have to contend with a murkier residue, lingering, as we saw in Chapter 3, from adherence to the long-established culture of protecting Britain's countrysides for consumption by particular groups. This means the 'new' objectives of thriving communities and empowerment need to swim against the established tide of land release and development restraint. We see the practical implications of this conflict later in the chapter.

The second part of this specification issue is that policies that neatly map onto the objectives are not always easily defined, or always feasible in terms of existing resources. This is both a technical issue and a political one. It is a technical issue in that it takes time and effort, for instance, to understand rural housing market dynamics and identify appropriate solutions (Coombes, 2009). Sometimes, it is tempting to take short cuts and to imagine that the market dynamic could be somehow altered. The desire to close rural markets to adventitious purchasers, and especially second home buyers, is a recurrent theme in rural housing debate, though it was shown in Part II that there are many types of purchasing and occupancy activity in rural markets. Closing the market to one type of buyer is more likely to encourage other types of interest than to assist local 'target groups', and may have unforeseen consequences of the type experienced in the Lake District in the late 1970s. It is also a political issue as deciding to expend resources to identify and define appropriate policies requires a commitment. A commitment that, the evidence would seem to suggest, has foundered against others. As we see later in this chapter, the data point to the objectives of maintaining vibrant rural communities being faced down by objectives of protecting key class interests.

This is in fact an instance of a third specification issue – that there may be conflict between objectives. We can illustrate this particularly well with the overarching goal of sustainable development. As we saw in Chapter 5, the Brundtland Report (WCED, 1987) strove for a balancing of society's economic, social and environmental objectives. If, as is often the case, economic or social objectives run counter to those of environmental protection, hierarchies for deciding which should take priority are not well articulated. And in the absence of any clear articulation, particular vested interests will generally see to it that their interest tops the pile. Thus, boosting profitability by moving employment from high-wage, high-employment and environmental protection to low-wage, low-protection contexts is seemingly as legitimate globally, post-Brundtland, as it was before. And denying low-cost rural housing development in the name of environmental protection or 'village conservation' is, it would seem, as legitimate an interpretation of planning for housing in rural Britain in 2009 as it was in 1959, 1969 or 1979 (Cameron and Shucksmith, 2007).

Acting out policy

An implementation gap exists because the rational model of decision-making suits a world of monopoly authority (political and administrative). There have been a number of critiques of this perspective (see, *inter alios*, Pressman and Wildavsky, 1973; Gregory, 1989), with some important strands looking at the motivations of public servants as budget-maximising managers (following Tullock, 1976) and as street-level bureaucrats (following Lipsky, 1980). Much of this work also contends that decision-making ultimately reflects the exercise of power. The most influential development of this idea was by Lukes (1974), who identified three dimensions of power – the power to take decisions, the power to avoid having to take decisions and the power to influence views on what decisions should be made. As we see shortly, Lukes' ideas have found resonance in research from the 1980s onwards.

Thus, it is suggested that rationalism's world view of powerful government cannot be applied with any real accuracy either to any of Britain's countries, or to sister states in the EU or OECD. Rural societies in these countries provide no exception. Their contemporary contexts are of a multiplicity of authoritative agents, each with their own preferences and interests, and each with differing abilities to control local policy agendas (Goodwin, 1998). It follows from this that discussions of how decisions are made are discussions of the 'art of government' (as Plato originally defined governance) or, indeed, governmentality, which, following Foucault (1991), draws attention to the ways citizens are shaped to meet governments' aims and to the organised practices through which subjects are governed (Mayhew, 2004). There is a wealth of research that identifies these relationships in rural Britain, with examples of its application being to agriculture (Winter, 1996; Murdoch and Ward, 1997), housing (Woods, 1998) and homelessness (Cloke et al, 2000a; 2000b; 2000c), community economic development (MacKinnon, 2002) and forestry (Stanley et al, 2005). Does the concept of governmentality help explain land release for housing in rural Britain?

Choices on land: decision-making in rural Britain and its impact

Britain's spatial planning systems should, in principle, ensure that all areas have an adequate provision of housing given what is known about their current and likely future populations. It is the policy of each nation's government (WAG, 2002b; DCLG, 2006b; Scottish Government, 2008b) that planning should ensure that adequate amounts of land are allocated to meet any identified shortfall. Need should be assessed and provision should be made at the level of housing market areas, which are defined with respect to people's living and work location choices (Coombes, 2009). Thus, planning tries to relate to people's locational decisions and it takes as its starting point functional geography rather than arbitrary administrative boundaries. This strategy, bound up with planning reform in the 2000s, seems eminently sensible. However, housing market areas frequently connect smaller village locations to larger settlements, possibly some distance away. These locations are functionally linked. The larger settlement, perhaps a market town or a larger sub-regional centre, may well be a source of employment for people living in its rural hinterland. The smaller village locations may be located within its travel-to-work area, but this is only a travel-to-work area for some residents. The housing market area may reflect the movements of a mobile minority who commute to jobs in the town. But the linking of these different areas may not express the behaviour of other residents, including those working in village-based jobs or those who are retired and economically inactive. For these people, the village is a discrete market, or perhaps linked into a local network or similarly sized settlements contained within a single parish. The implication of the housing market area, drawn up on the basis of 'reliable data', is that future housing provision will occur in the larger towns where services and employment can be more easily provided. When new social housing is provided, *for the village*, it will be in the larger town. Likewise, when new sheltered housing is provided, the town will be viewed as the most sensible location. Local residents growing old in the village, or in need of affordable housing, will find themselves 'catered for in' or 'displaced to' – depending on your point of view – the town. At the same time, the village will come to be dominated by more mobile and affluent commuting households, and the only older residents will be those, with money, moving in to retire. Planning policy across Britain tends to favour development in the largest settlements first, larger towns second and in smaller settlements last. Government in England has adopted this stance most explicitly, advocating a sequential test that formalises the urban preference, and insisting on sustainability appraisals of local development frameworks that essentially redline villages as inherently unsustainable. Regional planning also plays its part in ensuring that development is concentrated up the urban hierarchy, as noted in Chapter 6.

Image 10.1: 1990s' housing in Wellesbourne, Warwickshire. The village was designated a 'key settlement' in the 1970s and grew dramatically. It has become a focal point for development that is rarely permitted in neighbouring villages, which have rapidly gentrified. © Nick Gallent

This stance seems also to fit the wishes of some vocal interests opposed to new housing development in the countryside. It also fits the world view of more mobile residents – especially commuting households – who often project the value of mobility on others, arguing in favour of concentrated development in larger centres, and of directing younger or older villagers to these locations where their needs will be more easily met. Their logic is that social networks will not be disrupted as former villagers, seemingly 'displaced', will maintain their social contacts and will be able to service any need to return to the village, for work or for family reasons, by purchasing a car (DEFRA, 2010).

In the light of this logic, local groups – often made up of more mobile residents – regularly campaign against the allocation of land for new housing (including affordable housing) in smaller village locations. Opponents of individual proposals and schemes often project their views up the planning and political hierarchy to such an extent that it is easy to believe that the entire countryside is conservative and development-averse. Woods (1998) documents how anti-development campaigners forced a local authority in south-west England to lobby against meeting new house-building targets. Murdoch and Lowe (2003) show how the CPRE has questioned house-building targets at national level and joined local campaigns against development. Looking at Scotland in the early 1990s, Shucksmith et al (1993) found that the most significant influence on national policy was the professional ideologies of the civil service elite. Professional planners' opposition to house-building in the countryside saw some challenge from housing professionals, creating stalemates in some instances. At the local level, policies were also the outcome of a struggle between individual councillors acting 'parochially' on behalf of their constituents, sometimes landowners and farmers who wished to promote development for personal gain, and planning officials opposing rural residential schemes. Moir et al (1997) compared professional attitudes to new housing development in some remote rural areas of Scotland with other rural parts of the country. Whilst there was some evidence of a more relaxed attitude in the former, many authorities were found to be adopting a strongly protectionist stance. Comparing Scotland and England, Satsangi and Dunmore (2003) found that planning was more often frustrating affordable rural housing provision than facilitating it. Drawing on evidence for rural areas across England, Sturzaker (2009) concluded that those with power in the planning process exercise it to prevent affordable housing development, often influenced by vocal lobbies wishing to see the countryside preserved.

There is then a high degree of consistency in studies of housing land provision in rural Britain – despite national governments acknowledging under-supply, and despite well-intentioned local planning policy, attempts to secure more housing are commonly hindered by well-orchestrated campaigns and by well-organised local elites. The dimensions of power identified by Lukes (1974) are seen in the organised practices and shaping of interests and actions – the governmentality of rural housing provision – which evidently have an adverse impact on the availability of land for housing in rural areas and on the supply of new housing in Britain's countrysides. This bottom-up pressure on supply finds some agreement with national policies that, irrespective of the rhetoric, are keen to place strict limits on development in smaller village locations.

Note
[1] The other key protagonists were Glen Bramley (1993a, 1993b, 1996, 1998, 1999; Bramley et al, 1995) and Sarah Monk and Christine Whitehead (1996, 1999; also Monk et al, 1996) replied to by Evans (1996; see also White and Allmendinger, 2003).

ELEVEN

Private house-building

The provision of new housing in rural Britain has, apart from during a very short period, been the result of private sector activity. Councils, housing associations and other registered social landlords have of course commissioned new housing but have done little direct building themselves. The structure, conduct and performance of the private house-building industry therefore has a crucial bearing on supply and, particularly, on supply responsiveness. In both academic and policy commentary, there are commonly critiques of the industry for its ways of working and for the quality of its outputs. Yet, particularly in the thin markets that typify many rural housing systems, there can be significant constraints on what the builder can provide. This chapter explores the nature of private house-building in rural areas. It also looks at issues of rural housing quality, asking whether design is demand responsive, and sensitive to local context, or whether rural areas suffer the same variants on standardised housing designs seen in urban and suburban locations. Lastly, it examines the possible role that self-build or self-directed housing might play in Britain's countrysides.

The house-building industry and the housing development process

Housing output across Britain is dominated by a relatively small number of players who build speculatively. This is confirmed by data presented in Tables 11.1a and 11.1b, which also list the 'top 10' companies by turnover. But for the housing markets of rural Britain, outside of peri-urban areas – that is, in less accessible and remote areas – speculative building by the *volume builders* is rather less common. Instead, new housing in these locations is more regularly supplied by local or regional builders (some of whom are also subcontractors to the volume builders; see Satsangi et al [2000, 2005] for local market evidence in Scotland). Volume builders, as the name suggests, typically build in large volumes. This is what allows them to minimise the cost per unit of their output and, *ceteris paribus*, maximise the profits from development: essentially, they enjoy scale advantages. Local and regional builders, on the other hand, are rather more likely to build to order, or to produce bespoke housing, than they are to build on the anticipation of sale. Whilst the volume builders can (afford to) hold significant land banks, local builders do not.

In contrast to the fairly extensive literature on Britain's volume house-builders, there is very little that looks specifically at small-scale operations. Nicol and Hooper (1999; see also Wellings, 2006) reflect on the major changes in the structure of the industry in the previous two decades, focusing on concentration through merger and takeover, and the increasing dominance of large companies.[1] Such processes have acted to further marginalise the smaller firms. In Scotland, this has happened to an even greater extent than in Britain as a whole. Gibb (1999) notes that whilst in 1995 Britain's top 25 builders accounted for just under half of total output (46 per cent) the proportion in Scotland was 72 per cent. However, at the same time, he noted signs of a move towards de-concentration in Scotland in the 1990s. In the mid-2000s, a survey of developers in that country (SBE et al, 2007) suggested that Scottish-based companies tended to have smaller annual outputs (average 193) than UK-wide producers (average 605). However, this and other studies have not elucidated the building practices or the experiences of smaller companies and, for this reason, the examination of house-building practice in rural areas presented in this chapter focuses mainly on the larger providers and on general changes in the structure of the industry, as it potentially affects housing production in the countryside.

The data in Table 11.1a chart the process of consolidation since 1991: the number of developers delivering very small numbers of homes has declined. The largest companies make a very considerable contribution to the British economy (Table 11.1b), which is amplified if one includes the multiplier effect through the production supply chain. Housing construction is a critical component of Britain's economy. Therefore public investment in supporting the industry has been a crucial part of government's strategy to lift Britain's economy out of the 2008 to 2010 credit crunch and recession.

As a consequence of scale, volume builders are also more likely than local companies to negotiate options on land and only complete purchase of that land when planning permission has been secured (Adams and Watkins, 2002) and when the market conditions are right to instigate development. The purchase price, however, is usually somewhere between the value with, and the value without, full development permission (appraisals of development potential will suggest a price to the buyer, but the landowner will also have a view on the land's value that may not be its actual current use value: essentially, these parties negotiate a price at the option stage). Land speculation, and profiting from land purchase (often through the process of strategic land banking to capture inflationary gains in land values), is a crucial part of the speculative house-building process and the subject of periodic critique (see, for example, Ball, 1983; Barlow, 1999; Gibb, 1999). Summarising that literature, Adams and Watkins (2002: 131) argue that this aspect of speculation 'has generated an undue reliance on inflationary increases in land value as a source of profitability' and limits competition: larger builders can buy counter-cyclically and mitigate, if not rule out, new entry to the market. It may, as the Royal Town Planning Institute noted in 2007, act as a brake on housing supply, as the focus of speculation is placed on capturing inflationary gains from land markets rather than the production of housing itself.

Securing or buying land for development is clearly a vital, visible phase of house-building. For the speculative builder, however, it is highly unlikely to be the first. Housing development has been characterised as a multi-staged process (see Barrett

Table 11.1a: Concentration in British house-building

Year	No of houses	No of companies building 1–10 houses	No of companies building 11–100 houses	No of companies building 101–500 houses	No of companies building 501 houses or more	Total number on NHBC register	% output by largest builders
1991	19,662	7,069	1138	111	37	28,017	47%
1996	12,032	5,098	941	105	37	18,213	58%
2001	10,044	4,255	825	94	35	15,253	62%
2008	12,854	3,573	641	80	31	17,179	55%
2008 as % of 1991	65%	51%	56%	72%	84%	61%	–

Note: Number of houses is number of houses started in that year.

Source: NHBC (2009)

Table 11.1b: Britain's biggest house-builders by turnover, September 2009

Rank	Company	Turnover (£ millions)
1	Barratt	3,555
2	Taylor Wimpey	3,468
3	Persimmon	1,755
4	Bellway	1,150
5	Berkeley	992
6	Galliford Try	717
7	Redrow	650
8	Crest Nicholson	544
9	Countryside	518
10	McCarthy & Stone	457

Source: Contractjournal.com (accessed 5 February 2010)

et al, 1978), shaped by different forces, set within sometimes complex institutional and regulatory frameworks, involving a vast array of actors, and moving through a series of interlinked events (see, for example, Ball et al, 1998; Ball, 2006) of which viability appraisal is critical. Development is triggered by a 'maturing of circumstances' (Goodchild and Munton, 1985), which makes it possible to replace an existing use with one that is more profitable or socially valuable (Cadman and Austin-Crowe, 1991). Maturation could involve a change in planning policy or status, though it is normally taken to mean the move to viability as a result of market shift: the development of land happens when the necessary investment of time and money will yield an acceptable profit. This reality means that within the development process, the calculation of viability through residual valuation is critical (Millington, 1988; Harvey, 1996; Golland and Blake, 2004).

Undertaking a residual valuation involves calculating how much revenue a development will yield after development costs so that the maximum amount that can be paid for the land can be determined: this is the residual, surplus or leftover. The developer will subtract anticipated costs (construction, loan finance, marketing, professional and planning fees and normal profit, calculated as a percentage of operating cost) from anticipated revenues (the number of houses multiplied by their mean price, less tax liability). If this is negative, the project is not viable. The amount by which it is positive is the amount the developer can afford to pay for the land (again, the *residual* or surplus). For projects that are perceived to be higher risk, developers will seek to generate a bigger surplus, perhaps to cover the costs of higher interest rate charges. Given the relationship between potential market revenue, construction costs and risk, small sites in fairly remote rural locations or constrained infill sites – with potentially high development costs – may be unattractive to larger builders. In contrast, slightly bigger greenfield sites, in better connected rural areas, on which homes could be built that would find a market amongst, for example, relatively affluent commuters or early retirees (see Chapter 7) may be much more attractive. In some instances, competition will ensue between potential developers, with landowners therefore able to exploit a seller's market.

However, it is generally the case that development opportunities in rural areas come forward on much smaller sites that those typically found in cities and larger towns, making them less attractive to the volume builder. In turn, this means that the potential contractor market is thinner, slowing down the supply response to arising demand and ensuring that prices reflect product scarcity. In essence, more limited interest in exploiting rural development sites contributes to general affordability problems. The thinner contractor market also means that rural *social* housing procurement is generally less able to benefit from the scale economies and wider contractor competition found in urban Britain (see Chapter 14). Housing development is either slow to come forward, or when it does come forward it is costlier.

Has policy attempted to address specifically rural supply issues? In large part, the answer is no. In the 1990s, the government housing agency for Scotland, Scottish Homes, earmarked securing the provision of low-cost home ownership in rural areas as a channel for subsidy via the Grant for Rent and Ownership (GRO) programme. Private developers were eligible for a capital grant to reduce the valuation gap and bring sites to viability. However, few rural market schemes came forward.

The other response has been to stimulate the interest of volume house-builders in rural Britain by identifying sites for more substantial development. For example, the English government has been promoting 'eco-towns', new settlements of between 5,000 and 15,000 houses, or large schemes in market towns. The aim, with the eco-towns, was to create new settlements that had good transport links, could be easily keyed into existing infrastructure and where the latest technology for lightening the ecologic footprint of development could be showcased. The aspiration was that eco-towns would, as far as possible, be zero-carbon (Cooper, 2007). Government's eco-towns programme quickly became bogged down in a debate centred on the process of selecting sites. In 2008, 15 sites (from a long list of 57) were shortlisted and in that same year, the DCLG issued a draft Planning Policy Statement on Eco-towns that was arguably intended to weigh against local opposition. A view that government was trying to bully communities and local councils into accepting eco-towns quickly developed. Indeed, local opposition played a big part in ensuring that only four of the 15 sites were judged to have real potential to host an eco-town (DCLG, 2009d). However, the scepticism surrounding this flagship of Labour housing policy did not abate, with Arnold (2009) suggesting that the project is dead in the water and Morris (2009) arguing that the remaining schemes risk becoming a 'car dependent joke'. In 2009, Rob Cowan perhaps best captured the mood in the planning profession within a single cartoon (Image 11.1).

Image 11.1: 'Progress in planning – eco-towns' © Rob Cowan, Urban Design Skills

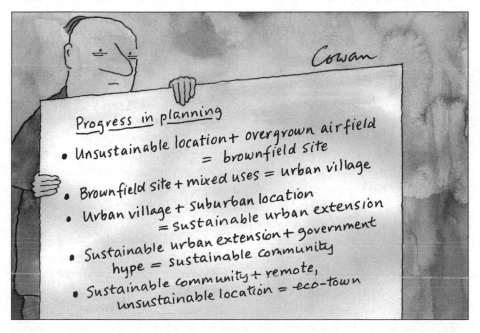

Eco-town development, alongside past attempts to grow 'key settlements' (Cloke, 1979), and the priority on expanding market towns (Cameron and Shucksmith, 2007), offers a means of addressing housing demand in rural areas that attracts the interest of volume builders but does not tackle the problem of housing supply in smaller village locations. Jenkins (2008) described eco-towns as 'the greatest try-on in the long and dazzling history of property speculation'. It is certainly true that large companies were behind many of the proposed schemes, and saw the programme as a means of building at volume in more rural locations. But these new towns (as many opponents label them) and proposed expansions also fit with government's revised view of planning for housing as occurring across strategic market areas. If villages are tied functionally to market towns (or to future eco-towns) then it will make sense to direct housing to these bigger settlements (see Chapter 10) on sustainability grounds. The corollary of this is that the door is firmly shut on development in villages and hamlets and the prospect of such development is cast as inherently unsustainable. However, this can be read as part of a wider strategy to placate sections of the rural population who are resistant to development and create a context in which 'affordability' can be addressed across strategic areas by the private sector. Resistance to larger development schemes parachuted into open countryside, or bolted onto existing towns, suggests, however, that this strategy is not without its own problems. But the most pressing problem is that it does not address the full range of rural needs, or tackle the ongoing social reconfiguration of smaller rural communities. In fact, it serves only to fuel this process.

There is also a question mark over the ecological case for concentrating development. Echenique et al (2009) suggest that policies attempting to compact the city and in favour of concentrated rather than dispersed developments may magnify carbon dioxide emissions rather than reducing them.

By supporting smaller-scale extensions to existing settlements of all types – cities, towns *and* villages – Scotland's Sustainable Communities Initiative appears to have won considerably more support (Tiesdell, 2009). Although newer, it seemed in 2009 to have been beset by none of the implementation troubles of the English programme. However, although not part of any national government initiative, Scotland has not been immune from new settlement proposals: Owenstown in South Lanarkshire is, at the time of writing, at project inception stage, with its promoters aiming to recapture philanthropic and community-centric ideals inspired by its Robert Owen-led near-neighbour, New Lanark.

Developers across Britain's countrysides acknowledge the difficulties associated with small-scale rural housing schemes. This acknowledgement is being expressed at the current time in strong support for initiatives and programmes that promise to deliver large numbers of homes on greenfield sites. Preference for near-urban green fields is well-documented (Adams and Watkins, 2002), making rural fringe locations prime targets for speculative development. Government in England, in particular, has been trying to tap into this preference but has also brought forward policies and programmes that acknowledge the greater viability and achievability of *accessible* rural sites. It is worth remembering however that there is a case for facilitating development not only in pursuit of profit, but in instances where that development is socially valuable (Cadman and Austin-Crowe, 1991). This happens, in a piecemeal way, through policies designed to promote the delivery of affordable housing as we shall see in the next chapter. However, there is certainly a case to incentivise additional general house-building under circumstances where risks are high or viability is unclear if it can be shown that this is of potential social value.

'Little boxes on a hillside ...'?

Given the above context and difficulties it is not surprising to find that rural Britain has rather lower rates of house-building than urban Britain. Expressed crudely in relation to total population, the difference in Scotland has been around 10 per cent since the mid-1980s (Satsangi, 2008). Across England, new dwelling completions rose by 22 per cent between 2002/03 and 2005/06. However, between 2003 and 2005, rural completions fell by 3.9 per cent (Shucksmith, 2007b). New rural house prices are higher than in cities and large towns (and affordability, expressed in terms of the link between prices and wages, is generally lower). This results from differences in effective demand, and also reflects the fact that house-builders regularly build for the high end of the market[2] in rural locations as they need to recover the higher build costs associated with smaller rural sites. We return to this point in Chapter 16, where it is noted that 'starter homes' are more commonly delivered for open market sale in larger centres.

At the same time, Britain's house-building industry has faced sustained and often highly critical scrutiny of the quality of its outputs (see Carmona, 2001; Leishman et al, 2004), raising questions about the conduct and performance of the industry. Besides the critical issue of housing quantity, across urban and rural locations, there are persistent concerns over the quality of homes delivered by the private sector, both in terms of their visual appeal and their build and space standards. In particular, critics contend that private production relies on a limited number of housing designs and that design solutions – both in terms of the homes themselves and their layout – from one location are inappropriately transported to another. Pattern-book designs are rolled out across the length and breadth of Britain, but what might work well in a particular part of Surrey may stick out like a sore thumb on the Isle of Skye, and the desirability of replicating 'Brookside Close'[3] a thousand times in different locations is being increasingly questioned (as is the quality of all 1980s' and 1990s' built red-brick development). Carmona et al (2003) argue that new homes are often insensitive to context and fail to contribute to any sense of place. House-builders claim to build for the market, supplying the products that buyers want. However, because they offer limited choice, and because they strictly control what is built through their market dominance and monopoly over strategic land banks, what sells is a *fait accompli* rather than an expression of consumer tastes. Development often fails to respect its landscape context. Larger developments may often suffer, in design terms, from limited 'legibility' and 'connectivity', either because of unwillingness to provide better infrastructure or because economic considerations result in poor layouts and site cramming. Whilst these issues are undoubtedly generic, Owen (1999, 2002a, 2002b) has highlighted specific concern over the perceived 'homogenisation' of rural England, sometimes expressed through pattern-book architecture and the loss of village character or distinctiveness. Such concerns have prompted many communities (around 600 to 700 across England) to produce 'village design statements' (VDSs) which set out the special architectural characteristics – if there are any – of residential and other buildings within villages. Hughes (2006) notes that there was some enthusiasm under the pre-2004 planning system to adopt these design statements as 'supplementary planning guidance' attached to development plans. For instance, 14 per cent of villages in the Kent Downs Area of Natural Beauty produced VDSs that were subsequently adopted; making community design concerns a material planning consideration. Anecdotal evidence suggests that this enthusiasm has been maintained with the introduction of the Local Development Framework (LDF) system, especially as there is no requirement to test the 'soundness' of design statements before a planning inspector: they remain 'supplementary' to the development framework.

The build and space standards of new homes are also frequently problematic. Internal space and sound insulation are often poor in comparison with older homes or public-sector housing (Karn and Sheridan, 1994). Homebuyers regularly complain about work quality and finishes, with new occupants commonly drawing up extensive lists of 'snaggings' and referring complaints to the National House Building Council. However, such critiques are general and have not been spatially disaggregated. It is not unreasonable to assume that many smaller, high-value and bespoke rural developments are likely to have fewer problems and compare favourably with older properties blighted by defects and often of below tolerable standard or 'non-decent'[4] (DCLG, 2007b). There are specific quality problems in new rural housing relating to the utility of homes for elderly or disabled occupants. Builders have shown some reticence to meet more stringent building regulations (Imrie, 2004) and in some rural locations, where development costs are higher, these may be an added disincentive to build new homes. It is also the case that the slow rate of replacement of rural homes may undermine attempts to deliver housing choices matched to the needs of older people (see Chapter 7).

How does the house-building industry respond to criticism of its products? The stock response is that these products sell and must therefore satisfy the needs and preferences of buyers. It was noted earlier, however, that limited choice in the housing market – combined with limited supply – makes the purchase of what is available a *fait accompli*. House-builders also point out that *routinisation* of production, and therefore a standardised product, has an economic rationale, as in other industries (Nicol and Hooper, 1999): it keeps costs down and ensures that homes are more generally affordable. Designs also reflect the conservative tastes of consumers, and producers see inherent risk in moving away from the market standard. The view is that if buyers want something different, with more space, and which is bespoke rather than 'off the shelf', they will be able to find this in the higher end of the market. Builders have been particularly scornful of what they see as elitist critiques of current layouts. Whilst architects and urban designers would prefer greater innovation in housing typologies, builders maintain that real people, especially real people with children, want to live in closes and cul-de-sacs where traffic speeds are lower and children are commensurately safer. With respect to work quality, the defence tends to be that on-site supervision and post-completion inspection systems have become more stringent in response to some past problems and the increased expectations of homebuyers.

Another stock response is that house-builders operate within a regulatory framework that generates particular outcomes. They are guided by building regulations and by national and local planning policy. Reductions in floor space standards, for example, are a consequence both of densification policies and of the way the land market is regulated. Building small homes is a means of upping densities and ensuring affordability, though neither of these planning priorities appears to have as significant an effect on floor spaces elsewhere in Europe as in the UK (Gallent et al, 2010). Planning authorities are the arbiters of design quality. Whilst the extent to which planning really influences housing design is debatable, there is of course some truth in all of these claims. However, there is also some passing of the buck. The products of the development process, both in terms of their quantity and quality, are determined by the interaction of market forces with regulatory priorities, and the motives and objectives of different actors in that process. Because of this complexity, housing development is inherently laden with risk. It is no surprise, therefore, that the industry attempts to standardise its products, making programme and cost targets, rather than design innovation, its top priority (Nicol and Hooper, 1999).

However, a counter-argument is that a range of product and process innovations would allow house-builders to tackle quality concerns without increasing costs. Ball (1999) argues that it is the structure of the industry that militates against innovation and encourages conservatism. There is also too great a focus on land speculation as opposed to the core business of building homes, as was noted earlier in this chapter, though the planning system itself tends to encourage this focus. Any significant shift in the types of homes being built in Britain would involve a move to more modern construction methods and away from the ubiquitous red-brick box that for many people is a symbol of all that is wrong with housing development in Britain's countrysides. Apart from the homebuyer 'conservatism' alluded to by the volume builders, there are other practical barriers to the use of modern construction methods in housing. Gaze et al (2007) highlight both the barriers, and drivers, to construction methods that would fundamentally change the look of rural housing (Table 11.2). In contrast to what is wrong, however, Image 11.2 highlights what is possible in contemporary rural housing design.

Self-build and self-directed housing

The general structure of the house-building industry means that it is not always attracted by or suited to smaller projects. For this and other reasons linking to individual preference and the tradition of 'self-help' in many rural areas, there is an increasing role for self-build and self-directed housing in Britain's countrysides. The former term is now strongly associated with one-off projects of the type showcased on Channel 4's *Grand Designs* and can suggest occupancy by those with bigger budgets. Indeed, Barlow et al (2001) identified a growing interest in self-build amongst more affluent households. Nevertheless, the profile of people who undertake self-build reveals a very diverse range of socio-economic characteristics. The majority of households tend to be middle-aged or older, and already own their home, or the bulk of the equity (National Self Build Association, 2008). However, self-build remains in some instances an option for households with more limited means, and a smaller proportion of self-builders comprises younger, less well-off, households. 'Self-directed' housing projects spring from local collaborations that often involve linking up with a social housing provider or tapping into grant funding. These are community-led projects in which the future occupants of homes co-ordinate the construction process and often have a direct hand in it (Image 11.2a). A number of self-directed schemes in Scotland have benefited from public subsidy and have made a key contribution to the well-being of some fragile communities. Amongst the range of benefits accruing from such development, for communities and individuals, is the avoidance of standardised products. Those directing the schemes tend to have significant input into the design process, also matching the specification of new homes to their own needs.

Table 11.2: Using modern methods of construction in housing: drivers and barriers

Drivers	Barriers
Housing shortages	Capital costs
Skills shortages	Concern over working alongside traditional
Quality	methods
Revisions to building regulations	Design difficulty
Government and environmental	Planning
initiatives	Lack of experience and reluctance to innovate
Waste reduction	Dominance of land in the house-building process
	On-site skills and product capacity constraints
	Transportation
	Lightweight construction
	Site-specific constraints
	Client scepticism

Source: Adapted from Gaze et al (2007)

However, although self-build has the potential to play a greater role in the provision of housing for people on lower incomes in rural areas, this potential is, to a large extent, stymied by a number of difficulties and barriers. Indeed, Morgan and Satsangi (forthcoming, 2011) noted in Scotland that although financial incentives for self-build can be a cost-effective policy tool, this approach to delivering housing is likely to make a numerically small contribution overall. Part of the issue is a cultural one (Rosnes, 1987). Although the popularity of self-build has grown steadily over recent decades in Britain, this has been from a very small base. An overview of the sector in 2008 highlighted that about 12 per cent of new-build in Britain is self-built. This figure compares poorly with other European states,

Canada, the United States, New Zealand and Australia. Fifty to 60 per cent of homes in the Scandanavian countries are built in this way, whilst over 80 per cent of housing in Austria is via self-builders (National Self Build Association, 2008). In addition to cultural influences, barriers within the British context relate to practical issues. It is difficult, for instance, for self-builders to compete with volume builders for land. However, the potential of self-build in smaller communities in rural localities relates to its ability to take advantage of single plots of land, which would otherwise be too small for development by housing associations. A difficulty here is a very familiar one: planning restrictions in rural areas have led to a dearth of such sites being made available. Further, where small plots are available, there still remains the issue of lower-income households competing with more affluent groups, even where the intention is to undertake a self-build scheme. Woof (2009) highlights that a significant step forward for self-build in small communities lies in the recognition of the need for affordable housing in principle in such settlements, not linked to the identification of specific sites within the LDF.

The success of individual self-build schemes highlights the way that perseverance by individuals and groups at local level can overcome such difficulties, often linked with support from local authorities. For example, a scheme of 12 self-build houses at St Minver, Cornwall, was developed using a Community Land Trust, with the assistance of an interest-free loan from the then North Cornwall District Council (Cornwall Community Land Trust, 2009). In another instance, a group of families who clubbed together to develop a self-build scheme in Hockerton, Nottinghamshire, were also supported by planners in Newark and Sherwood District Council who were receptive to the eco-friendly approach the families were taking (National Self Build Association, 2008).

The nature of the development industry, its motives and the context in which it operates are key determinants of housing outcomes. The context in rural areas is varied, but generally very different from urban and suburban areas. In near-urban hinterlands, there is often intense competition for housing land. Further afield, in remoter rural locations, this competition dissipates and small parcels of developable land will often fail to stir the interest of volume builders. Development costs, and associated risks, tend to be higher. Developers will counter such risks by concentrating on high-end development: but larger detached properties with a bigger price tag may only find a market amongst commuting households or retirees, and such buyers will still prefer better-connected locations. This means that in more isolated areas, fewer companies may be interested in developing sites, unless there is a prospect of wealthier buyers being attracted to that location. Here, self-built and self-directed housing has a potential role in sustaining the balance and vibrancy of communities, so long as it is associated with economic opportunity. But in general, rural housing strategies across Wales and Scotland, and especially across England, have focused on concentrating development. This is justified in terms of its supposed sustainability, and it also creates opportunities attractive to volume builders. But perhaps most importantly, it squares with the

Image 11.2: Examples of contemporary rural housing developments

a) Self-directed single house, Portree, Isle of Skye © Dualchas Building Design, 2010

b) Three house development, Dornie © Dualchas Building Design, 2010

c) Single private house, Invergarry © Dualchas Building Design, 2010

current process of planning for housing in rural areas: to tie small settlements to bigger centres and to address the 'local needs' of villages within these centres. However, this strategy is accelerating social change in Britain's countrysides, creating socially and economically unbalanced communities, and perpetuating reliance on piecemeal 'tactical' interventions that seek to deliver against local needs. These interventions, examined in the next two chapters, need to be viewed against a tide of rural gentrification affecting many areas and an urgent need to open villages up to their 'fair share' of development opportunity (Bramley and Watkins, 2009).

Notes

[1] Their focus was specifically on firms producing at least 1,000 units per annum.

[2] For example, in the more rural council areas of Scotland from 2003 to 2006, new-build prices adjusted for size were higher than in the more urban areas (Scottish Government, 2007, Appendix 2). The English House Condition Survey (DCLG, 2007b: 48) reveals that homes in rural England are generally bigger (with more floor space) and more expensive than in England as a whole.

[3] A fictional cul-de-sac of detached red-brick houses used in a 1980s' and 1990s' soap opera bearing the same name.

[4] Forty-three per cent of all rural homes were judged 'non-decent' in 2007 compared with 29.6 per cent in suburban areas and 41 per cent in all urban and city locations (DCLG, 2007b: 64).

TWELVE

Planning and affordable rural housing

An important tactical solution to the shortage of reasonably priced housing in some locations is the use of the planning system to procure affordable homes through development control. An obvious answer to the basic question of how affordable housing (affordable to median local wage-earners) should be provided, where it is needed, is surely through some sort of subsidy on construction cost, whether the land to be built on is in private or public hands. Essentially, part of government's 'welfare' spending should go towards the provision of affordable homes.

This obvious model of direct provision was the norm for much of the 20th century, with the state (through local authorities) using taxpayers' money to build public housing. Political support for this approach drained away during the last decades of the 20th century: right-wing governments, in particular, felt that full-cost subsidy for house-building by the public sector was an inherently inefficient means of providing cheaper housing. Also, because land costs can account for a significant proportion of total build costs (typically one third since 1945, but this will vary depending on the size of a plot and the number of homes to be built), it was felt that switching to land subsidy (paid for by landowners through some sort of tax on land value uplift and development profit) could be a means of reducing the burden on taxpayers (but not of course on landowners), whilst achieving the same level of overall affordability. Before looking at how this is achieved, and with what success, it is important to understand the evolution of this approach. Its origins are rooted with those of the planning system itself.

Why a land subsidy?

The 'planning and affordable housing' approach – based on land subsidy extracted from development permissions and often, but not always, coupled with a construction subsidy – is the product of two policy developments during the 20th century: the first is the move from comprehensive and direct to indirect provision of affordable housing; the second concerns the opportunities arising from the planning process to contribute to this indirect provision.

Direct to indirect provision

For much of the 20th century, housing policy emphasised a supply-based response to housing demand. This meant the direct provision of public housing serving general need. This response, formulated at the end of the 19th century but not rolled out on any significant scale until after 1919, used taxpayers' money for large-scale house-building programmes. Inevitably, these programmes reflected the different needs of major cities, smaller towns and the countryside: the large housing estates eventually built in urban areas were not replicated in more rural areas, but the model of provision – local authority-led and reliant on direct capital investment – was the same.

This is not the place to rehearse the full history of shifting party political ideologies and how they shaped housing outcomes (numerous texts do this already – for example, Mullins and Murie, 2006), although it is pertinent to note that during the interwar years and then again after the Second World War, both Labour and Conservative governments extended capital funding for council housing. The Conservatives, however, tended to do so less enthusiastically and, from the end of the 1950s, favoured private housing provision, and made specific attempts to grow the private rented sector through a programme of legislative deregulation. By the mid- to late 1960s, the housing policies of the major political parties had begun to converge, and both the Conservatives and Labour shared a desire to move away from mass public housing provision. This was given momentum by evidence in the early 1970s that the UK had a surplus of new homes and also by the realisation that public spending needed to be reined in.

Although it was a Labour administration that began sharp cuts and redirection in public spending on housing in the mid-1970s, the 1979–97 Conservative governments had a particular appetite for withdrawing from council provision. The Housing Act – and corresponding Tenants' Rights Etc (Scotland) Act – introduced in 1980 gave secure council tenants the 'right to buy'[1] their homes at a discount; placed restrictions on future public building; and left housing associations to deliver most affordable housing. Its plan was to create a housing system in Britain that emphasised home-ownership whilst also providing an affordable housing 'safety net' for households unable to buy their own homes, either on the open market or through the right to buy council tenancies. This represented a move to a demand-based welfare model: support would henceforth be provided to those households who sought it out and could demonstrate a clear need.

Furthermore, the Conservatives believed that local government should *facilitate* the provision of affordable housing by other agencies, and that the way in which provision was taken forward should encourage innovation and cost-efficiency (HM Government, 1987). The Housing Acts of 1988 emphasised the importance of public, private and voluntary sector collaboration in future non-market housing provision, with local authorities cast as 'enablers' of housing association development, part-funded from private sector borrowing and, eventually, from planning gain arrangements. From 1974, housing associations had received generous capital funding: but after 1988, the government wished to 'stretch' the sector, giving it access to *some* public money, but also encouraging it to find innovate ways to bridge the funding gap. Hence, direct provision of affordable housing by government gave way to indirect provision, led by a private–voluntary partnership arrangement.

In the 20 years since the 1988 Acts, affordable housing providers have been constantly adapting to stricter and ever-evolving funding rules. They have needed to maximise use of their remaining grant support (part of affordable housing programmes for the respective nations), combining this with other forms of public subsidy and with private borrowing. But rather than relying on grant receipt and money from the banks, almost half of all affordable housing delivered is 'procured' through the planning system,[2] though in the context of declining overall supply (Crook et al, 2006; and see later discussion) and a geography of provision weighted towards areas of higher land values (Newhaven Research, 2008: 3).

Delivery through planning (as a community 'gain') has evolved into an important approach to supplying affordable housing across Britain. Planning gain itself had evolved over the previous four decades from the failure of successive governments to construct a viable system of taxing private capital gains from land value uplift accruing from the grant of planning permission. This was the second key policy development.

How is this procurement possible?

The power to grant or deny permission, based on development plan policies, was handed to local authorities in 1947 and, from that date, planning control became a key driver of land values. By the 1990s, a unit of land with residential development permission in 'the vicinity of Reading' (in South East England) was between 250 and 500 times more valuable than a piece of agricultural land of equivalent size (Evans, 1991: 854). Planning generates a potential for significant development profit and, since 1947, government has sought ways of harnessing the value uplift conferred on land through the grant of development permission. It is these attempts to tax value uplift that have shaped the planning system's contribution to the indirect provision of mixed-funded affordable housing, called for by the Conservatives in 1987.

Six years before the 1947 Acts, the Uthwatt Report (Ministry of Works and Planning, 1941) had discussed the concept of 'betterment', arguing that there ought to be a tax on the land value gains associated with planning consent. This idea was taken forward in the 1947 Town and Country Planning Acts as a development charge, or a 100 per cent tax on land value gain accruing on the grant of planning permission. The instigation of this system prompted an immediate debate: how should uplift be calculated? And related to this, exactly when should the 'before' and 'after' land valuations be conducted? And, most significantly, what impact might this charge have on the market for land and therefore on Britain's post-war economic recovery? Would the charge stifle development and growth? The debate raged and the charge was abandoned. It was resurrected, however, with the creation of a Land Commission in 1964, which introduced another betterment charge on private land sales. The same concerns over operation and growth arose again, and again the charge was abandoned (in 1970). And then for a third time, in 1974, an incoming Labour government created another betterment charge – this time branded the 'development land tax' – which was scrapped on Labour's departure from power in 1979.

All three attempts were accompanied by heated debate over the appropriateness of a single UK charge, centrally administered, that sought to tax capital gains and cost the impacts of development and ultimately supply, in a centralised way, the infrastructure needed to support growth. Fears over economic impact, over the potentially complicated nature of the system and over the centralised (and therefore locally unsympathetic) manner in which charges were to be levied put paid to these different attempts to tax land value uplift. Because of these fears, Cullingworth and Nadin (2002: 26) argued that 'it seems unlikely that the issue [of betterment] will return to the political agenda in the foreseeable future'. It did return, however, in the form of a proposed 'planning gain supplement', which became embroiled in the same debates and was abandoned.[3]

This storyline provides a critical context for the emergence of a *locally* negotiated planning gain approach (sidestepping the controversies accompanying the search for UK-wide systems) in the 1970s, which eventually became the primary means of delivering affordable housing with limited or no public subsidy.

In England and Wales, the 1971 Town and Country Planning Act allowed local authorities to enter into agreements with applicants, imposing obligations on developers and requiring them to deliver community gains as a price of receiving planning permission (the gain was viewed as a *local* levy on land value uplift, and negotiated in the context of *local* conditions). In Scotland, the 1972 Town and Country Planning (Scotland) Act established equivalent powers. During the 1970s and 1980s, some local authorities argued that one such gain could be affordable housing: that a community's need for such housing could be delivered through development control. They experimented with this approach but little headway was made, largely because it was not accepted that the need for such housing was a material planning consideration.

But this position shifted in the late 1980s in line with government's thinking on innovation and, more importantly, cost-efficiency. It was soon established that local planning gain could be a source of indirect subsidy for affordable housing, written into DoE and Welsh Office Circulars on planning and affordable housing in 1991 and a revision Planning Policy Guidance Note 3: Housing (then applying to England *and* Wales) a year later.

How has it worked?

The basic approach has been to use the development control process to negotiate, with private interests, for the inclusion of affordable homes within speculative developments. The planning system is deployed as a lever, generating a land-cost subsidy for these – often 'social rented' – homes. 'Local needs policies' (explored further in Chapter 13) have been written into local development plans, and continue to be written into Development Plan Documents (DPDs) in England and Wales (introduced by the 2004 Planning and Compulsory Purchase Act) and

Development Plans in Scotland (rooted in the 2006 Planning Etc (Scotland) Act, which updated the 1997 Town and Country Planning (Scotland) Act). These policies have resulted in two broad approaches.

First, a general approach involves the negotiation of affordable housing contributions from developers within sale housing schemes, on the basis of Section 106 Agreements[4] (1990 Town and Country Planning Act) or Section 75 Agreements (1997 Town and Country Planning (Scotland) Act). Affordable housing is treated as a gain (for the community) and is specified as a requirement within the Section 106 or Section 75 agreement written into a planning permission: in England and Wales, the requirement typically ranges from 20 to 50 per cent of total units depending on evidence of need (Crook et al, 2006: 354) and site viability; a study by Newhaven Research in Scotland suggests that local authorities make more modest requests north of the border, typically in the 5 to 25 per cent range (Newhaven Research, 2008: 27–30). The inclusion of affordable housing is an obligation imposed on the developer, and will be factored into how much the developer is willing to pay for the land. On the basis of a residual valuation (see Chapter 11), the developer or land buyer will calculate a surplus (anticipated market revenue less estimated development cost), which becomes the maximum amount that can be paid for the land (without affecting viability). The cost of meeting the planning obligation is subtracted from the surplus and hence this cost is borne by the landowner, though the cost may be shared through the negotiation of sale terms. Sometimes the developer builds these affordable homes (a specified number or proportion) and then sells them to a housing association at a cost that reflects the saving on land cost borne by the landowner. This saving represents an indirect subsidy, or the 'additionality' generated through the approach. In the best-case scenarios, this subsidy will partially or completely substitute for grant-funding, which can then be diverted elsewhere, perhaps to a location where less significant planning gains are possible. The general approach means that social housing is provided as part of a mixed development and is funded through planning gain, private sector borrowing and public subsidy. It forms part of a 'mixed funding package' as opposed to 'direct funding' of the type that was central to the production of affordable housing during much of the 20th century.

This approach was re-endorsed within English policy guidance in 2006, although there has been some refocusing of attention on the need for 'intermediate' – *between* market and social – housing. Planning Policy Statement 3 (PPS3) indicated that within Local Development Documents, planning authorities should set targets for the provision of affordable housing (DCLG, 2006b: para 29) to be delivered with a mix of direct finance and 'developer contributions'.[5] This target should be informed by strategic housing market assessments, which should also drive an area's market housing strategy with its aim of achieving broader affordability across the housing market.[6] The approach to seeking developer contributions remained largely unaltered from earlier policy. The real change introduced by PPS3 related not to affordable housing but to affordability and the need to align approaches with an understanding of changing market conditions, 'managing delivery' in such a way as to prevent under-supply from driving price inflation and decreasing access opportunities.

Policy was updated in Wales in the same year, with TAN 2 also placing a new emphasis on intermediate housing, alongside social rented provision (Welsh Assembly Government, 2006a: 4). Similarly, local housing market assessments (LHMAs) featured prominently in the revised guidance, with the TAN calling on local authorities in Wales to 'understand their whole housing system' (Welsh Assembly Government, 2006a: 6), thus enabling them to design effective planning-led affordable housing policies.

Revision of Scottish Planning Policy (SPP) for housing was completed in 2008 with the issuing of a new SPP3 (Scottish Government, 2008b). Like its English and Welsh counterparts, the Scottish policy statement places a new accent on understanding housing market dynamics, delimiting housing market areas (HMAs) and formulating more 'holistic strategies' that balance concern for market housing with policies for different social and intermediate products. However, it is in some ways a less complete document than PPS3, leaving the detail of delivery to associated advice notes (PAN74 *Affordable Housing* and PAN72 *Housing in the Countryside*) and a separate SPP (15) on *Rural Development*. Significantly, and in contrast to corresponding guidance in England, SPP3 seems to open the door to 'new housing outwith existing [rural] settlements', which 'may have a part to play in economic regeneration and environmental renewal' (Scottish Government, 2008b: 24). The associated PAN74 (Scottish Executive, 2005a) restates support for the general approach of procuring affordable housing through the planning system. Noticeably, however, neither SPP3 nor PAN74 (nor indeed PAN72) makes explicit reference to the second approach to securing affordable housing through agreements.

Originating in southern England, this second approach – the permitting of exceptional planning permissions for housing on land that would not normally be released for this use – was intended to be, and remains, a solution to affordability issues within or adjoining small village locations. It involves the granting of 'off-plan' permissions, often on agricultural land outside a village's development boundary. A partnership between the local planning authority, a registered social landlord, the landowner and a developer can progress a scheme involving: the release of land at less than full development value; the construction of 'local needs' housing for less than market cost (because of the land value subsidy); the transfer of these homes to a housing association; and renting of the homes to households in need, at a price they can afford, or offering them to local households on an intermediate tenure basis.

Following local experiments with the granting of exceptional planning permissions in southern England in the 1980s, on the back of Section 52 agreements (Gallent, 1997), simultaneous circulars were issued in England and Wales by the DoE and the Welsh Office, which gave official backing to the approach. Scottish exceptions remain in the experimental stage, and have so far been confined to a few areas including the Scottish Borders Council, which has adopted a comparable approach under the auspices of its *Housing in the Countryside* strategy (Scottish Borders Council, 2008). However, despite the potential to use the exceptions policy in Scotland, as set out in PAN74 (see Shiel et al, 2007), there seems to be reluctance to invest effort in policies that are 'unlikely to provide an answer to the scale of the site availability problem which has become evident, and are not particularly compatible with the preference for a plan led system and a clear policy framework on houses in the countryside' (Shiel et al, 2007: 46).

The success of the approach, where it operates, hinges on whether landowners can be encouraged to part with land at a price nearer agricultural than full development value. Research has shown that where there is uncertainty over a planning authority development strategy, or its intentions for a particular site are unclear, owners will hang on to all land in the hope that one day it may be earmarked for market housing (Gallent and Bell, 2000).

In the past, the approach was viewed as idiosyncratic: as out of step with plan-led policies. However, policy in England has emphasised that a 'rural exception site policy' can be one way of 'allocating and releasing sites solely for affordable housing' (DCLG, 2006a: para 30). The exceptions approach differs from the general approach in that it deals with small sites that would not normally be used for housing, because they are subject to restraint policies. Despite these differences, both approaches rely on the influence of planning on land prices and therefore total development costs. The cost of building new homes is reduced and this reduction is passed on to occupants, making the homes more affordable.

There have been local innovations on these broad approaches, though all are predicated on the need to reduce land cost as a means of achieving affordability. Some of these innovations are examined later, following a brief assessment of the overall contribution of planning and affordable housing policies to the supply of affordable housing. There is some bias here towards England. This is in part due to a paucity of unit-contribution assessments for either Scotland or Wales, and less consistent use of affordable housing policies in Scotland[7] (Shiel et al, 2007: 51). However, some comparisons are possible.

Delivery through planning: what has its contribution been?

Figures on the total contribution of these mechanisms to the supply of affordable housing in England can be drawn from Housing Investment Programme (HIP) returns: these are reports of local housing delivery provided annually by local authorities. They reveal, for example, that total output (that is, completions from all sources) of all affordable housing in England fell from nearly 45,000 units in 2000/01 to around 33,000 in 2004/05 (Crook et al, 2006: 359). These figures combine planning gain contributions with direct (grant-funded) provision and, according to Crook et al, 'the most obvious implication of these overall figures is that Section 106 has been unsuccessful in maintaining provision against a background of falling grant levels' (Crook et al, 2006: 359).

Over the same period, Section 106 completions doubled (from just over 9,000 to 18,000 completions). As grant funding to housing associations declines, a greater *proportion* of affordable housing output is generated through planning gain, but the absolute Section 106 output does not make up for the overall decline in supply. There is also great variation in terms of what can be achieved through planning gain from place to place, including a significant urban bias. A stronger market in southern England (and therefore greater incentive for the private sector and landowners to bring forward development, and accept larger planning contributions) meant that strategic sites in the South East region and in London contributed 10,000 completions to the 18,000 unit total in 2004/05. In contrast, the combined total of the North East and North West regions was fewer than 1,000 units.

Image 12.1: Affordable housing in Keswick, Cumbria © Sue Kidd

In Scotland, it has been noted by Newhaven Research that local authority effort – and subsequent Section 75 contributions – also tend to be focused in areas of higher land values (Newhaven Research, 2008: 3) and more acute development pressure. Data from the Scottish Government show that the total volume of affordable housing *consents* grew from 5,670 in 2005/06 to 6,892 the following year, falling back to 6,767 in 2008/09. However, over the four years examined, almost three quarters of these consents were not connected to planning gain arrangements: the actual figures ranged from 64 per cent in 2008/09 to 78 per cent in 2006/07 (Scottish Government, 2009b).This suggests that a lower proportion of affordable homes in Scotland are procured through the planning system and that this proportion is becoming steadily smaller.

In Wales it has been revealed that 'Local Authorities only secured between £14m and £20m worth of affordable housing through Section 106 Agreements in 2005-6' (Welsh Assembly Government, 2008b: 1). In Scotland, the Newhaven Research study for the Chartered Institute of Housing (CIH) concluded by asking whether 'it is beyond the wit of Scottish stakeholders to devise a system that can generate far more gain for far less pain than the present policy framework currently delivers' (Newhaven Research, 2008: 64). It seems certain that there is more faith in this approach in England, compared to either Scotland or Wales.

Economic conditions over time are critical, making it difficult to predict the future contribution of Section 75 or Section 106 negotiations to the total output of affordable housing.This is because affordable housing is piggybacked on general development.When the economic conditions for development are favourable, there is likely to be a steady output of affordable homes secured as a condition of planning permission (assuming that planning authorities are willing and able to extract as much from the system as possible). During the period of economic prosperity and strong house price growth between 2000/01 and 2006/07, planning gain made a significant contribution to the overall supply of affordable housing in England (Crook et al, 2006). But it was predicted that a downturn, or recession, might have a potentially catastrophic impact on supply (Centre for Cities, 2008; Hetherington, 2008). In the aftermath of the global banking crisis, which began to bite during 2008, there were real drops in construction activity[8] alongside clear difficulties in securing private finance for new HA schemes (CIH Scotland, 2009: 4). Both prompted governments to bring forward recovery and rescue packages (DCLG, 2008a; Scottish Government, 2008c) and led to calls for a return to direct public-sector provision (House of Commons Council Housing Group, 2009; Orr, 2009). These were heeded in Scotland through investment in new council housing in 2008/09 and 2009/10 and in England's 2009/10 local authority new-build (LANB) programme. An increasing number of commentators believe that the current system of procuring affordable housing through planning is too vulnerable to economic shocks (Gallent et al, 2010), delivering fewer affordable homes at those times when need is at its greatest.

The land question

Reliance on planning to deliver affordable homes in rural areas has long been problematic, because the amount of land available for development and hence the total volume of new-build is low – especially in and around villages – for reasons outlined in previous chapters.The 'flow of land' and the state of the market are defining factors in the success, or otherwise, of this approach (Crook et al, 2006: 371).With regards to the general approach, land-flow is a critical obstacle, with general restraint policies being reinforced by local reactions against housing development, and with these reactions underpinning an 'environmental rationale' in decision-making.

Image 12.2: Affordable housing making use of local materials, Keswick, Cumbria. Where schemes are part direct-funded, they must adhere to the HCA Quality Standards. Affordable housing schemes therefore have better build and space standards than comparable private development. © Sue Kidd

In England, the Commission for Rural Communities noted a decline in housing output that pre-dated the economic downturn. In 2003, private enterprise added 56,556 permanent dwellings to the rural housing stock: in 2005, the figure was 54,707 (CRC, 2006: 32). Provision by social landlords increased from 3,978 to 4,570 dwellings during the same brief period, perhaps compensating for a small part of the reduction in private provision. But overall, rural housing output fell from 60,688 units to 59,290. Arguably, these short-run variations provide weak evidence of a supply crisis in rural areas, though judged against year-on-year increases in demand, they present a worrying trend. Before the downturn, new dwelling completions in England increased by 22 per cent (between 2002/03 and 2005/06): but between 2003 and 2005, rural completions fell by nearly 4 per cent (Shucksmith, 2007b).

In 2004/05, roughly a third of all affordable homes (12,000) were provided in rural areas (including acquisitions to the stock). But for analytical purposes, these 'rural areas' include: 'significant rural' areas that may have as little as 26 per cent of their population in rural settlements; 'rural 50' areas, which can be semi-urbanised; and 'rural 80' areas, which are predominantly though not entirely rural. It is very difficult to say precisely how many affordable homes were provided in villages and areas of dispersed settlement as opposed to larger centres. However, half of the 12,000 homes were delivered in 'rural 50' and 'rural 80' areas. Assuming planning gain accounted for half of this half then 3,000 units may have been procured through exceptions and as a contribution of smaller speculative developments: though this may be an optimistic assessment given the realities of land supply and viability in villages.

As shown in Appendix 1, the Scottish Government uses a different method of settlement classification, separating settlements by size and by travel time to a major urban centre. Its analysis of the location of 26,000 affordable housing consents for 2005 to 2009 shows that 22 per cent were in small settlements in accessible and remote rural Scotland. A further 7 per cent were in small towns in remote rural Scotland and 66 per cent in urban areas. However, for affordable housing with some form of developer contribution (7,200 houses), 42 per cent were in small settlements in accessible and remote rural areas and small towns in remote areas, suggesting that developer contributions were more frequent in rural than in urban areas (Scottish Government, 2009b). It is important to note, however, that these data refer to consents rather than housing completions.

Two obvious conclusions can be reached at this point. First, planning has a potentially big role to play in delivering affordable housing, though the size of its contribution is dependent on economic conditions and land supply. Second, land supply has been the critical factor in limiting the supply of affordable housing in rural areas. Supply has the usual drivers: economic, environmental and social. The social driver has been particularly potent. At its core is a perception of what is desirable and acceptable, expressed in an environmental rationale for planning and a rejection of housing in and around villages on sustainability grounds. Taylor (2008: 151) was critical of the way generic sustainability appraisals result in a red-lining of villages, arguing that the rules applied to areas of concentrated population are inappropriate in much of the countryside: there should be greater flexibility in the application of its principles in the countryside so as to reflect a concern for the social composition of smaller settlements and for the well-being of rural communities. This same issue was picked up at the end of the last chapter.

Apparent acceptance of this view prompted *The Sunday Times* to announce the government's intention to 'bulldoze rural housing curbs' in England (Oakeshott, 2009). These rumours preceded the publication of the government's response to the Taylor Review (DCLG, 2009a), which, when it arrived, failed to live up to its billing. Government's response to the majority of Taylor's recommendations was one of broad acceptance – most points raised were 'generally agreed'. However, there was also an insistence that local planning was already sufficiently flexible.

Government in England seems to be saying that it has provided rural councils with the means to facilitate the provision of rural housing, it agrees broadly with the recommendations of the Taylor Review, and it hopes that councils will deliver against rural needs. There is little sense of change afoot in the response, although there are a few notable exceptions including reference to the possibility of providing landowners with incentives to 'come forward to provide land for rural exception sites' (DCLG, 2009a: 29). References to greater flexibility can even be read as a guarded criticism of local planning, which has hitherto been inflexible, guided not by government's policy frameworks (which are clearly up to scratch, in government's view), but by local resistance to development. This response perhaps betrays a fear of radical change (and its political consequences), adding up to an almost apologetic call for local authorities to do more (if they can) within a framework that aims to limit growth in smaller village locations. That is not to say that in the light of the review, some authorities will not think again about housing land in villages. However, additional innovation as opposed to a more systematic approach seems the most likely outcome and this is unlikely to provide a convincing 'answer to the scale of the site availability problem' (Shiel et al, 2007: 46) in many rural areas across Britain. Land for housing will remain the critical impediment to rural housing supply and also a brake on those interventions designed to deliver affordable housing for local need.

Innovating 'grant-free' models

Prior to the 2008–10 credit crunch and recession, when it was believed that a greater volume of contributions could be extracted from private enterprise and the land market, the DCLG (2006a: 2) set the goal of increasing 'the scope for achieving development without grant'. Echoing the sentiment of the 1987 Housing White Paper, it noted that 'local authorities can also improve delivery through creative use of their own resources, or by working effectively with other providers. They may be able to provide homes directly if resources are available, or through Housing PFI [Private Finance Initiative]. They may also give planning permission or other support including land or money to new providers to help them deliver innovative grant-free models' (DCLG, 2006a: 3). This goal may have been revised in light of the recession, with more rather than less public money being spent on affordable housing, and certainly less faith in the unremitting rise of land values. However, there are instances where grant-free delivery of affordable housing is possible, so these are worth some attention.

Research by Douglas Birt Consulting (2004) for the Housing Corporation has drawn attention to a number of ways that less restrictive planning can aid the development of grant-free affordable housing (Douglas Birt Consulting, 2004: 5). The examples cited included: affordable homes mixed within commercial, non-residential development; building micro-flats; key-worker housing on public employer land (with development on NHS estates seen as particularly important); and shared-equity initiatives that are less reliant (than social renting) on construction subsidies. Whilst some models and outcomes have been derided as cheap, inadequate homes masquerading as affordable ones – especially micro-flats – there have also been positive examples of innovative delivery.

Auchincloss (2008: 16–17), for instance, outlines the approach taken by THF Ltd in Cornwall. The objective of this private developer is to provide 'affordable housing to local people without public grant and [to keep] it available for low-income groups in perpetuity'. The purchase of land at below market value is the critical factor, and government in England has agreed to consider sanctioning incentives to landowners (DCLG, 2009b: 29). THF Ltd sells its homes at a 'price equal to the entire cost of delivery including land, construction costs and planning and professional fees. The figure is typically between 60 and 70% of open market value. There is no in-built profit margin' (Auchincloss, 2008: 17). Its only return is a shared ownership rent of just over £1000 per annum, payable by the occupier. Combined with mortgage payments, it is estimated that homes built by the company are affordable to households on an income of around £25,000 a year. Planning obligations are used to restrict occupancy to local residents unable to buy under normal market conditions. A similar model could be adopted by community land trusts (see Chapter 18). Such models fit evolving government thinking north and south of the Border (DCLG, 2006a; Scottish Government, 2007) and, 20 years on but under overtly different policy ideologies, represent an extension to the 1987 Housing White Paper's goal of innovating supply solutions that limit direct public responsibility.

The future

At the beginning of 2007, the task of predicting the future contribution of Section 75 and Section 106 policies to the production of affordable housing would have seemed a much simpler task than at the time of writing (2009/10). Despite overall falls in the supply of affordable homes, the number secured through planning was growing, and, in England, one could perhaps imagine Section 106 eventually paying for almost all social rented and intermediate tenure homes given the advent and growing success of grant-free delivery.

A lot changed from 2007 to 2010. The banking crisis, which became apparent in 2008, became a full-blown recession. Applications for residential development in Britain fell to historically low levels and developers mothballed many of the sites on which they had existing permissions. Housing completions were well below the national governments' targets, despite succour from accelerated capital investment programmes.

In 2007, the system that had evolved over the previous 20 years seemed to be paying dividends. In 2009/10, there is a questioning of its fundamental principles. Although house prices had fallen, the affordability of homes had not increased. This is because the falls were associated with the reduced availability of mortgage credit. As unemployment rates climbed alongside mortgage defaulting, and as house-building faltered and bank lending ground to a halt, the need for affordable housing was rising once more.

Although arguably specific to the here and now, this experience raises fundamental questions over the logic of relying on growth and general development to meet the nations' needs for affordable housing. And there were calls for a return to direct public sector house-building: during past recessions, public expenditure on house-building programmes had provided a means of cushioning the construction industry from downturns, keeping many of its skilled workers in paid employment.

But it is in rural areas where, even during the good times, the planning system has failed to deliver a sufficient supply of affordable homes.[9] This is because the approach relies on an adequate supply of land for development. Governments appeared to be inching towards an acknowledgement of this fact, but the economic downturn meant that even with a relaxation of planning rules, developers may be reluctant or unable to grasp new opportunities. Achieving a steady supply of affordable homes in the countryside may require governments to do more than flag up existing flexibility in the system. It may need to lead a radical reappraisal of land policies in rural areas, playing a crucial role in bringing about a culture shift. It may even need to countenance a return to direct investment and public building at more than just an experimental scale.

Notes

[1] The sale of public housing – and implicit support for tenure transfer as a route to owner-occupation – under discretionary policies (local authorities able to sell but not obliged to do so) was already significant when the Conservative government gained power in May 1979, and had been growing steadily since the 1967 Housing Subsidies Act and the subsequent 1975 Housing Rent and Subsidies Act, which allowed sitting tenants of local authorities to purchase equity shares in their council homes (see Gallent and Tewdwr-Jones, 2007: 58–9).

[2] Caution is needed in interpreting data. Data for England are reasonably comprehensive and have been used extensively in work by Crook and colleagues (various dates). Data for Scotland and Wales are not as full, though it is clear that the contribution of planning gain in these countries has generally been lower (see Newhaven Research, 2008; Welsh Assembly Government, 2008b).

[3] The idea was resurrected as a Community Infrastructure Levy (CIL), introduced for England and Wales by the 2008 Planning Act to run from April 2010 (after the time of writing this book). It was designed as a local levy: to pay directly for 'community infrastructure' and to contribute indirectly to sub-regional projects. Government's intention was that CIL would run in tandem with Section 106 policies, though planning contributions would be scaled back where an authority decided to set a charge linked to development permissions.

[4] In 1991, Section 106 (along with Sections 106A and 106B) was substituted by Section 12(1) of the Planning and Compensation Act of that year, but these obligations continue to be known as Section 106 Agreements.

[5] This phrase is widely used in planning policy but, as suggested earlier, it is rather misleading.

[6] Further discussion of this approach and its consequences in rural areas is provided in Chapter 11.

[7] Levels of usage in Wales have been broadly similar to those in England. A study by Gallent et al (2002a) showed that more than 80 per cent of English and Welsh rural authorities seek to negotiate for quotas of affordable housing using Section 106 agreements (Gallent et al, 2002a: 469). However, only a third of Welsh authorities had granted planning exceptions compared to 70 per cent of authorities in England (Gallent et al, 2002a: 470).

[8] For example, England saw the number of completions by private enterprise fall from just over 150,000 homes in 2007 to fewer than 108,000 in 2008; completions by private enterprise in Scotland fell from 21,640 to 17,860; the corresponding figures for Wales were 9,110 and 8,950 (all figures sourced from DCLG, Live Tables, 6 February 2010). In February 2010, the National Housing Federation predicted that the amount of housing delivered by the private sector in 2009/10 would be at its lowest level since 1923 (Morris, 2010).

[9] That is not to say that there have not been local success stories and many examples of innovation (Gallent et al, 2002a).

THIRTEEN

Targeting 'local' needs

One of the most revealing tactics for addressing housing supply pressures in rural areas is the selective targeting of 'local' needs. It involves giving priority access to 'local people' – households with a 'local connection' or those working locally – for new homes, whether these are for rent, for shared ownership or for outright purchase. Priority access to specified groups is often a requirement, written into a planning obligation, where affordable housing is delivered through an exceptional permission or secured as a planning gain within a private development. In some instances, occupancy conditions have been attached to all new housing developments in an area. The local planning authority, which has 'enabled' the scheme through its development control function, has a responsibility to ensure that housing for local need fulfils this purpose in perpetuity, or may believe that – because land supply in the next planning period will be limited – all new housing should serve the local market.

The tactic is revealing for two reasons: first, because it highlights the indirect nature of the public response to the need for affordable housing; and, second, because it shows how authorities attempt to address the specific needs of a part of the housing market without increasing general supply and thereby mustering local support for development. Because of broader planning constraints, and the external interest that new market homes could attract, authorities will not release land for general development, but instead restrict the occupancy of a high proportion of the housing they do permit. This constraint on general supply serves to protect the rural resource, but also focuses external market interest on existing properties. The dilemma is not an easy one to solve and government has long resisted calls to build new public housing on land especially earmarked for that purpose (ACRE, 1988), though opportunities may arise to provide homes for local need, or for key workers, on land owned by a local authority or another public body.

There are several key areas of concern relating to this topic. First, there is the inevitable controversy that surrounds giving priority to 'local people'. Second, the effectiveness of the tactic, noted above, is also keenly disputed. Third, if used too widely and readily, giving priority to local needs can impact on the general supply of housing and have a range of potentially undesirable consequences. Fourth, who should be given priority? The question of who is 'local' is perhaps easier to resolve than the question of whether the case for special treatment should be merely 'ancestral' or whether there should be a pressing economic case for supporting specific groups. There has been an evolution of thinking on this issue from the late 1970s, stretching from support for agricultural labour to an apparently broader priority on 'essential' workers, which for many commentators, has not become broad enough and continues to act as a brake on the diversification of rural economies. And finally, to what extent can the tactic be used to widen the social mix and create more 'sustainable' rural communities? These issues are briefly examined in turn.

The favoured few

Access to the direct housing products of the public or voluntary sectors has always been restricted. Getting a council house in many areas involved (and still involves) joining a waiting list and having your needs assessed against those of others on the same list. Particular attributes may see you move up or down this list, including being married, having children, working close by or having lived in an area for more than a specified number of years. The fact that the local authority was spending public money on performing a welfare service justified having some means of judging the relative needs of different applicants and making appropriate choices. The same was true of housing association tenancies, particularly between 1974 and 1988 when association projects were often fully funded from the public purse (that is, between the creation of a full capital grant support system and the move to mixed funding for association schemes: see Chapter 12).

This form of 'needs-based' allocation of social housing has run into heavy criticism. It has failed, for example, to deliver against the needs of newly forming households who have not yet accumulated sufficient points to warrant assistance under the system (Shucksmith and Philip, 2000: 47). It also stands accused of concentrating marginalised households in what can become sink areas (Marsh and Mullins, 1998: 755), whilst 'choice-based' allocations or lettings – which place less emphasis on normative measures of need and allow applicants with fewer points to take up tenancies in less popular areas – can create 'communities with a wider social mix' (Abbott, 2005: 4). Such criticism, however, often draws on experience in urban areas. But one accusation that seems to have greater currency in rural areas concerns the role of local councillors in seeking to support or protect what they see as local interests. Shucksmith and Philip (2000: vi) draw on previous research to assert that 'councillors in rural areas may operate in a more paternalistic or clientelist manner than elsewhere, placing emphasis on their role as local representatives and as articulators of the interests of those constituents who contact them': what should be a normative allocation process can be subject to political interference and 'unaccountable discretion' (see Pawson and Kintrea, 2002: 648).

At the time of writing, waiting lists – or registers that are 'shared' or 'common' between social housing providers – still provide the entry point for households seeking assistance, though this assistance is no longer paid for solely with public money. Sometimes there is an element of land subsidy levered through the planning system (with costs being met, primarily, by landowners), which is mixed with grant funding from the Homes and Communities Agency (in England), the Welsh Assembly or the Scottish Government; or sometimes new affordable housing schemes are grant-free (but may still utilise public land assets). Because different sectors have some input into the production of affordable housing, competing claims can arise over who should be seen as 'local' and as 'in need'. There is often broad agreement between the public and voluntary sectors, but private providers may take a different view, questioning the choices of their not-for-profit partners. The example of landowners wanting family members or employees to benefit directly from their 'philanthropy' (especially on exception sites) is a case in hand, and an issue raised by Taylor in 2008. Indeed, government in England proposed in November 2009 to incentivise landowner participation in exceptions schemes by creating a 'referral system' (DCLG, 2009b: 11) in which 'employees or members of the family of the landowner' – who have a 'local connection' – can be nominated to occupy new homes on the exception site. The issue was also raised in the context of the Scottish Government's Rural Homes for Rent scheme, announced in 2008, under which private or community landowners making their land available for affordable housing developments became eligible for capital assistance (although no explicit reference was made to family members in the scheme's model allocations policy; Scottish Government, 2008e). Incentives for landowners are now increasingly a key part of rural affordable housing schemes.

More broadly, however, there has been a questioning of the use of occupancy agreements where housing is delivered through the market, where planning gain or an exceptional permission has been the sole means of reducing the build cost (by taking out much of the land cost). In these circumstances, the rationale of favouring households who just happen to live in the vicinity of the scheme has been questioned and contrasted with past initiatives whose logic seemed more clear-cut: to provide homes for agricultural workers or to build council houses (with public money) in areas where labour demand existed but where market housing had become too expensive. The basic criticism is this: it makes no sense, on equity, welfare or economic grounds, to preferentially assist local people in areas where there is no labour demand; it would make more sense to direct assistance to locations where there are jobs and other opportunities. In most instances, planning policy does the latter (not perhaps because of the economic logic, but because development land opportunities are scarce in villages), but there is a weight of feeling in rural areas (though not articulated in these terms) in favour of ancestral rights – that local homes should go to local people and that where the open market inhibits this 'natural justice', the planning system should intervene to sort things out.

Debate surrounding this issue was triggered by the 'local needs' policies that took root in the planning system around 1990 in England and Wales. The first draft of Planning Policy Guidance note 3 (PPG3) (1988) made no mention of procuring affordable housing through development control, but a redraft in 1989 caused something of a stir by suggesting that a community's need for affordable housing should be seen as a 'material planning consideration' (DoE, 1989: para 25) and that 'local arrangements' should be made with regards to the 'release of small sites within or adjoining existing villages which would not otherwise be allocated for housing' (DoE, 1989: para 28; see also Gallent, 2000: 129–31). These instructions were then transferred into two planning circulars (7/91 and 31/91 for England and Wales, respectively) and the final draft of PPG3 in 1992. Some legal experts took issue with these 'local needs' policies. Hutton, for example, writing in the *Journal of Planning and Environment Law*, commented that such policies 'unfairly advantage those on low incomes who, by good fortune, live in rural areas' (1991: 311). His point was again about the missing link between homes and jobs, whether occupants would in fact be key or essential to the local economy, or whether they were merely the 'favoured few'.

Landowners can be reticent to release land for rural exceptions: because they hope land will one day command full development value; because they believe that homes built may not be secured as affordable in perpetuity; or because they have no direct control over who will benefit from their goodwill, though this may now change. Hutton is yet to respond to the suggestion that landowners will be able to refer friends and family to be housed on exception sites.

Local successes

There is, of course, a broader objective in mind when those unable to compete in the open market are given assisted access to housing: to promote social mix and avoid the total gentrification of villages. It may also be the case that those nominated to occupy homes in the latest shared ownership or social rented housing scheme have other good reasons to remain in the village: perhaps they have caring responsibilities, or will be cared for in some way by nearby family members. It could also be the case that the parish or community council has argued for more local housing for reasons of protecting 'community interest', positing, though probably not in these exact words, that 'intensive emotional ties' are maintained through residency – in close proximity – of kinship groups, and that it is through these ties that the lifeblood of the community flows. Avoiding what some see as the decimation of 'community' is a rationale often at the heart of local needs policies and, in this respect, schemes that have appeared to protect this community interest might be judged a success, bringing 'stability' to villages (Cumbria Rural Housing Trust, 2004).

Many local authorities have developed local needs policies. In North Norfolk, the prevailing view is that local people need choice, but that market processes often limit the choices available. Research in the district in 2002 suggested that local buyers are excluded from many villages as a result of a combination of retirement, second home pressure and a lack of job opportunities. This means that they must widen their search for homes (and, of course, jobs), often ending up in their 'third or fourth area of choice'. The local authority developed standard local needs approaches: allowing the development of isolated dwellings for agricultural workers and applying Section 106 conditions to new affordable housing and also to homes sold to sitting tenants through the right to buy. Its view was that these were successful where they were applied, though application was not broad enough and therefore residential choices were still primarily driven by the market. In an ideal world, the authority would have liked to have seen local buyers treated preferentially by the mortgage market (offered lower rates, perhaps subsidised by the state), though it also recognised two counter-forces that limit what is achieved through local needs policies. First, residential choices cannot be solely driven by the availability of housing: access to jobs is critically important. Whilst planning can create opportunities for enterprise and investment, it offers no guarantee of outcome. Businesses will make their own choices, expanding or contracting as economic forces dictate. It is fanciful to suppose that the planning system has absolute power to determine local outcomes. Second, there is local expectation that the system cannot live up to. People have a strong desire to 'live very locally to their home area', but sometimes the wisdom and realism of this expectation needs to be questioned rather than simply accepted and responded to. The success of local needs policies in North Norfolk does not lie in blindly anchoring local communities to villages, but in sensitive and integrated application: tying homes to jobs and ensuring that affordable housing is retained in perpetuity.

The same research made similar findings across England. In Suffolk Coast, for example, the local authority had a similar attitude to local needs policies but had encouraged more widespread take-up of shared ownership opportunities. Its officers noted the 'resentment' amongst local people that stemmed from being 'forced' out of villages and shunted to nearby towns. This resentment, however, was aimed more at the perceived causes of this displacement (second home purchasing and retirement) than the authority's apparent inability to formulate an effective response. In East Lindsey, it was recognised that a strengthening economy does not always counter this pattern of displacement. Growth in the area's tourist industry was first seen to strengthen the position of local households, creating additional jobs and providing people with the means to buy their own homes. But as growth associated with tourism continued, more incomers arrived in what was seen as an 'up and coming' area: some took advantage of lower house prices whilst others were attracted by the coastal location and proximity to the Wolds AONB: local needs policies have been developed belatedly, as a response to the area's economic success and the effect of this success on local people, whose new jobs in a burgeoning tourism sector still do not pay enough to compete in the strengthening property market.

Have these controls over occupancy provided a lasting and fundamental answer to the needs of these communities? Are they now 'more sustainable'? Authorities recognise the need to link economic development to the availability of housing, but often this link is difficult to plan for and to 'get right'. Jobs that are provided may be low paid and not empower local people; and sometimes investment may advantage incomers with a different skill set. This means that a combination of planning policies and local needs restrictions may still cause a separation of households from jobs and services. Local needs policies may, to some extent, achieve their goal of creating a more socially mixed community, but may also isolate assisted households within communities where there are not the right kinds of jobs or services. Perhaps it would have been better to have questioned residential aspirations in North Norfolk and to have viewed displacement in Suffolk Coast as a natural process of socio-economic restructuring. Accepting this market view means accepting some element of gentrification as an inevitable feature of rural change, avoiding a situation where the assistance rendered is out of step with economic reality.

In a report to the Scottish Government, Satsangi and Crawford (2009: 7) argued that, besides issues of 'legality and legitimacy', local needs policies run the risk of undermining development viability leading to a stagnation in the housing market which may compound difficulties in the wider economy. As well as the risk of fostering a mismatch between jobs and homes, 'there must also be concern about whether' this type of 'policy of restraint fits with the primacy … attached to improving national and local economic growth rates' (Satsangi and Crawford, 2009: 7).

Undesirable outcomes

This potential disjuncture is one undesirable outcome. There are also others. Whilst occupancy controls are often used selectively (as in the examples given earlier), and only applied to particular schemes where there is some proof of need (and usually where these schemes have some element of public or land subsidy), they have occasionally been used more generally and applied to all new development in an area. The justification tends to be that the amount of development land that will come forward in the next planning period is limited and should therefore be exclusively reserved for local need. The most regularly cited case of such general application is that of the Cumbria and Lake District Joint Structure Plan, which was referred to in an earlier chapter and which was studied by Capstick (1987) and Shucksmith (1981, 1990b). The Lake District Special Planning Board (LDSPB) sought to use the Section 52 provisions of the 1971 Town and Country Planning Act to control the occupancy of all new housing built within the Lake District National Park. Essentially, the Joint Structure Plan (LDSPB, 1980) issued by the LDSPB and Cumbria County Council stipulated that all new housing would have to be built for local need and that Section 52 would be used to ensure that it could only be occupied by 'local people' in perpetuity. The Lakes were (and continue to be) attractive to commuters, retiring households and second home buyers. House-builders were used to supplying this market and to enjoying the profits that this generated. They were not at all happy with this interference and many chose not to continue building in the Park (and could not do so because of declining viability and the risks associated with a shrinking market), but to move their operations outside the jurisdiction of the LDSPB. Despite the land allocations of the council, their policies had impacted on the 'marketability' of land and caused a reduction in house-building consequent – fundamentally – on reduced development viability (see also Satsangi and Crawford, 2009: 7). This was the first consequence.

It was also the case that the demand that was no longer catered for by new-build did not simply disappear. Holidaymakers, commuters and soon-to-be pensioners were still looking for homes in the Lakes, but now focused their efforts on the second-hand market. These two trends – reduced production of new homes and more intense, focused competition for older property – combined and added up to one thing: higher house prices. The big losers in all this were newly forming, local households. The big winners were existing property owners who were happy that the planners had chosen to concentrate and accentuate existing patterns of wealth in the area.

Eventually, in 1983, the Secretary of State for the Environment intervened and deleted the policy from the Joint Structure Plan, implying that it represented undue interference in the operation of the housing market, and had failed to fulfil its intended purpose. One practical difficulty that occupancy controls cannot overcome is that they can only operate within a section of the housing market: they have no influence over transactions in the second-hand market so tend to concentrate buyer interest when applied too generally or rigorously to new development. Hence they can 'distort' the market by causing an intensification of demand, whilst reducing interest in new development opportunities. However, this experience in the past has not dampened enthusiasm for wider use of occupancy controls today.

In 2002, the Pembrokeshire Coast National Park Authority (NPA) and Pembrokeshire County Council placed a Joint Unitary Development Plan (JUDP) on deposit (PCC and PCNPA, 2002). The plan contained a policy (Policy 47) stipulating that in 26 'sustainable communities' new residential development would not be permitted unless it were explicitly connected to a 'need for residential development for local persons' or 'an essential need to live within the sustainable community'. In effect, all new housing must be for 'local need' or meet the needs of 'essential workers'. The policy aimed to close the door on speculative development in some of the National Park's most desirable villages.

In the context of the 1990 Town and Country Planning Act (Section 106), and advice contained in Planning Policy Wales (issued in March 2002: Welsh Assembly Government, 2002a) at that time, it was generally accepted that it would normally be appropriate for local policies, and development control decisions, to favour particular categories of potential occupant including 'local people' and 'essential workers'. But because the Pembrokeshire policy was to be so widely applied (like the Lakes policy 20 years before), there was a concern that it would be *ultra vires* (that is, beyond the granted power of the local authorities involved) and could run contrary to the 1998 Human Rights Act. This was the initial response of the Welsh Assembly Government in Cardiff, which called on the NPA to ensure that all such policies were tied explicitly to local evidence and not applied generally (echoing the opinion of the Secretary of State for the Environment in 1983). Legal advice was sought by the authority, which subsequently embarked on an intense programme of evidence-gathering in order to justify Policy 47. The authority commissioned an evaluation of likely impact from a team of academics (Tewdwr-Jones and Gallent, 2002), who referred back to the work of Shucksmith in the Lakes. They drew parallels and inferences from the attempt by the LDSPB to prioritise local needs through the use of a Section 52-based policy, concluding that *blanket restrictions* could have a range of unintended economic, environmental, social and housing market effects.

These might include indirect discrimination against first-time buyers, with the policy helping some directly but reducing the likelihood of others being able to access homes. This was the experience in the Lakes. It was also suggested that where homes were offered to local buyers on an intermediate tenure basis, these buyers might have difficulty in securing mortgage credit (at favourable interest rates) as prospective lenders could be concerned about the onward sale of homes subject to occupancy restriction.

There could also be an impact on the local construction industry with many potential construction sites subject to planning, denying developers the opportunity to build for the general market. Arguably this impact could be limited as builders would continue to concentrate development in larger centres and on sites unfettered by restrictions. But this then raises the question of *who* will develop affordable homes if private sector interest wanes and development viability reduces as a result of an enforced tightening of the market for homes in small village locations. Perhaps more philanthropic providers will come forward, or community land trusts will take the strain. This certainly appears to be the English government's current hope.

There is also an impact on potential migrants, who are arguably being discriminated against. Although migrants are sometimes stereotyped as seasonal residents or retired downshifters – who either consume nothing, and erode local services, or who consume more than they contribute – many incomers invest in the local area. They invest directly in their homes, they pay local taxes and they often devote their time and effort in the development of local communities. As Gallent (2007) puts it, they 'dwell' in rural communities in a variety of ways and many make a clear financial and social contribution. Local needs policies, if they are too pervasive, can be read as a rejection of migrant contribution and this in itself is problematic, given the acknowledged contribution that migrants make to rural economies and communities, particularly through their association with new micro-businesses (Bosworth, 2006).

However, there are potential benefits to the local area: existing homeowners may reap a financial reward; restrictions on house-building may inflate the value of local property, encouraging owners to borrow and spend, perhaps by improving their homes. They will benefit personally, as will the local economy. Likewise – and because of these same restrictions – there may be a slowing of land-take for new development, bringing environmental rewards (if development is viewed as having an inherently negative impact on environmental quality).

Returning to the first point, the policy will inevitably directly help some local households: this seems certain. The impact on other local households (the wider pool of those in need and existing homeowners) is more debatable. Authorities developing these types of policies tend to focus on direct consequences, viewing

broader concerns as academic or uncertain. There is also another reason why 'local needs' are established as a priority in local plans: resistance to development. Building under the banner of local needs is far more palatable than 'indiscriminate' construction. Therefore, local needs policies should not only be seen as a form of targeted assistance, but also as a means of delivering housing numbers.

Agricultural labour, local connections and essential workers

The constant return to the 'occupancy' solution, not only in Pembrokeshire but also elsewhere – back in the Lakes, in Cornwall and across Britain – is not down to sheer pig-headedness, but a struggle with fundamentals: rising demand for homes, limited land coming forward through planning and a local need that cannot be met within a constrained market.

But behind this strategy, several attendant debates rumble on. First, how should local planning authorities define 'local connection'? Should the focus be on ancestral rights or needs tied to employment? And second, to what extent should the needs of agricultural or essential workers be prioritised, and are current priorities right, in the context of restructuring rural economies? There has been a long, drawn-out debate on the nature of localness. Three decades ago, Mark Shucksmith catalogued some of this debate, looking at the different interpretations of the term 'local' for policy purposes. He argued that attaching acceptable meanings to the terms 'local' and 'need' is a critical challenge for planning policy (Shucksmith, 1981: 17), adding that doubts and uncertainties surrounding definitions of local (from a specific village, from a cluster of villages, from a district, and then, of course, what does 'being from' entail: being born somewhere, having a family connection, working in a village or area?) and of the nature and ethics (Rogers, 1985) of need make the idea of 'local needs' a 'very rocky foundation on which to build policy' (Shucksmith, 1990b: 66). This practical and moral uncertainty (should the hand of planning be making such 'personal' judgements?) is frequently sidestepped through pragmatic application: 'local need' is used as a sweetener, with the label often taken to denote a 'politically acceptable rate of housing development, rather than a social concept of need' (Shucksmith, 1990b: 64).

The body of literature on what constitutes 'need' is extensive, though common sense suggests clear daylight between 'demand' with its economic inferences and 'need', an understanding of which normally builds on Needleman's (1965) definition: the extent to which the quality and quantity of homes 'falls short of that required to provide each household or person in the population, *irrespective of ability to pay* or of particular personal references, with accommodation of a specified minimum standard and above', with the italicised part often seen as the most crucial (Needleman, 1965: 18).

The debate over agricultural and essential workers is perhaps simpler and can be summarised as follows. Safeguarding the needs of agricultural workers is anachronistic given fundamental shifts in the nature of rural communities: the

priority that farm workers once enjoyed should be transferred to those who are 'essential' to modern rural economies. This debate has been played out in planning policy and particularly in the shift from PPG7 to PPS7 in England, the revision of TAN6 in Wales and the replacement of NPP15 with SPP15 in Scotland. During each of these shifts it was argued that the definition of an 'essential worker' should be revisited, or the needs of agriculture should be reconsidered in the light of economic change, and that there should be a consequent review of the functional and financial tests that need to be satisfied if agricultural or essential worker exceptions are to be made.

There is an ancillary debate, albeit one that has receded, over local authority responsibility to house former farm workers who have lost their tied homes on cessation of employment. A responsibility to rehouse farm workers was created by the 1976 Rent (Agriculture) Act, which remains in force. The more pressing issue is who is 'essential' to the rural economy, and how should this be acknowledged within the planning system.

It needs to be recognised that there is a wider, generic policy concern for key and essential workers. This often means key public sector workers and those providing what are considered to be essential services: so nurses and some other types of health worker, teachers, and police and firemen often fall into this category. But these are not given priority to housing in specified locations (below a borough or district level) – rather they benefit from general priority and support and may have preferential access to new social housing or may be able to take advantage of low-interest or interest-free government loans designed to augment their capacity to acquire mortgage credit. When we talk about essential workers in the countryside, our concern is more specific, and often about whether planning policy will permit one-off developments designed to allow an essential worker to reside in a very specific location.

England perhaps wrestles hardest with this issue, with Scotland and Wales developing policy that is more sensitive to economic restructuring in the countryside. In England, PPG7 seemed to grudgingly acknowledge that new homes might be needed for 'agricultural and forestry workers' in open countryside, but added that 'normally it will be as convenient for such workers to live in nearby towns or villages as it will be for them to live where they work. This may have domestic and social advantages as well as avoiding potentially intrusive development in the countryside' (DETR, 2001: Annex 1, para 1). A clear emphasis was placed on restricting development, with government questioning the real *need* of anyone to live in more isolated locations. The guidance went on to note the 'substantial reduction in agricultural employment' (para 3), adding to the sense that the guidance was really about questioning the extent of need rather than providing clear direction to planning authorities. In fact, its opening four paragraphs did little more than reiterate government's presumption against such development, highlighting the risk of abuse, and emphasising its concern over the 'genuineness' of agricultural and forestry need.

In fact, the guidance offered in PPG7 to English authorities was much maligned for two reasons. First, it seemed to create an intentional stalemate: it opened the door to isolated residential development, but then rejected as false the need for such development as a result of wider economic change. And second, it failed to acknowledge that this change could itself generate a need for other forms of essential worker housing, not confined to the farming or forestry sectors.

Planning Policy Statement 7 (PPS7)[1] paid lip service to this issue. Its annex on the same subject was given an extended title – 'agricultural, forestry and other occupational dwellings' – and the restrictive tone found in its forerunner was somewhat lessened, though it still highlighted the preferred logic of 'workers [living] in nearby towns or villages, or suitable existing dwellings' (ODPM, 2004: Annex A, para 1). PPS7 noted that 'there may ... be instances where special justification exists for new isolated dwellings associated with other rural-based enterprises' (para 15) before emphasising that applications for other occupational dwellings would be subject to the 'same stringent levels of assessment'. This meant, amongst other things, that the business to which the dwelling was connected must be viable, and there must be a 'functional need' to live in close proximity: for example, the need to deal with emergencies, or to provide 24-hour care to animals. The latter conditions need to be reinterpreted for non-farming businesses.

A significant criticism of the guidance was its failure to provide detail: to give examples of the types of rural businesses (other than farming) that might generate a need for occupational dwellings. Applicants have struggled to meet the strict criteria set out in planning policy, unless their businesses share some of the key characteristics of farming. For example, stud farms and horse-riding centres have animals and can therefore reasonably propose a need for someone to be close at hand, offering persuasive animal welfare arguments. But other businesses essential to the rural economy are unlikely to satisfy PPS7's functional tests, and so essential workers in rural areas remain agricultural workers despite the decline of farming activity. The policy is predicated on the goal of preventing development in the open countryside unless the case for development is so compelling that an authority could not reasonably oppose it.

A lasting contribution to sustainable communities

There are a number of crucial debates that come together around the issue of local need. It is clear, however, that development in the countryside is seen as an exception rather than a rule. Beyond settlement boundaries, the case for one-off additional homes must be compelling and decisions running contrary to the general presumption against residential development are rare. Even development within and adjoining villages is infrequent: this is partly a result of local resistance but also because of a paucity of land unfettered by planning. In this chapter we have argued that the priority given to local needs – via the planning system – is about judicial use of limited land resources and also about mustering support around development. Where local needs policies have been applied they have delivered *individual* opportunities to reside in a certain location, satisfying perhaps a particular family's desire to be close to friends and relatives or to have a home in the village where they have a strong, established family connection.

But for every household benefiting from such local policies, many others are obliged to move away, not only because of a lack of suitable accommodation, but also because of inadequate services and insufficient diversification in the rural economy. Government's attitude towards 'essential workers' – that they would be better off moving to a nearby town – is often extended to 'local people' wishing to live in smaller villages and hamlets. The social and economic logic is simply not accepted. Planning policy guidance implicitly rejects the economic case for living in the countryside and plays up the social benefits of town life.

Planning authorities, for their part, continue to 'struggle with fundamentals' – a powerful 'environmental' rationale driving the planning system versus rampant demand for rural living. Local politicians need to steer an uncertain path: between the need to deliver homes for local people, and the need to place strict limits on development. In this context, a focus on local needs policies seems to provide a tactical solution. But these policies are not providing the homes that rural communities need: the real issue seems to be land for growth, not linked to individual aspiration, but to wider community objectives, driven by a fundamental concern for the social composition of the countryside and of rural communities. The targeting of local needs, above any other policy or approach, is symbolic of the tension between development and conservation in the countryside.

Note

[1] Some parts of PPS7 dealing with economic development have been replaced by PPS4: Planning for Sustainable Economic Growth (DCLG, 2009c), though the annex on 'agricultural, forestry and other occupational dwellings' contained in PPS7 is unaffected.

Part IV
Tenure and policy intervention

FOURTEEN

Social renting

Renewed support for direct housing provision by local authorities, noted in Chapter 12, appeared to be gaining momentum in policy and academic circles in the early years of this century (Monk and Ni Luanaigh, 2006). In the rural context, having a wider variety of mechanisms available is valuable, not just an attempt to lever a higher rate of non-market housing into communities, but also to provide alternative ways of overcoming the inherent difficulties of developing affordable housing in such localities. Despite post-1990s' policy exhorting a range of social rented and intermediate options in developments (for example, DCLG, 2006a), such intermediate housing products seemed to have very limited presence in smaller settlements (Hoggart and Henderson, 2005). Furthermore, a narrow focus on home ownership in national policies scarcely extended viable housing options for people on lower incomes in rural localities. Monk et al (2006) used the notion of 'housing staircases' to highlight how the lack of available properties at lower prices in many rural communities caused affordability problems for households on lower incomes. Also falling prices do not necessarily ease affordability problems. The following section considers the issue of housing affordability and the net need for low-cost housing in order to provide a context for the discussion on the role of social rented accommodation in rural localities.

In 2007, England's Commission for Rural Communities (CRC, 2007a) calculated the affordability of market housing in the smallest settlements in terms of the ratio between household incomes and house prices (Table 14.1). Wilcox (2007), however, has pointed out that it is not sufficient to look at house prices alone as a measure of affordability and that analysis of this issue needs to consider the capacity of households to pay market rents. This conclusion chimes with the findings of Bramley and Watkins (2009) in relation to the relative affordability of private rents in many rural localities, and their call to address not only the supply of homes for sale, but also the supply of homes for rent from a mix of landlords.

Scotland and England have the benefit of calculations by Glen Bramley and others on the level of net needs for affordable housing in these countries. Bramley and Watkins (2009: 194) argue that their analysis of affordability in urban and rural local authorities in England reveals that rural areas have:

> as good a case for extra affordable housing investment as urban areas, in proportion to their demographic scale. However [their analysis] does not support the more extreme view that rural areas have a greater relative need.

Table 14.1: Ratio of household income to house prices, England, 2006

	Village, hamlet and isolated dwellings	Town and fringe	Urban >10k residents
Less sparse	8.9	7.2	6.8
Sparse	9.1	8.6	7.1

Note: The definitions of 'sparse' and 'less sparse' are discussed in the Appendix.
Source: Commission for Rural Communities (CRC, 2007a)

However, Bramley and Watkins' (2009) analysis at the level of urban and rural wards also showed that, away from London, net need for affordable housing was greater in rural areas, especially inaccessible rural areas, and less in urban areas. Nevertheless, if London is included in such calculations, there is very little difference in net needs between urban and rural areas. There was some variation across England in these results: in the South the difference between urban and rural areas was slight, in the North and the Midlands, rural needs tend to be more acute. In Scotland, the total need for *additional* affordable housing in 2005 was calculated at just over 8,000 units per year (Bramley et al, 2006). An analysis for the Commission for Rural Communities estimated that the total need in the rural areas of England (settlements with fewer than 10,000 residents) was for over 30,000 affordable homes per year (Roger Tym and Partners and Jordan Research, 2006). By drawing on housing needs assessments undertaken in Wales' nine most rural authorities between 2000 and 2004, the Joseph Rowntree Foundation (JRF, 2008) has been able to make a strangely accurate estimate of the net annual shortfall in the supply of affordable homes, of 3,803 units. There is certainly little apparent evidence for an improvement in the affordability of housing in rural areas contained within the latest fall in house prices since 2008, partly due to the crisis in mortgage lending, but also the gap between low incomes (in many rural areas) and the availability of accommodation at the lower end of the market. Spedding (2009) pointed out that in spite of falling house prices, the ratio of average house price to average household income in rural areas improved by just 0.1 points between December 2007 and December 2008. Across all rural areas, the average household would still need more than seven times its income to purchase an average home, compared with 6.3 times household income in an urban area in the same region. Monk et al (2006) point out that getting an increased *supply* of housing that is affordable to lower-income groups is the crucial issue, whether this housing is for purchase or for rent. In this context, it is social renting that has, and continues, to play a crucial role for groups on low incomes.

The role, potential and perceptions of social renting

The history of developing social renting in rural areas can be summed up in two words: inertia and resistance. Inertia, because of the myriad practical difficulties of developing social renting in small communities; and resistance as a result of cultural and political opposition to the notion of a vibrant social rented sector in the countryside. Case study research has shown the way that delivery mechanisms and local governance structures have combined in different localities to produce varied outcomes in terms of the amount of social rented stock that exists (Newby, 1979; Dickens et al, 1985; Long, 2005). In spite of the innovation and hard work taking place at local level, national averages tell their own story. Tellingly, the analysis by Bramley and Watkins (2009) concluded that the key feature of the rural housing problem in rural areas was one of *supply*, rather than affordability, highlighting the constrained size of the social rented sector and low turnover of properties as critical barriers to housing access. This neatly summarises the predicament in smaller village and hamlet locations, where the supply of social rented options is particularly constrained and house prices tend to be relatively high. This conclusion also provides an explanation for the persistence of the problem of limited access to housing for lower-income groups in rural localities across housing market cycles. The dearth of social rented stock in the rural communities of Wales, England and Scotland compared with urban areas is conveyed in Tables 14.2 to 14.4.

Tables 14.2 and 14.3 present data on the tenure profiles for the rural areas of England and Wales in 2001. Use of the Scottish Household Survey allows the tenure pattern in 2007 for Scotland to be shown (Table 14.4). The tables are not directly comparable because of different classifications of urban and rural areas in Scotland compared with England and Wales.

Table 14.2: Tenure of households in Wales, 2001

		Owner-occupied (%)	Social rented (%)	Private rented (%)	Other (%)
Sparse	Urban >10k residents	57.4	24.4	15.8	2.4
	Town and fringe	64.6	19.0	13.4	3.0
	Village, hamlet and isolated dwellings	75.3	10.2	11.8	2.7
Less sparse	Urban >10k residents	70.4	19.5	8.0	2.0
	Town and fringe	72.9	17.7	7.3	2.2
	Village, hamlet and isolated dwellings	78.4	11.3	8.0	2.3

Note: The definitions of 'sparse' and 'less sparse' are discussed in the Appendix.
Source: JRF Commission on Rural Housing in Wales, from 2001 Census.

All three tables reflect the range of challenges to the provision of social rented accommodation that exist in rural localities, and which have historically led to lower levels of provision than in urban areas. Just over 10 per cent of the stock in villages, hamlets and dwellings in England and Wales was rented from social landlords in 2001. Even though Scotland has traditionally had a more buoyant social rented sector than Wales or England, nevertheless, proportions of social rented accommodation are far lower in rural areas compared with Scotland's urban areas. Commentators have noted the difficulties of providing social rented accommodation in rural localities, as well as the localised outcomes resulting in higher than average levels of provision as a result of the particular impact of dominant power relations (Dickens et al, 1985). But however provision is affected by local politics, all rural areas have been washed over by the 'right to buy', which has reduced the overall volume of social rented accommodation. Furthermore, subsequent policies have failed to bring about sufficient new–build social rented accommodation in the smaller communities across Britain and have acted to reduce the overall volume of social housing (Hoggart and Henderson, 2005).

Table 14.3: Tenure of households in England, 2001

		Owner-occupied (%)	Social rented (%)	Private rented (%)	Living rent-free (%)
Sparse	Urban >10k residents	69.9	16.2	11.8	2.1
	Town and fringe	67.7	17.8	11.8	2.7
	Village	72.8	10.6	13.0	3.6
	Hamlet and isolated dwellings	71.0	4.6	18.7	5.7
Less sparse	Urban >10k residents	66.8	21.1	10.2	1.9
	Town and fringe	76.5	14.5	7.1	1.9
	Village	77.7	10.3	9.2	2.8
	Hamlet and isolated dwellings	77.6	4.9	13.2	4.3

Note: The definitions of 'sparse' and 'less sparse' are discussed in the Appendix.
Source: State of the Countryside Report, 2005, from 2001 Census.

Table 14.4: Tenure of households in Scotland, 2007

	Owner-occupied (%)	Social rented (%)	Private rented (%)	Other (%)
Large urban areas	61	27	10	2
Other urban areas	67	26	7	1
Accessible small towns	71	24	4	1
Remote small towns	65	27	7	2
Accessible rural	76	13	8	3
Remote rural	72	14	11	3

Source: Scottish Household Survey Annual Report, 2007, Table 3.4

In spite of increasing constraints upon the current right to buy council housing,[1] especially in rural areas – and the fact that tenants in England do not have the right to acquire housing association property in settlements of under 3,000 residents – the overall stock of social rented dwellings continues to fall, as supply has abjectly failed to keep pace with sales. Furthermore, the changing role of former social rented housing that has been sold as a result of the right to buy has also been highlighted. It is not until this former rented stock is sold on that the repercussions for lower-income groups become clear. An analysis of resales by Chaney and Sherwood (2000) – in a rural part of the East Midlands of England – showed how the changing role of this stock marked a sharp break with the past and had accelerated the changing socio-economic composition of rural communities in their case study area. Further evidence collected as part of the Rural Affairs and Environment Committee Report highlighted the use of resold former social rented accommodation as second homes in some parts of Scotland (Scottish Parliament Rural Affairs and Environment Committee, 2009). It is notable that the bricks and mortar subsidy used to develop social rented housing, as well as the huge discounts in price made available to former sitting tenants as part of the right to buy, have ultimately contributed to a stock of housing that has enabled second home owners to enjoy a rural lifestyle.

It is this historical context that severely constrains the role that social renting can play in rural areas and limits how stakeholders might respond to discussions about the future potential of this sector. Such discussion has taken place against the backdrop of shifts in the roles that different tenures are playing. A survey for the Chartered Institute of Housing (CIH, 2009) suggested that demand for owner-occupation was not what it had once been amongst younger households. How far these views might change if, or when, there is an upswing in the market remains to be seen. Maclennan (2007) argued that at the national level in England, it was likely to be the private rented sector, and not the social rented sector, that would pick up younger households as a preferred housing destination. But due to the constrained rental options open to younger households on lower incomes in many rural localities, in both the social and private sectors, people have few choices other than to move to urban areas. This issue will be returned to in the next chapter.

A focal point for recent debates about the future of social renting in England has been the review of social housing by John Hills (2007). A dominant theme has been how to reconfigure the housing 'offer' to provide a greater degree of choice and flexibility of accommodation for low-income groups. However, the various proposals that have been put forward need to take account of the particularities of different types of housing market, including how the social rented sector works in rural areas (Murie et al, 2007).

One facet of this distinctiveness is the role that social rented housing plays in rural communities. Much of the debate on a future social rented sector within policy circles has focused upon developing mixed communities by introducing alternative tenure choices in urban localities dominated by social renting. However, in many villages the opposite is the case. It is only the presence of social rented housing (but with the addition of housing provided by private landlords who have been so minded as to let accommodation on low rents in some rural localities) that has enabled the maintenance of socially and economically diverse populations, albeit in sometimes highly polarised communities. The irony of this policy emphasis has not been lost on a number of commentators with respect to rural localities in which it is social renting that has held the key to sustaining mixed communities (Shucksmith, 2007b).

A further aspect to these debates has been how to achieve a balance between a safety-net function for the social rented sector compared with a much more 'aspirational' role: as a tenure of choice. Fitzpatrick and Pawson (2007) suggested that in areas of high demand the tensions between fulfilling a safety-net function and achieving a wider 'tenure of choice' role are irresolvable without a large increase in the size of the sector. The safety-net function of the sector is exemplified by its crucial role for homeless people who meet eligibility criteria for help. The same authors (Fitzpatrick and Pawson, 2007: 164) asserted that the role of the social rented sector in Britain, with regard to homelessness, made it 'unique across the developed world in providing a legally enforceable right to long-term housing for certain "priority" groups'. This role has particular challenges for housing providers in relation to the management of access to social renting in rural areas.

To some extent, these tensions are played out at the level of individual settlements in terms of striving for a balance between allocating according to priority need and meeting the housing aspirations of households who can demonstrate some connection with communities where local letting policies apply (an issue that was explored more thoroughly in Chapter 13). Milbourne (1998) highlighted how the range of housing providers in rural areas of Wales can lead to diverse outcomes for people depending on the access criteria being applied. Nevertheless, the fact remains that the proportion of social rented lets to homeless households in both Wales and Scotland increased substantially from 2003/04, although this percentage fell in England. Fitzpatrick et al (2009) draw attention to the extent to which allocations to homeless people are 'squeezing out' other households who want social rented accommodation, and this theme is examined further in Chapter 17. The fundamental problem in many rural localities where the supply of social renting is so low is that not only will the sector struggle to broaden its appeal as a wider tenure of choice, but that it can currently barely cope with its narrower safety-net role. The conclusion is that in many rural localities the social rented sector is simply not large enough for it to perform the roles either expected of it or that are hoped for.

There is also the issue of how different housing options are perceived. A challenge for providers in widening the appeal of social rented accommodation is overcoming the cultural resistance to social renting that leads to the stigmatisation of this sector, and the perception that it is a 'tenure of last resort' that people only access if they must. How far this notion really bears up to the views and experiences of people who live in social rented accommodation in rural localities is unclear. Although Bevan et al (2001) found mixed views amongst social rented tenants, the range of experiences suggested considerable satisfaction with renting from housing associations in rural areas. Instead, the stigma associated with social renting appears more closely linked with the views of other residents in rural settlements, including community representatives on local councils (Milbourne,

2006). In particular, the latter research noted concerns about the potential for anti-social behaviour and 'importing' people from other areas who may have no link with the 'host' rural community. However, another factor that hinders greater fluidity and flexibility between tenures is a practical one.

In areas of very high housing demand, the various elements of the housing system become disconnected from each other. People who rent cannot afford intermediate housing options and people in intermediate housing remain trapped there because they cannot afford open market prices. Hickman and Robinson (2006) looked at patterns of increasing fragmentation and differentiation within the British housing system, and the impact of these processes on the social rented sector. Social renting also performs diverse roles in different rural localities, in part connected with regional variations in housing markets. The situation in rural areas within the North of England is complicated by the relationship with the nearby metropolitan areas. Attempts to 'engineer' demand within low-demand urban areas – by containing development in surrounding areas – looks to have had very negative consequences for the housing opportunities of low-income groups in these rural areas, as the capacity to develop new social renting is constrained through sub-regional planning policies. Monk et al (2006) highlighted the example of Harrogate District, which had a low housing quota allocated to it via the Regional Spatial Strategy in an attempt to mitigate the impact of low demand in parts of Leeds.

Low turnover in re-lets

It is not just the supply of new housing, however, that has a significant impact upon the role that social renting can play in rural areas, but also the level of turnover in existing stock. The flow of re-lets is not just a function of the low level of stock in rural localities, but also the nature of how the social rented sector is being used by different groups of the population. Intense demand for social rented housing in the South of England plays out not only within urban cores, but also in surrounding rural areas. Monk et al (2006) drew upon a rural case study in Suffolk to highlight the combination of a large excess of demand over supply, and the impact of low turnover. The potential for a positive outcome in terms of how people matched their housing, employment, social and other needs could be reduced because of a poor geographic match between where these disparate elements and vacancies occurred. The demand for such housing was such that people had to be prepared to take any offer that was made to them by the housing provider for fear of losing their place at the head of the queue for housing. Rugg and Jones (1999) drew attention to the difficulty, for young people especially, in trying to match housing with employment in rural areas. Retired people are not constrained in the same way, and Monk et al (2006) noted the popularity of housing outcomes in rural locations for this group. A further problem with the very limited availability of social rented stock is finding another available home within reasonable proximity if there is a change of household circumstances that necessitates a move. A particular constraint in rural localities is when families outgrow the number of bedrooms available.

Choice-based lettings offer one way of providing a greater degree of flexibility for people, and a number of agencies have grappled with combining this approach with local lettings policies in rural localities. Nevertheless, whilst choice-based lettings have provided greater transparency in the process of applying for social renting, the issue of supply remains more insoluble: in high demand rural areas applicants have a long wait ahead of them if they are choosy about where they wish to live.

Coping with low demand

In other instances, low demand for social rented accommodation can also present challenges for housing providers in rural schemes as well as in urban areas. Difficulties with letting social rented accommodation have been highlighted in rural former coalfield communities in the North East of England (Bevan et al, 2001), and also areas of economic decline in parts of rural Wales (Milbourne et al, 2006). However, this issue is more to do with neighbourhood effects than tenure *per se* (Hickman and Robinson, 2006). The differing roles of social rented accommodation in localised, but very different, housing markets has also been noted in Cumbria. Intense demand for accommodation in and around the Lake District can be contrasted with lower demand in parts of West Cumbria. In the latter area, social rented accommodation has been linked with regeneration, helping to stabilise the decline of settlements (Blenkinship and Gibbons, 2004). This latter research noted that a feature of some low-demand rural areas was churning within the social housing stock. However, increased turnover within social housing in rural areas should not necessarily always be viewed as a negative development. Research on rural social housing based in the South West found that an increased turnover reflected a changing, but no less valuable, role for social rented housing within rural housing markets (Forrest and Murie, 1992). As well as providing long-term accommodation, it was found that social housing was increasingly performing an important role in allowing households on lower incomes to continue living in rural communities during periods of crisis such as the breakdown of a relationship, or eviction from privately rented accommodation. Similarly, Bevan et al (2001) found that housing association accommodation was playing a vital role in rural communities in enabling households to access social rented housing at a time when they also often needed to maintain social networks. For example, households moving on from a relationship breakdown valued the chance to live in social housing close to family and friends. Social rented housing was thus performing a role in mitigating wider impacts associated with sudden changes in the personal and economic circumstances of households.

Social renting, rural services and community well-being

An additional role for social rented housing has been in helping to sustain local services in rural communities (Blenkinship, 2004). However, the power of tenure may have been overstated in this regard, such that people who live in social rented accommodation will be predisposed to certain courses of action in the public sphere. Monk and Ni Luanaigh (2006) caution against ascribing too much to the impact that social rented accommodation can play. Instead, their research in the West Midlands found that social rented tenants were no more or less likely to use local services than occupiers of market housing. What was important was that new housing developed in smaller communities could help sustain services, rather than being a particular tenure. However, this situation is likely to depend on the type of rural locality. In areas of high environmental amenity, market housing is likely to attract second and holiday home owners and, in these situations, it is the fact that social rented accommodation will be occupied on a permanent basis that is significant. The same authors also point out that there has been too much of a focus on measuring impacts that are readily quantifiable, such as how much people make use of local services, rather than critical dimensions of people's lives. It is in helping to sustain personal social networks where the wider value of a social rented option in rural communities appears to lie, but which requires more qualitative approaches to uncover. Instead, where social renting can have a broader impact upon rural communities is connected with the attitudes and input of social housing providers. Murie et al (2007) contend that one of the more aspirational roles for the social rented sector in the future will be in relation to regeneration and civic renewal. A number of studies have highlighted the wider contribution agencies have made to rural communities with respect to social and economic regeneration (Oldfield King Planning Ltd, 1997; Countryside Agency, 2003). A much stronger focus on community-led processes leading to social rented housing delivery has also become part of the policy landscape with the encouragement given to Community Land Trusts (see Chapter 18).

Delivering social rented homes

Whilst the social rented sector plays diverse and significant roles in many rural communities where it is present, these roles are limited and mediated by the severely constrained supply that exists in most localities. A further distinctive aspect of the social rented sector in rural areas is the experience linked with the process of supplying new units. A recognition that the development of social rented housing has to be 'done differently' in rural areas has led to specific and innovative approaches to this issue.

The complexity involved in working within smaller rural communities is not only revealed by the nature of the approaches adopted by agencies, but also the range of stakeholders involved (Milbourne, 2006). This complexity has led to the creation of specialist roles that are unique to the rural context. Rural housing enablers operate in a facilitating and brokering role, with the task of finding a way through the various barriers and challenges that exist. Indeed, the Rural Housing Policy Forum described enablers as 'the essential prerequisite' in acting as intermediaries between all the disparate elements and agencies required to deliver the successful development of affordable housing in rural areas (Best and Shucksmith, 2008: 9). However, similar to the uneven spread of housing association activity, whilst truly innovative approaches have developed in some areas, coverage remains patchy. The development of good practice has certainly raised the potential for extracting the maximum efficiencies from within the constraints imposed by the current policy framework. However, such efforts should not deflect attention away from the fundamental weaknesses at national levels in getting sufficient numbers of social rented accommodation into rural communities. Instead, there is the danger that innovation and initiative remain locked into the areas where good practice has developed. The limited resources available means that the current approach of pragmatic opportunism, where agencies take the line of least resistance through local governance structures, and other obstacles such as site availability seem to take precedence over matching supply with assessed needs.

A considerable aspect of this resistance is around the pervasive influence of residents who attempt to stymie social rented developments within villages through the control of parish councils (Gallent et al, 2002b; Yarwood, 2002). Bevan et al (2001) noted parish councils refusing to cooperate with rural housing enablers in the face of evidence of relatively high levels of housing need within their communities. However, resistance to developing social renting in villages is not just about NIMBYism. Hoggart and Henderson (2005) also pointed to the reluctance of housing agencies to develop schemes in smaller communities, highlighting the limited response of housing associations to the needs of smaller communities. However, to be fair to a number of housing associations, the situation appears to be more fragmented than this in terms of their response. Whilst the housing association movement has maintained an overall urban focus, nevertheless, a number of specialist housing associations have evolved with a specific remit to develop in rural communities. It is important to recognise the positive impact that these agencies have had, despite regular shortcomings in capacity or coverage. In the Scottish context, for example, Satsangi (2006) argued that the failure to supply sufficient social rented housing was down, primarily, to inadequate funding and an incomplete network of housing associations operating in rural areas.

Furthermore, Lavis (2007) has argued that in England there has been a gradual shift in the mindset of agencies towards developing social rented accommodation in smaller rural settlements. An outcome of the 2008 Housing and Regeneration Act was the creation of a new agency to oversee investment, the Housing and Communities Agency (HCA). Rural interests have been pressing the case for keeping rural housing very much on the new agency's agenda, primarily through the Rural Programme of its predecessor, the Housing Corporation. The rhetoric of the new agency has been to emphasise its commitment to developing in rural communities, exemplified by the establishment of a Rural Housing Advisory Group to maintain this focus. Nevertheless, an acknowledgement of the problem has not yet translated into a scale of provision commensurate with estimates of need. An example of this issue can be seen from the Rural Programme, which explicitly recognises the requirement to target rural communities with fewer than 3,000 residents. However, Hoggart and Henderson (2005) highlighted that of the 17,000 settlements with populations of less than 3,000 on the Housing Corporation's list, only a fifth had benefited from the programme up to that date. Although DEFRA has suggested that the rate of investment going into the supply of affordable housing in rural areas matches population shares between urban and rural districts, this analysis is at local authority level, and it is not clear from this how far investment has been directed towards larger settlements, including urban areas of these districts rather than smaller communities. Research by ECOTEC (2008) suggested that smaller communities receive a lower rate of investment than their population shares warrant. Notwithstanding some increase in the Rural Programme, commentators in the early 21st century argued that there was still a need for an accelerated investment in rural communities, pointing out that settlements with populations under 10,000 house 19 per cent of the population, but only receive 10 per cent of new affordable housing supply (Affordable Rural Housing Commission, 2006). A similar situation in Wales was illustrated by a survey by the Wales Rural Observatory (2005) which found that 85 per cent of responding community councils in settlements of 4,000 people or fewer had not had any affordable housing development by social rented landlords (housing associations and local authorities) between 2000 and 2005, with no provision in responding councils with populations of 400 or fewer (with the proviso that there was a significant non-response to their questions from community councils).

Chapter 12 put forward the case for a return to direct provision by local authorities as an alternative to mechanisms within the planning system. The complexity of delivering in rural areas in terms of the variety of agencies and stakeholders involved also suggests room for diverse ways of securing social rented accommodation in rural localities, drawing not only upon housing associations but directly by local authorities. In England, the 2008 Housing and Regeneration Act brought about significant changes for local authorities, not least the ability to work with the private sector to secure new supplies of social rented accommodation. Local Housing Companies raised the prospect of new council housing in rural areas in the future, although the recession stalled activity in all of the pilots. Moreover, as with many initiatives, it remains to be seen how far the focus of attention follows historic patterns and is directed towards urban areas. At present only one of the 14 pilot Local Housing Companies (in England) has a rural focus. Nevertheless, there were signs that local authorities might be given scope to develop social rented accommodation in the future if the national Housing Revenue Account were to be reformed to enable authorities to retain rental income.

In Scotland a number of local authorities were given the opportunity to develop again, boosted by three rounds of direct investment from the Scottish Government. A number of rural councils planned to build new council housing in smaller rural communities, dovetailing with housing association developments there and in their larger settlements. In England, the 2008 Housing and Regeneration Act opened up the potential for private sector providers to not only develop but also manage social housing as well. As will be seen in Chapter 15, this idea was taken a step further in Scotland, with a new potential role for the private rented sector in rural areas.

The future of social rented housing

The chronic shortage of accommodation for people on lower incomes leads to a focus upon how the small stock of property that does exist outside of the market sector in rural localities can be used most effectively to meet the needs and aspirations of as wide a cross-section of the population as possible. Debate about how the future social rented sector might provide a better housing 'offer' for people has considerable resonances with the particularities of rural locations. To borrow a phrase from the literature on universal design and lifetime homes, a key principle that is emerging is enabling 'flexibility in use'. The principle of universal design relates traditionally to the way housing should be sympathetic to the lifestyles of as wide a range of the population as possible. The aim is to make a home easier to use and have the capacity to be readily adapted as a household's needs change over time. The wider intention is to supply accommodation that can provide flexibility in use across different occupants over time. However, discussions about accommodation for low-income groups also emphasise that flexibility should extend to how a property is occupied on the basis of tenure. People should have a range of choices open to them: a multi-instrument approach for households on low incomes, which stands in contrast to a rigid focus on single-tenure solutions (Cole, 2007; Maclennan, 2007). This approach is not just about providing a range of social rented and intermediate units on a development. Instead, how individual properties might be used should not be determined by whether they belong to a particular tenure or another, but by individual households, based on their own needs and aspirations. Murie et al (2007) highlighted the value of enabling people to remain living in their homes, even if they want to shift from renting to owning or vice versa. At the time of writing, the idea of tenure-neutral developments was being pursued in rural localities in Wales, with a housing association retaining control over a property to enable occupancy to interchange between renting and owning according to the circumstances of the residents. All Section 106 and rural exceptions sites were being delivered on a tenure-neutral basis in Monmouthshire (Monmouthshire County Council, 2009). One of the difficulties identified by Monmouthshire County Council (2009) was ensuring that the funds were in place to enable housing providers to buy back the property if the occupier wishes to sell. The problem comes back to the practical difficulties of replacing social rented housing in rural communities.

Providing flexibility for households on low incomes also extends to the roles that all rented housing plays in rural housing systems, be that from private landlords or non-market providers. Renting in rural areas, whatever the type of ownership, plays various roles in meeting the needs of low-income households. However, within the new policy context of a mixed economy of providers, it is also important to hold on to the distinctive features of social compared with private renting. There has been a call from some quarters to move to short-term tenancies in the social rented sector. However, the limited housing options that are available to low-income households who cannot afford owner-occupation in rural localities, but who wish to remain living in these areas, can include a range of very insecure living arrangements such as winter lets, caravans or staying with friends or family. Further, whilst some private landlords play a highly significant role in meeting the needs of households on low incomes, there is evidence to show that a higher proportion of people are made homeless in rural areas through private tenancies coming to an end than in urban areas. The social rented sector provides one of the only sources of long-term security of tenure for people on low incomes who can access it in rural areas, and this is an attribute that needs to be strongly defended.

Note

[1] Early in 2010, the Scottish Government announced its intention to remove the right to buy for new tenancies.

FIFTEEN

Private renting

A key theme from the previous chapter was that the provision of a wide range of options to rent or buy, or to acquire property on an intermediate basis, would help to facilitate access to housing for lower-income groups in rural localities. Part of this range of options stems from the privately rented sector (PRS). From the 1980s onwards, policy-makers have tended to see the valid contribution that private landlords can play in terms of delivering affordable housing solutions. Perhaps an ideal scenario in the future would be one in which the question 'Which tenure does a housing provider belong to?' would become increasingly irrelevant, with greater attention given to the quality of the housing and management service provided by individuals and organisations, whatever their background. At the same time, the PRS of the early 21st century performs particular roles within the housing system, and the extent to which these roles are distinctive from, or complementary to, the social rented sector needs to be recognised. Further, the PRS in rural localities has developed in different ways from the sector in urban areas and these differences also affect the particular sub-markets of local housing systems that the sector is operating in. The profile of the PRS has also been shaped by its history and it is to these issues that the chapter now turns.

Trends and legislative responses

Across Britain, the decline of the PRS over the course of the 20th century was spectacular. From being the dominant source of general needs housing at the start of the 20th century, it collapsed both numerically and proportionately in comparison with other tenures. Commentators have highlighted the main reasons for this decline. The sector was subject to heavy regulation with respect to both rents and security of tenure over most of the last century (Scanlon and Whitehead, 2005). Moreover, private renting compared unfavourably with both owner-occupation and social housing in terms of taxation and subsidy, contributing to a lack of investment in new-build for the sector (Kemp, 2004). As a result, the PRS fell from over 90 per cent of the total stock in 1919 to around 9 per cent by 1991.

The legislative context changed significantly in the 1980s with attempts to revive the sector, first, with the 1980 Housing Act and, then, more significantly, with the 1988 Housing Act, which introduced Assured Shorthold Tenancies to England and Wales. Similar developments took place in Scotland with the introduction of assured and short assured tenancies in the 1988 Housing (Scotland) Act.[1] These tenancies allowed for a minimum rental period of six months, after which a landlord could give two months' notice to quit. The Act also abolished regulated rents for new lets, removing another disincentive for landlords to invest in rental property. Further reforms were introduced by the 1996 Housing Act, which meant that tenancies set up after February 1997 were automatically on an assured shorthold basis. An accelerated possession procedure was also introduced, which made it easier for landlords to evict tenants if they had legitimate grounds for regaining possession. A key development therefore was that the revival in private renting was underpinned by a dramatic reduction in security of tenure for tenants. Whilst the sector became more attractive for landlords, the issue of security of tenure marks perhaps the most significant difference between this sector and social renting.

In addition to the changes in legislation in the 1980s and 1990s, Rugg and Rhodes (2008) put forward three other reasons for the upturn in the size of the PRS towards the end of the 20th century. One reason was the impact of the slump in house prices in the early 1990s, with a number of householders unable to sell their properties and choosing to let them out instead, as well as existing landlords expanding their portfolios by buying up repossessed properties at auction. Other factors included an expansion of demand groups for private rental accommodation, as well as the increased availability of finance from 1996 through buy-to-let mortgages. At the time of writing, there are signs that reduced credit availability and depressed house price inflation (if not actual deflation) are increasing the number of properties in rural areas being let out, rather than being made available for sale. There is of course nothing new here: trends in private renting have traditionally run counter-cyclical to the market for house purchase.

Within the context of this overall dramatic decrease in the size of the sector over the course of the 20th century, there was a very large variation in the extent of decline in different rural localities. Long (2005) highlighted that there was a combination of specific reasons in particular rural localities that hastened the decline of private renting, including: the contraction of the workforce in agriculture, and thus the need for tied accommodation; high prices from the sale of former private rented accommodation fuelled by increasing demand from in-migrants; and also a shift into holiday lets (see also Bowler and Lewis, 1987). Spencer (1997) highlighted that many landowners capitalised the assets of housing formerly used by their employees, often to reinvest in other aspects of their businesses.

However, the PRS in other rural localities proved more resilient. In England, for example, 21 per cent of households in rural villages and hamlets in the North East live in the PRS (Rhodes, 2006). At a finer level of analysis, this feature is more striking still. Research on local housing markets in parts of rural Scotland highlighted far higher concentrations of private rented accommodation. For example, a study of communities in parts of Dumfries and Galloway showed localities where over 40 per cent of households were living in the PRS (Craigforth Research and Consultancy, 2006). This trend may reflect that the PRS in some rural areas is underpinned by landowners who have motivations that run counter to the treatment of rental property as trading stock on the open market. As will be seen later in the chapter, a number of landlords have traditionally provided a source of accommodation to local households in some localities. Landlords have also retained their portfolios in order to preserve the integrity of their landholdings (Bevan and Sanderling, 1996).

Trends since the 1980s suggest that the PRS in rural areas has proven less responsive to regulatory change and to market developments such as the growth of buy to let: it did not grow in the 1990s at the same rate as private renting in towns and cities (Rhodes, 2006). Nevertheless, it is important to consider the base from which any growth has taken place. In some rural localities at least, the proportion of households renting privately has remained relatively high. In terms of national averages, the PRS in each of the countries in Britain remains proportionately larger in rural areas than in urban areas (Hancock 2002; Houston et al, 2002; Milbourne et al, 2006). Part of this is due to the continued significance of tied accommodation and housing provided rent-free. Nevertheless, whilst tied letting is a significant characteristic of the rural privately rented sector, it is necessary not to overstate its importance. The large majority of landlords with rural properties let them on the open market.

A theme that has run through trends within the PRS over the last century or so has been the quality of a proportion of accommodation for let, in both urban and rural areas. In rural localities the poor condition of accommodation provided by many private landlords in the 19th and early 20th centuries was noted in a number of reports and studies (Savage, 1919; Gauldie, 1974), and this issue in parts of the sector has continued to the present day. One consequence of this historical legacy is the extent to which parts of the privately rented housing stock comprise very old dwellings, and it is the quality of this stock that limits the potential role of the modern privately rented sector. Houston et al (2002) noted that in Scotland some of the worst standards were apparent in cottages on large rural estates either in the tied sub-sector or open market lets.

Another legacy of the decline in agricultural tied lettings has been the number of empty dwellings in rural areas. Landowners may have been reluctant to sell these properties as this would impact upon the integrity of their landholdings and potentially disrupt other aspects of their businesses. A policy focus has been to develop a variety of mechanisms to encourage bringing such properties back into use for general needs housing (Cairncross et al, 2006; Flint and Currie, 2009). In Scotland, policies have involved housing associations taking on the management of properties through Lead Tenancy Schemes and also Rural Empty Property Grants. The Rural Homes for Rent programme (introduced in 2008) has also offered grants to private and community landowners to renovate and let empty houses as well as develop new housing.

Current roles

In spite of the small size of the PRS in relation to owner-occupation, there is a variety of roles that the sector performs. Indeed, the complexity of the sector is reflected in the number of distinct sub-markets that exist. A review of the PRS in England, for example, identified 10 sub-markets, including:

- young professionals;
- students;
- the housing benefit market;
- slum rentals;
- tied housing;
- high-income renters;
- immigrants and asylum seekers;
- temporary accommodation; and
- regulated tenancies
  (see Rugg and Rhodes, 2008: iv).

As highlighted at the start of the chapter, the balance between these various roles varies not only between urban and rural areas, but also between different rural localities.

It is also important to consider the relationship between the PRS and the other tenures and how far shifts from the 1990s onwards have altered the roles that the different tenures perform. Maclennan (2007) has highlighted the reducing accessibility of owner-occupation for younger households and the fact that it is not the social rented sector but the PRS that has picked up these households. This feature of the housing system has drawn increasing attention from analyses of affordability in housing markets, with access to the PRS attracting a more prominent role (Wilcox, 2007; Bramley and Watkins, 2009). Rugg and Rhodes (2008) highlighted this shift in the roles played by different tenures for younger age groups in England. In households where the household reference person was aged between 25 and 29, 59 per cent were owner-occupiers in 1993/94. By 2006/07 this figure had dropped to 48 per cent. Instead, the proportion of this age group living in the PRS had grown from 19 per cent in 1993/94 to 32 per cent in 2006/07.

However, it appears that the PRS in rural areas is not performing this role to the same extent for younger age groups. Rhodes (2006) identified that single-person, non-pensioner households in England and Wales were less likely to be living in rural villages and hamlets (19 per cent) compared with urban areas (29 per cent). The evidence from Scotland is more striking. Strachan and Donohoe (2009) showed that just 4 per cent of rural private tenants in Scotland were aged below 25, compared with 46 per cent of urban tenants. Further, 46 per cent of private tenants in rural areas of Scotland were aged 50 and over, compared with 11 per cent of urban private tenants. Thus, whilst trends at national levels point to the PRS providing an increasingly important housing destination for young people, this is not happening in rural areas to the same extent. Urban areas may be performing a key role here in providing housing opportunities for younger out-migrants from rural areas. Certainly, not all young people want to remain living in rural areas and, for some, the most attractive aspect of their village is the bus stop and a ticket to the nearest town or city.

Ford et al (1997) categorised young people in rural areas of England as 'committed stayers', 'committed leavers', 'reluctant leavers' and 'reluctant stayers'. Where housing stress is most apparent is in the difficulties that young people who are committed to remaining in rural areas experience in meeting their accommodation needs in the privately rented sector, and also the proportion of young people who leave rural localities not because they want to, but because they cannot match their housing and employment requirements (Rugg and Jones, 1999). Pavis et al (2000) found that young people who were reliant on private renting in rural areas of Scotland felt that accommodation in this sector was often too remote for their needs, or of poor quality. A further pressure on the housing stock in some rural areas is also apparent where accommodation is used for second homes or holiday lets, rather than as permanent residential accommodation, including private lets. In these localities, housing options appear not only very constrained, but also more insecure. Households who wish to remain in these types of area are more reliant on short-term options such as winter lets, or options such as staying with friends or family. One option in these types of area is to convince owners to convert holiday cottages into longer-term residential lets, and Iona stands out as one example of where this has happened.

A further difficulty in rural areas is the profile of the housing stock. Smaller accommodation for single people, especially flats, is far less common than in urban areas. Instead, the rural housing stock tends to be composed of detached or semi-detached dwellings. Indeed, a significant trend in high-demand areas has been the conversion of smaller dwellings into larger units, including knocking through semi-detached cottages to form one large house. An issue here could be the dispersed or intermittent nature of demand for accommodation from young people across rural localities. Where demand for accommodation has been geographically concentrated in rural areas over a short space of time, private landlords have responded. An example here is the area of Breckland, in East Anglia, where the number of Houses in Multiple Occupation (HMOs) went up from 40 in 2002 to 480 in 2006 (Audit Commission, 2007), in response to the demand from migrant workers in this area (see Chapter 9 for a fuller discussion of housing and migrant workers in rural areas).

A characteristic of the PRS is mobility amongst its residents and the level of churn in terms of the length of tenancies. Again, the pattern in rural areas shows that the PRS is playing a different role from that in urban areas. Strachan and Donohoe (2009) showed that the PRS in rural areas of Scotland was performing a long-term, or a lifetime, role in terms of people's housing. Evidence of a longer-term role was also evident in England. Rhodes (2006) found that 56 per cent of tenants in urban areas of England were resident at the same address as one year earlier compared with 64 per cent of rural tenants.

In addition, the PRS in rural areas of Britain was also more significant for households with children. Families with children comprised 27 per cent of the Scottish PRS in rural areas, compared with 15 per cent of urban PRS households. This pattern was replicated across rural areas of Wales (Welsh Assembly Government, 2002b), and also England. For example, Rhodes (2006) found that 21 per cent of the PRS in rural villages and hamlets in England comprised couples with dependent children, compared with 11 per cent of the urban PRS.

Perhaps the key issue here is the profile of landlords in different rural areas and the extent to which property is let close to market rents, or at a lower level with a view to providing accommodation that is more affordable to households on lower incomes. The presence of large landowners in particular rural localities appears to be crucial here and it is important to get underneath the general averages across all rural areas and recognise the diversity of renting in housing markets at a finer scale of analysis. A useful framework for analysing the heterogeneity of rural areas is the analysis presented by Marsden et al (1993). These authors put forward the notion of the English countryside as differentiated by the balance of power held by various networks of stakeholders and actors in local housing markets. This analysis helps to understand the PRS because of its identification of pockets of rural England characterised by paternalism. It also so happens that the focus of much of the research on the PRS in rural areas has dwelt upon the stock of property let by landowners (Bevan and Sanderling, 1996; Satsangi, 2002).

Crook and Hughes (2003: 18) highlighted that some landowners in their role as private landlords performed a 'quasi-social' function in parts of rural Scotland, where their rent-setting policies and letting strategies were motivated by concerns about local community cohesion and social welfare. In part these motivations stem from a perspective of 'stewardship' not only in relation to wider land use, but also social relations. Satsangi (2002) also noted that in Scotland these landlords often let their properties at below market rents to people with a local connection to the area. The research by Satsangi (2002) found that landowners perceived their contribution in terms of providing rental housing as complementary to that of the social sector, rather than as a substitute for it. In particular, there was a reluctance to let to people on Housing Benefit. Discussions with landowners in England suggested mixed views on this matter (Bevan and Sanderling, 1996). Whilst many landowners emphasised their stewardship role, others highlighted the higher rents that could be derived as a result of the legislation in the 1980s. These latter views pointed towards a weakening of traditional attitudes in response to a greater marketisation of rental housing delivery. Nevertheless, research in both Scotland and England going into the 21st century shows the overall resilience of traditional views on renting. It also throws into sharp relief the way that new forms of Conservatism in the 1980s, exemplified by Thatcherism, washed over these rural areas, which were characterised by much more traditional conservative values, and the impact of these changes on the strategies of landlords who let property in rural areas.

In contrast, a different picture emerges in rural localities that are not dominated by landlords who let with social objectives in mind. Information drawn from local housing market assessments points to the difficulties that households on low incomes may have in trying to gain access to the segments of the PRS where properties are let much more in line with market rents. Monk et al (2006) highlighted the difficulties that households faced in their case study areas in finding, and affording, private rented accommodation. In this respect it is also necessary to consider access to private renting in terms of the flow of lets, rather than just the size of the stock. Turnover in any one locality, and hence availability to households looking for a home, is likely to be low, given the relative size of the sector, the proportion of the stock available to the general public and also the longer length of tenancies in rural localities (Rugg and Rhodes, 2008). A further difficulty arises from entry costs to the PRS in the form of requirements for rent in advance, and/or deposits.

Another barrier that households face is a result of the profile of the local labour market in rural areas. A feature of many rural areas is not high unemployment, but low incomes resulting from seasonal and low-paid work in the primary and service sectors. These households can get caught between market rents that are unaffordable relative to their incomes, but also the tapers that exist for people in employment when trying to apply for Housing Benefit. However, even households on incomes that are low enough to be eligible for full Housing Benefit can experience difficulties affording rents. In 2008 a new system for assessing entitlement for Housing Benefit was introduced, termed the Local Housing Allowance. In some parts of Britain the way that rural and urban areas are assessed together within a single rental market (termed Broad Rental Market Areas) in order to determine the level of rent that will be eligible for Housing Benefit can leave some households with a shortfall between the amount they receive in Benefit and the rent charged by the landlord. Centrepoint (2009) highlighted that young people in rural parts of Northumberland were struggling to find privately rented accommodation they could afford because relatively expensive rural areas were assessed with cheaper urban areas such as Blyth and Ashington. However, it is important to recognise that the nature of this issue varies across the country. Around Cambridge, the situation is reversed compared with the example of Northumberland. Households claiming Housing Benefit struggle to pay for accommodation within the city, which is more expensive than the surrounding rural areas that also comprise its Broad Rental Market Area (Cambridge City Council, 2009).

However, the financial constraints on households are only one facet of the difficulties that households face in gaining access to privately rented accommodation in rural areas. Attitudes of landlords towards tenants on Housing Benefit can limit the rental housing options of low-income households, in part stemming from preconceptions of landlords towards households who claim Housing Benefit, but also disincentives due to the way that Housing Benefit is administered. On the other hand, the diverse roles the PRS plays are evident from numerous schemes around Britain that help homeless people to access privately rented accommodation. The very limited options in terms of social renting or specialist emergency provision for homeless people in rural areas mean that a number of agencies in both the statutory and voluntary sectors have focused attention on using the PRS in rural localities, such as supported lodgings.

Future prospects

There are increasing signs that the ideological dogmas that have hampered the development of housing systems in rural areas at the level of national governments are attenuating with respect to renting either in the social rented sector or with respect to private renting. Devolution has had a role to play here. The idea that private landlords cannot be trusted to provide rented housing solutions on the same basis as providers of social rented accommodation is set to be severely tested in Scotland following the introduction of the Rural Homes for Rent Scheme in 2008. Under the scheme, rural landowners across Scotland, including community buyout groups, are able to apply for housing grants to help them build new affordable homes for rent on their land. Five million pounds has been made available over three years for the scheme. As well as meeting eligibility criteria, the landlords have to sign up to grant conditions in terms of how the housing is developed and managed. The turn of phrase 'private social landlord' that has been put forward by the Scottish Rural Property and Business Association represents a verbal collision between tenures that would have been an anathema to national policy-makers in the 20th century. Instead, as Malpass (2009) has noted with respect to changes in England brought about by the 2008 Housing and Regeneration Act, policy seems to have jumped back an entire century, borrowing from housing systems at the end of the 19th century in terms of potential providers. The 2008 Housing and Regeneration Act allows for public *and* private agencies to develop and manage affordable housing. Ironic, then, that people in many rural areas are still living in purpose-built privately rented accommodation constructed by landowners over a century ago to house their workers. As such, it is a positive step in helping to break down and blur the boundaries between the rented tenures. That said, there is no place for naivety or complacency. A welcome development in policy has been a recognition of the need for regulatory regimes that have the teeth not only to winkle out rogue elements from within the privately rented sector, but also to combat incompetent or ignorant management practices. The key outcome here appears to be about achieving a balance between enabling the business of renting to grow, whilst protecting residents and also reputable landlords from unsavoury elements that continue to plague parts of the sector.

A feature of the PRS is its diversity, not just in terms of the roles that it plays but the extent to which these roles coincide, or not, with the needs of people in rural communities. Kemp and Keoghan (2001) have argued that the function that the PRS performs in housing markets can be characterised as one of increasing complexity, reflecting key shifts in society such as the break-up and reformulation of households over the life course. A distinctive characteristic of part of the sector in some rural localities is in meeting the long-term needs of tenants, especially families. At the same time, tenure arrangements can lead to insecurity in others parts of the privately rented sector.

A further layer of complexity relates to the changing roles of other tenures, and the movement of households between them. For example, on the one hand, the social rented sector provides a crucial safety-net function for households who become homeless because of the loss of private rented accommodation, which is a significant reason for homelessness in rural localities (see Cloke et al, 2001b). On the other, private renting provides an affordable alternative for households who cannot access social rented accommodation, as well as providing a lifestyle option for people seeking the peace and quiet of a remote location in rural areas (Strachan and Donohoe, 2009).

Perhaps the most significant issue is that across the nations of Britain, the PRS is strongly characterised as a sector for young adults. However, this chapter has emphasised that the sector within rural localities does not feature significantly as a housing destination for this age group, and that private renting is performing a variety of other roles instead. Debates about the affordability of owner-occupation or the availability of social rented housing in rural areas are perhaps missing the point as far as young single people are concerned: it is the role that the PRS performs that is the key.

Note

[1] Scotland's equivalent to the 1980 Housing Act was the 1980 Tenants' Rights Etc (Scotland) Act.

SIXTEEN

Rural low-cost home ownership

Although no country of Britain is yet entirely a 'nation of homeowners', each has seen a movement in this direction for several decades. The level of home ownership in Britain as a whole is one of the highest in Europe, built on (until the 2007/08 credit crunch) accessible mortgage credit and fuelled by a house-building sector that has perfected the art of erecting identical starter homes (almost invariably two-bed semis) on greenfield sites up and down Britain. In some rural markets, levels of private ownership come very close to 100 per cent, as a result of: early movement away from private renting; high levels of take-up of the right to buy; decades of counter-urbanisation, which has brought salaried commuters, retirement migrants and second home owners to many rural areas; and an economic transformation that has seen seasonal workers, lacking the income and wealth to buy their own homes, supplanted by newcomers who rarely choose to rent their homes. Notwithstanding some local differences, this general picture is repeated across England, Scotland and Wales, with home ownership becoming by far the most dominant tenure, sometimes to the detriment of households unable to compete in more exclusive markets.

Successive governments have lauded the personal and social benefits of owner-occupation to the extent that its expansion has become an ideological goal fixed within most party manifestos. These governments have frequently come to the electorate with grand plans to 'expand home ownership': to give those still 'locked into renting' or languishing in social tenancies the opportunity to buy a home of their own. The biggest strides towards Eden's dream of a 'home-owning democracy' were made by the Thatcher governments during the 1980s, which began by giving council tenants the right to buy their homes from local councils before embarking on an ambitious programme of public stock transfer to the housing association sector. The Conservatives transformed the possibility of local councils releasing stock for private ownership – instigated in the 1950s – into an obligation to extend a 'right' to sitting tenants. In the countryside, this policy rapidly depleted an already dwindling supply of rented accommodation.

But Thatcher was adamant in her view that ownership was the aspiration of the vast majority of UK households, and that government should do everything in its power to make this aspiration a reality. This was the personal angle: government stepping in to help support individual preferences, to encourage self-sufficiency and responsibility, and also to create a secure focus of personal investment. There were also broader social, economic and political goals. First, there was (and is) a belief that stronger communities can be built on the back of personal investment in that community; people become real stakeholders and come to share common concerns over noise, nuisance and tidiness as well as acquiring a real stake in the local area.

Second, there was a belief in the economic efficiency of owner-occupation (for the state) as pressure is lifted from public house-building programmes. This claim of efficiency has been hotly disputed since the early 1980s as many owner-occupiers have needed rescuing from ownership that is only marginally affordable, and some have ended up homeless and claiming Housing Benefit. Governments have needed to fund mortgage rescue schemes at considerable public expenditure cost in the light of difficult economic conditions that had underpinned a sharp rise in mortgage defaults and home repossessions. There were 12,800 repossessions across Britain in the first three months of 2009, compared with 8,500 in the first quarter of 2008 (Council of Mortgage Lenders, 2009). Owner-occupation, especially when it is at the margins of affordability, can be costly to individuals and to the Treasury.

Finally, we are left with the political view: that Thatcher's strategy of increasing ownership through the dismantling of the welfare state was a means of weaning voters off Labour, and increasing the ranks of the grateful working classes who would subsequently vote Conservative. In England and Wales, this strategy showed dividends in general elections until the early 1990s. North of the border, however, it was an abject failure, as the number of Tory MPs fell from 22 in 1979, to 10 in 1987 and none in 1997. These national political trends reflect a continuance of the loss of faith in Conservative policy that started in the 1960s and 1970s; they are also linked to the resurgence of nationalism (Pilkington, 2002: 59) and to catastrophic episodes – notably the debacle over the Poll Tax – which firmly discredited Tory policy-making (Torrance, 2009). The economic policy of the 1980s was also widely seen in Scotland as the wrecking ball of the country's industrial heritage and catalyst of unemployment and impoverishment for which the Conservatives largely have not been forgiven.

Home ownership has become a fundamental part of personal and collective aspiration. Events that reveal the fragility of this system of personal ownership (and hence personal responsibility), including the credit crisis and recession of 2008–10, tend not to dampen overall enthusiasm for owning a home of one's own. Private renting is subject to clichéd attack: 'renting is dead money', 'you're paying someone else's mortgage' and so on. The Conservatives were successful in convincing a whole generation that all forms of social housing provide a safety net, presumably there to prevent failed owner-occupiers from hitting the ground too hard. Social renting is thus depicted as a transient tenure: something you do only if you must, and only then as a stopgap (Rowlands and Murie, 2008; Monk, 2009). The desire to increase home ownership – for a mix of reasons, but largely because increasing access to the tenure is popular – has gradually permeated social housing programmes. A distinction is made between affordable housing delivered for social renting (usually from housing associations) and for 'intermediate' tenure: newspeak for shared ownership or ownership that is low cost, gradually achieved via a part-rent/part-buy arrangement. This chapter looks at different routes to, and forms of, low-cost home ownership (LCHO) in rural areas. It reviews the evolution of approaches and their significance as a means of meeting rural aspirations and addressing housing needs.

From low-cost home ownership to HomeBuy

What is meant by the term 'low-cost home ownership'? It implies a means of reducing the cost burden on households who aspire to buy and occupy their own home. Strategies for delivering LCHO were developed in the 1980s. These were generally of two types: first, the promotion of 'starter home' developments; and, second, the development of shared ownership arrangements from which participants could 'staircase', in time, to full ownership. At first, such arrangements focused on new-build, but they have since extended to the purchase of second-hand property with the help of a shared ownership partner, normally a housing association. We begin here by looking primarily at the shared-ownership route, before considering starter homes in the next section and then the very latest approaches to opening up ownership later in the chapter.

Shared ownership

In 1980, Britain's Minister for Housing and Construction signalled the government's intention to launch a number of initiatives aiming to increase access to owner-occupation (Malpass and Murie, 1987: 286). Seven key initiatives began in the following year: the selling of council houses to sitting tenants[1] under the provisions of the 1980 Housing Act and the 1980 Tenants' Rights Etc (Scotland) Act; the sale of public land to housing associations with permission for starter homes; building starter homes on public land in partnership with private builders; improving homes for onward sale; selling unimproved homes for improvement by purchasers; building for shared ownership rather than outright sale, whenever feasible; and the use of local authority mortgage guarantee powers to facilitate downmarket (or sub-prime) lending by building societies (Malpass and Murie, 1987: 287). A significant portion of Housing Corporation capital funding was subsequently diverted to shared ownership schemes and to 'improvement for sale' (IFS: that is, the acquisition and rehabilitation of homes for onward sale to nominated households, often under shared ownership arrangements). During this decade and by 1989, around 36,000 homes had been provided under these arrangements (Birchall, 1992: 32).

Conservative policy on shared ownership built on an idea posited by Sir John Stanley in 1974: his pamphlet published by the Conservative Political Centre – *Shared Purchase: A New Route to Home Ownership* – outlined the means by which a Conservative government might fulfil its pledge to expand home ownership beyond the level achievable through obligatory council sales (Stanley, 1974). Indeed, the Conservatives 'hoped that shared ownership would complement the right to buy' (Balchin, 1995: 201). The first schemes were rolled out from July

1979 and confined to local authority (and some housing association) new-build projects. Following the 1984 Housing and Building Control Act (and the 1984 Tenants' Rights Etc Amendment (Scotland) Act), shared ownership was offered to council tenants unable to buy their homes outright, even with substantial discounts (Balchin, 1995: 202). The mould was now set: shared ownership provided an important route to low-cost ownership, and could be applied to new-build and existing homes. This path to ownership has evolved into numerous forms since the early 1980s. The advantages seem fairly clear-cut:

> it offers house hunters an opportunity to obtain accommodation in an area where other tenures are unobtainable or unsuitable; local authorities [or associations] are able to keep a degree of control over the allocation of housing and house prices; it is a means of creating a more socially balanced community; and once established it is possible that the balance can be maintained as each shared ownership property must be offered back to the housing authority [or association] when the occupier wishes to move. (Balchin, 1995: 202)

Indeed, such schemes – usually involving part purchase and part (subsidised) renting – seem to offer a good compromise between outright ownership and renting. In the late 1980s, however, some critics argued that too much shared ownership is a bad thing, often resulting in the inadequate provision of social renting opportunities for the very poorest households (Ball et al, 1988: 207). Policy in this century has emphasised the balance that needs to be struck between rental and intermediate tenures (DCLG, 2006a).

Striking a balance between tenures – as a means of achieving more balanced communities overall – has been a central objective of LCHO. Terry (1999: 25) notes that this form of ownership has not only been used by government to 'encourage people into home ownership earlier', but also as a means of freeing up social rented lettings and creating 'balanced' and 'regenerated' communities. However, in rural areas, and especially where the total volume of new-build is low, these broader aims have been difficult to achieve. Policy-makers have also faced the accusation of being far less concerned about creating such a balance in terms of 'social composition' in rural areas given the acknowledged difficulties of making smaller villages more mixed (Hoggart and Henderson, 2005: 181, 194).

Throughout its early history, shared ownership was confined to properties built or converted by a social landlord. Therefore, shared ownership opportunities followed the standard pattern of residential development, with concentration in market towns. But in 1983, 'Do it Yourself Shared Ownership' (DIYSO)[2] – a scheme whereby 'homes selected by households in need were purchased off the shelf by a social landlord and then leased to the applicants' (Shepherd, 1999: 35) – held out the prospect of greater access to affordable homes for households residing in areas with fewer new-build opportunities.

DIYSO was hugely popular, especially in the countryside, but this popularity led quickly to its demise. Because of spiralling costs, the Housing Corporation was forced to end its funding for DIYSO in 1984. For the next six years, government grappled with the combined effects of the right to buy and the apparent inability of its shared ownership policies to compensate for the loss of low-cost homes in the countryside. In 1990, a 'Rural Shared Ownership' (Policy F2-34/90; Housing Corporation, 1990) repurchase scheme was set up in England 'as government recognised the need for low-cost homes to remain available for local people' (Shepherd, 1999: 36): housing associations could use 'housing association grants' to repurchase equity bought by a householder through 'staircasing'. Further, for occupants who had acquired full ownership in designated rural areas – and in settlements of fewer than 1,000 residents – it became mandatory to serve notice on the partner housing association that they intended to sell their home. The association would then have six weeks to exercise a legal option to repurchase. The scheme was designed to ensure a retained supply of affordable housing in villages.

Two years later, the Housing Corporation revised this guidance (in F2-03/92; Housing Corporation, 1992), setting a limit on staircasing (in 'eligible rural areas') of 'at least 80 per cent of the property value' (essential on exception sites where homes must be retained in perpetuity) and extending the repurchase scheme to settlements of up to 3,000 residents. Because the total amount of affordable housing in rural areas is limited – restricted by the supply of developable land – a critical concern is that opportunities for this type of LCHO will be lost to communities because of the right of initial occupants to progress to full ownership and then sell properties on the open market. Throughout the development of these policies, restrictions have been set to prevent this from happening, and to ensure that shared ownership arrangements benefit successive occupants. This has been a key characteristic of rural shared ownership.[3]

Another model was provided until 2009 by the Rural Housing Trust (RHT)[4] (in England). It developed shared ownership schemes (usually on exception sites) without grant support. The grant-free nature of these schemes meant that occupants did not have the right to staircase to full equity: rather, the Trust was able to retain – and continues to retain – its share and an element of control over homes in perpetuity (a legal requirement on exception sites since 1991). This type of affordable housing – whether grant-funded or funded solely through planning gain – is of course only appropriate where local buyers can almost, but not quite, afford to purchase their own home (RHT, 2008). Of course, like any developer, the RHT could only progress schemes where there was land available to build on. Between 1989 and 2008, the Trust built roughly 430 homes in England under its grant-free model, making a modest contribution to meeting housing needs in rural areas.

Shared ownership is important, meeting the needs of 'single people, couples and families who would not receive priority help from their local authority housing department' (RHT, 2008: 1) and, when combined with a planning exception, it is a means of bringing forward the right kind of development, in the right locations, at an appropriate cost. The right to purchase back and golden share arrangements are important strengths where supply is constrained. But there are also key weaknesses.

First, the scheme is dependent on there being opportunities (i.e. land) for housing association new-build. Where these opportunities are limited, the standard approach to shared ownership will have a commensurately limited impact.

Second, shared ownership can be expensive depending on market conditions. It is not a full-subsidy solution, but is dependent on the ability of housing occupants to foot a big part of the total cost. Shared ownership arrangements helped 40,000 households in England between 1999 and 2005 (House of Commons Committee of Public Accounts, 2007: 10) but these tended not to be households drawn from the lowest income groups.

DIYSO dealt, in theory, with the issue of limited new-build, but not with the barrier of cost. In April 2006, all existing shared ownership arrangements were transformed into a single programme of 'HomeBuy' (comprising Social, New Build and Open Market HomeBuy). These are examined more closely towards the end of this chapter.

Starter homes

Today, the label 'starter home' is usually applied to small private houses built without subsidy (land or capital), but which may attract – and suit the needs of – young couples looking to set up home for the first time. Use of the label has generally lapsed, as starter homes in the 1980s quickly became associated with poor space standards, prompting developers to move upmarket (Karn, 1995: 114) and to offer more than the minimum product, which proved increasingly difficult to market as the decade wore on. That said, developers still build tiny units (often flats in central urban areas and the ubiquitous semis on greenfield sites), often labelling these 'affordable homes' (affordable by virtue of their limited plot size, though they may well have an equivalent per-square-metre cost) and causing – intentionally – general confusion over what constitutes 'affordable housing': something that is merely cheap because it is small, or affordable because there is some element of land or grant subsidy.

Government has usefully drawn a line between starter homes and affordable housing. It now states, categorically, that the latter term may only be used to denote social rented or intermediate housing (including shared ownership or HomeBuy products) that fits the exact definition set out in *Delivering Affordable Housing* (DCLG, 2006a). Small 'starter homes' or housing offered at below market cost are labelled 'low-cost market housing' (and local authorities are encouraged to plan for such provision in their local development frameworks). It is distinctly different from affordable housing, which is always housing – outside of the market – delivered with some form of subsidy that makes it more affordable, relative to market housing in the same area.

But the origin of the label can be found in the same package of initiatives launched in 1981: indeed, the most popular form of public–private or public–voluntary partnership in the early 1980s involved the sale of public land for the purpose of providing units for LCHO. This strategy inevitably lost momentum as public land banks were depleted, but speculators stepped in to meet the market demand for small homes for first-time buyers, usually concentrated on peripheral greenfield sites, relying on pattern-book designs, mixing two-bed semis with higher-end units: three- or four-bed detached with more generous front and back gardens, and sometimes double garages. But few red-brick, greenfield, speculative developments in the 1980s or 1990s lacked a generous proportion of starter homes.

Central government and local planning authorities were keen that private development should cater for a mix of needs and so, by the end of the decade, planning policy guidance on housing was calling on authorities to use their development control function to encourage a mix of smaller and larger family units. But for their part, speculative developers had a deeply vested interest in building very small homes: these form the first rung on the home-ownership ladder for first-time buyers, and without new buyers entering the market, there can be no trading up by established homeowners, no transaction chains and therefore no demand for bigger, more expensive properties. Speculators build for the market and also to keep the market moving: the supply of bottom-end products is essential to future business success.

But there is no reason why developers should pepper starter homes uniformly across the countryside. Rather, single points of entry into the market are provided by speculators, usually on strategic sites within market towns or in other larger centres. Here, there is often a concentration of starter homes, commonly arranged around cul-de-sacs and marketed at young, as yet childless, couples.

The reason for this concentration is obvious: it is guided by planning. Land allocated for housing in rural areas has been concentrated in larger settlements, often within or adjacent to designated key settlements in the past, and market towns today (Cloke, 1979; Parsons, 1980; Cameron and Shucksmith, 2007), focusing the process of middle-class gentrification in locations – often village locations – where development has been generally discouraged or where speculators build for the high end of the market. Thus planning has 'influenced the geographical impact of gentrification in rural areas' (Parsons, 1980: 17), with villages experiencing the biggest changes in their social composition, a process that has been amplified through a concentration of right-to-buy sales – together with a paucity of shared ownership opportunities – in 'smaller village locations' (Milbourne, 1998).

However, from a development point of view, many villages are simply not entry points into the housing market: they are high end (see also Chapter 11). And because of planning restrictions, any attempt to create entry points in these locations needs to be based on a circumvention of normal planning rules. This usually means allowing an exception, that is, an exception to normal regulations that produces an exceptional outcome – a home built for an individual or a household without substantial income or wealth. Speculators make most effective economic use of the land that is available. Creating entry points into the market is important, but can be most effectively achieved on cheaper greenfield sites adjoining less desirable towns. Without subsidy or circumvention of planning rules, prime village sites are closed to such development. This seems to make economic sense, and government has been keen to stress the social and personal benefits of town life (ODPM, 2004). Hence there is a degree of harmony between government's and the private sector's views of appropriate residential development patterns in the countryside, with both being driven by a market rationale, tempered by an acceptance of the need for planning constraint. These issues were given more detailed consideration in Chapter 11.

Equity sharing initiatives in the 2000s

There is a strong sense that different products cater for different parts of the market. This thinking was critical to the development of housing policy from the early 1980s. Starter homes have a part to play in market towns and in larger villages; general shared ownership is important in these same locations, with units often secured through planning on strategic sites before being offered to households on different tenure arrangements. The DIYSO scheme seemed to recognise, however, that new housing is not always available (or possible) in locations where there is, nevertheless, a need for low-cost accommodation. DIYSO was an important policy development in rural areas (given the constraints on residential development) as it seemed to offer new opportunities to rural households. Despite the expense of the scheme, government signalled its continuing support for the principles of DIYSO with proposals for the introduction of HomeBuy in 1998 (Shepherd, 1999: 37).

Introduced in April 1999, HomeBuy was seen as a new route into LCHO, designed to help lower-income households (but not the lowest) in England into home ownership. Under the scheme, purchasers were given an interest-free loan of 25 per cent of the purchase price of their home: as with DIYSO, government was using public money to subsidise home purchase and, as with DIYSO, beneficiaries were able to achieve full control of their home without a facility for public-sector repurchase. Jackson (2001) was one of the first researchers to review the operation of HomeBuy just 15 months after its introduction. He argued that 'making HomeBuy available to lower-income households would be expensive in subsidy terms', adding that 'people who buy under HomeBuy have considerably higher incomes than those who buy under Shared Ownership' and that 'HomeBuy is not flexible enough to cope with the wide regional variations in income-to-house-price ratios in England' (Jackson, 2001: 1). In other words, HomeBuy seemed to offer no solution to meeting the housing needs of households on low incomes but living in areas where house prices had accelerated well beyond the reach of local wage-earners. Instead, Jackson found that HomeBuy purchasers tended to earn considerably more than those households who had benefited through the DIYSO scheme. And because the subsidy rate was fixed (a loan of 25 per cent of property value), the programme was spatially inflexible: a household with an income of £25,000 could benefit substantially in an area of modest house prices, but would feel little benefit where prices were considerably higher. This meant that the scheme was not a route into LCHO in all areas: many households in rural England were left needing considerably more assistance, either some sort of heavily subsided DIYSO-type arrangement (as in Wales, see below) or new social rented housing.

The equivalent scheme in Scotland from 2005 has been 'HomeStake', now part of the wider 'LIFT' (Low-cost Initiative for First Time buyers), launched in October 2007 (Scottish Government, 2008d). The scheme is similar to HomeBuy in many respects. Like HomeBuy, it allows eligible households to purchase a share of a new-build or an old property (a 'New Supply Shared Equity Scheme' and an 'Open Market Shared Equity Pilot', respectively), though the mechanism for acquiring existing homes – and supporting this in more rural areas – was introduced tentatively (as a pilot) given the known cost risks associated with this type of shared ownership mechanism. At first, the open scheme was piloted in Edinburgh and the Lothians. It was then extended to seven further areas of high demand, including rural Aberdeenshire and Highland councils, at the beginning of 2008. In March 2009, it was announced that the scheme would be temporarily extended across the whole of Scotland in the light of the worsening economic conditions. The Scottish Government allocated £60 million of funding to the 'extended pilot' for the period April 2009 to March 2010 but also set strict local price ceilings on how much participants in the scheme are able to spend on a home. In the East Mainland area of Highland, for example, the maximum eligible price for a two-bed home was £70,000 in 2009/10. Ceilings have been set to reflect the bottom 25% (lower quartile) of homes sold and are reviewed regularly using data on the price of homes sold in each area (see Scottish Government, 2010). The Scottish Government was aware that this is a costly response to meeting housing need and – given land and property prices in some areas – it will not benefit all communities. For these reasons, it remained a pilot and a temporary measure ancillary to the 'New Supply' scheme, for which land subsidies can sometimes be generated through planning.

Innovative approaches have developed at the local scale, such as the mechanisms used to develop LCHO in villages by The Highlands Small Communities Housing Trust, Scotland. The Trust pioneered the use of Rural Housing Burdens, which is a shared equity, pre-emption right condition imposed on the title of the house plots that it sells. The mechanism ensures that, whenever the property is sold, the seller will be able to get back not more than 75 per cent of the open market value of the property (as assessed by the District Valuer) because the Trust retains its 25 per cent share of the equity.

Perseverance with the HomeBuy model – and its equivalents – is perhaps an indication that appropriateness to all market conditions and all types of location are not its primary considerations. HomeBuy is not a rural housing solution; or rather it is not a means of meeting the needs of all rural households. In line with its philosophy of different products for different groups, HomeBuy in England has been transformed (since April 2006) into a means of facilitating the purchase of social housing by existing tenants (Social HomeBuy), providing a shared ownership route for key workers and priority first-time buyers (New Build HomeBuy) and supporting the purchase of open market homes by key workers and other priority groups (Open Market HomeBuy, the successor to the 1998 scheme, and the equivalent of the open pilot in Scotland).

Government's commitment to HomeBuy is also a commitment to 'intermediate' housing solutions over social renting, where possible. To some extent, this reflects the reality of changed aspirations, post-Thatcher. But it also harps back to government's aim of flexible solutions, tailored to the circumstances of individuals. Many households are in an intermediate situation: not wanting to rent, but unable to buy.

Unfortunately, these intermediate schemes cannot always deal with the market and development contexts of rural areas. In Wales, one response has been to develop a different kind of HomeBuy: a scheme that is closer to shared ownership (DIYSO) than its current English namesake. This was introduced in 1995/96 by Housing for Wales and then carried forward by the National Assembly for Wales (now the Welsh Assembly Government).

In 2002, Gwerin Housing Association, operating in rural Monmouthshire, began entering into 50–50 shared ownership arrangements with rural households, jointly purchasing homes on the open market. In order to limit its expenditure, properties in the major towns – Abergavenny, Monmouth, Chepstow, Caldicot and Usk – were deemed ineligible, hence allowing the association to focus its resources on the area's villages. Gwerin was one of very few associations to develop a strategic policy for targeting HomeBuy (Welsh Assembly Government, 2007: 4). However, even this seemingly generous scheme is not without its shortcomings. In order for HomeBuy (dubbed 'rural HomeBuy' in some areas) to operate at all, it was necessary for the Assembly to set strict limits on the value of properties that could be purchased under the initiative, as is the case in Scotland, though the Scottish pilot has not 'red-lined' areas. 'Acceptable Cost Guidance' was written into the scheme, setting out the maximum share value that would be locally affordable, and hence the maximum value of a property that should be purchased under the scheme (Welsh Assembly Government, 2007: 5). But even with only a 50 per cent share of a property bought at apparently 'acceptable cost', many households are still unable to afford the combined cost of a mortgage plus a shared equity rent. In order to achieve costs that are acceptable to a full range of local households almost all purchases in predominantly rural districts have been 'in or near larger towns, rather than in rural villages' (Welsh Assembly Government, 2007: 4). This pattern might partly be explained by purchaser preference, but the cost of acquiring scarce rural housing is certainly an added factor.

Back in England, 'rural HomeBuy' is a derivative of the standard initiatives launched in 2006 or shared ownership arrangement (relabelled New Build HomeBuy) where staircasing remains capped at 80 per cent under the regulations introduced in 1992. Arguably, these schemes still fail to deal with the fundamentals of rural housing markets: in both England and Wales, they have widened access to home ownership in market towns without having any significant impact in villages. The picture in Scotland is slightly different, or at least less certain. An initial evaluation of the Open Market HomeStake pilot – the forerunner of the 'open' LIFT scheme – concluded its operation in 'different kinds of rural areas' needed to be tested further. Application of the approach seems to have a clear logic:

> In affordability terms quite a lot of rural areas appear to offer scope, often because of the coincidence of low incomes in work with quite high house prices. In some instances the practical limitations on new supply may imply that a scheme assisting access to the secondhand market may be of value (Bramley et al, 2007: 102).

As a practicable response, however, it is limited by its funding: is there enough public money available to create market 'entry points' for all eligible households in the most overheating markets, including some villages? It may well be prudent to expand the scheme during low points in the economic cycle (i.e. the recession of 2008–10), whilst there are attendant falls in house prices, but public expenditure may not be able to keep pace with demand once the market picks up.

Another model of equity sharing – the Rural Home Ownership Grant (RHOG) – was developed by Scottish Homes from 1990 and subsequently adopted by Communities Scotland and the Scottish Government. The RHOG is a means-tested capital subsidy, payable to people developing their own home or, in limited circumstances, for open market purchase. It was targeted on rural areas where there were recognised to be severe supply constraints. A grant of up to 40 per cent of capital cost was payable, with clawback arrangements should the user sell on within 10 years of grant receipt. Evaluation of the grant showed that it had provided a cost-effective mechanism in circumstances where other LCHO mechanisms would have struggled and that it had enabled the survival of some fragile rural communities (Morgan and Satsangi, forthcoming, 2011).

Rural housing aspirations and LCHO

Extending access to home ownership has been the primary goal of LCHO initiatives, and over a period of 30 years they have played a significant role in meeting the housing aspirations of a population weaned off social and private renting during the 1980s. At the time of writing, more than two households in every three in Britain are homeowners, and surveys in the different countries of Britain consistently suggest that 90 per cent of all households aspire to own their own home (e.g. House of Commons Committee of Public Accounts, 2007: 9). Rural households are no less enthusiastic about home ownership: and the desire to buy often lures local people away from villages, where the opportunities to do so are few, to nearby towns.

Villagers are split between two competing aspirations – to live locally and to buy. The realities of the planning system and of the land market create this choice (Chapter 11). LCHO is inherently difficult to deliver in villages where there is less land for development and second-hand housing is expensive. When affordable housing *is* delivered, it is often heavily dependent on land and direct subsidy in order to make it sufficiently affordable to those on the lowest incomes. This means that rather than struggling against fundamentals, and ultimately achieving very few affordable homes in villages, it is perhaps wiser to focus efforts in market towns. There are other policy drivers that make this the most likely outcome, including the belief in the inherent sustainability of concentrated over more dispersed development patterns.

The net result is an abandonment of these villages to market forces, and concentrated gentrification in some small village locations. This trend has been strongest in the most popular villages, where prices have risen sharply. Southern England and the commuter belts of major cities have perhaps been characterised most clearly by 'overheating' markets, though this is a generalisation. Elsewhere, pressure on the rural housing stock has also been acute, with some rural households finding themselves priced out of the market for homes to purchase.

LCHO clearly meets an aspiration and, in its various manifestations, is a means of widening access to home ownership. For a great many households it is a more popular tenure choice than private or social renting, but there is a clear desire for more LCHO opportunities to be made available in villages. This is evidenced in the popularity of DIYSO in England, rural HomeBuy in Wales and LIFT in Scotland. The fact that these schemes have sometimes been unable to deliver against aspiration is not down to inherent weaknesses in their design, but a result of spiralling rural property prices from the mid-1990s. High prices meant that neither the public sector nor the potential equity-sharers were able to purchase homes for a price that would be affordable, to individuals or to government. LCHO deals tactically with a core aspiration of UK households, but it does not address the more fundamental barriers to housing access in the countryside: planning constraint and a consequent lack of development land.

Notes

[1] The right to buy has arguably made by far the biggest contribution to LCHO. Jones (2007), for example, points out that it accounted for 90 per cent of LCHO in Wales between 1980 and 2007. It has been of comparable importance in England and Scotland. Whilst the focus of this chapter is on mechanisms designed to open up owner-occupation to a broader spectrum of households, the importance of the right to buy in extending ownership to former public sector tenants, and its overall contribution to LCHO, is considerable.

[2] In England only. Shared ownership schemes in the Celtic countries took similar forms, and had similar advantages and disadvantages.

[3] In Scotland, restrictions on the maximum percentage of value held by a purchaser were available through a variant model, shared equity.

[4] The Rural Housing Trust ceased to function in January 2009. Whilst the Trust retains equity shares in its shared ownership schemes, the 'difficult trading conditions' resulted in it winding down its development activities (RHT, 2009).

SEVENTEEN

Homelessness

Previous chapters have highlighted not only the roles played by different tenures, but also some of the mechanisms for bringing forward greater housing choice for lower-income groups. One of the costs of not providing sufficient housing is the number of people who fall out of, or can never gain access to, mainstream housing in the countryside. In this respect, homelessness represents the clearest expression of failure within rural housing systems. Homelessness thus represents a key indicator of social and economic stress, and demands attention to alleviate its condition. Yet rural homelessness has had to struggle to find a way into policy discourses or indeed into being recognised.

At the same time, homelessness is also much more than a housing issue, and reflects wider, deep-seated social problems such as poverty, exclusion, chaotic lifestyles and the way that society responds to vulnerability. Solutions to homelessness require not only access to sufficient housing options in mainstream housing, but also a range of specific housing and support options that facilitate prevention, as well as routes out of homeless experiences. This chapter provides not only a focus on the particular challenges for tackling homelessness in rural contexts, but also a consideration of the way that the very existence of homelessness in rural localities has been downplayed and marginalised.

The contested nature of (rural) homelessness

The scale of the problem is in itself an issue for debate. The way that homelessness is defined obviously has implications for the number of households that are included in measurements. The definition of statutory homelessness is often much more tightly drawn than those definitions used by lobby groups or academics. For example, statutory homelessness is defined as affecting:

> persons without any accommodation in the UK which they have a legal right to occupy, together with their whole household. Those who cannot gain access to their accommodation, or cannot reasonably be expected to live in it (for example because of a risk of violence), are also legally homeless. (Fitzpatrick et al, 2009: 6)

This statutory definition can be compared with the one used by Fitzpatrick et al (2009: 6) as:

> the situation of those sleeping rough or living in temporary or highly insecure forms of accommodation, such as hostels, night shelters,

women's refuges, bed & breakfast hotels, or staying temporarily with friends and relatives because they have no home of their own. Also people living in accommodation which they have no legal right to occupy (such as squatters or young people whose parents have withdrawn their 'licence' to remain at home) and those whose accommodation is so substandard or dangerous (for example, because of a threat of domestic violence) that it is not reasonable to expect them to stay there.

The difference between the official recognition of homelessness and the range of circumstances that can be argued as constituting a homeless experience opens up the category of hidden homelessness; those people who may have highly insecure or otherwise unsatisfactory housing arrangements, but who nevertheless are not owed a duty to be accommodated by local authorities under prevailing legislation. However, the way in which homelessness can be hidden in rural areas is more than an outcome of competing definitions. It also encapsulates social and cultural factors that heavily contest the presence of homelessness in these localities. One reason why rural homelessness has been so controversial is that it cuts to the heart of powerful images of what the countryside is thought to be about in popular culture. Chapter 2 discussed the pervasive influence of the rural idyll, and it is this notion that casts a large shadow over debates about homeless people in rural areas, not just in Britain, but internationally as well. Britain is not unique in the construction of these powerful images of rural areas and the way that homeless people are rendered invisible by these representations. Commentators elsewhere have drawn attention to the invisibility of homeless people within popular images of rural areas within the United States, Canada and Australia (Beer et al, 2003; Milbourne and Cloke, 2006; Skott-Myhre et al, 2008). Thus, although the notion of the rural idyll has developed along different trajectories in various countries, the term 'rural homelessness' is certainly contested within these respective cultures such that the latter can be rendered invisible within the former. However, a body of research (see for example, Cloke et al, 2002) has highlighted that putting the case for rural homelessness has been hampered by the way that the concept of the rural idyll masks such social problems.

Trends in rural homelessness

In the early years of the current century, trends in the pattern of officially recorded homelessness in the rural areas of England appeared to tell a story of policy successes. Statistics (see Table 17.1) show that overall homelessness rates in all areas of England, rural and urban, have been falling since 2002/03 (CRC, 2008a). Furthermore, homelessness rates in rural areas of England are much lower than in urban areas. Figures from the Commission for Rural Communities (CRC, 2008a) reveal that homelessness rates in 'Rural 80' authorities (that is, local authorities where over 80 per cent of the population live in areas classed as rural) were 2.1 per thousand total households, compared with a rate of 4.4 per thousand households in major urban areas.

Table 17.1: Homelessness per thousand households, England, by area type

	Rural 80	Rural 50	Significant rural	Other urban	Large urban	Major urban
2002/03	3.6	4.2	4.1	6.0	5.4	8.2
2003/04	3.6	4.5	4.4	5.9	6.3	8.4
2004/05	3.4	4.2	3.7	5.5	5.8	7.3
2005/06	2.7	3.1	2.9	4.2	4.1	4.7
2006/07	2.1	2.3	2.3	3.3	3.3	4.4

Source: Commission for Rural Communities (CRC, 2008a)

However, in contrast with the situation in England, research has shown that rates of homelessness in rural areas of Wales are similar to the rates experienced in urban parts of this country (see Table 17.2). It is also the case that studies in Scotland (Strachan et al, 2000; Milbourne and Cloke, 2006) and Wales (Milbourne et al, 2006) have identified an upswing in rates of homelessness in the rural areas of these countries. Based on research from Tribal HCH, the Scottish Executive compared the outturn and projections for four groups of councils, one group of which comprised mainly rural councils. The mainly rural councils experienced the highest rate of growth in homelessness between 2001/02 and 2003/04 (Scottish Executive, 2005b).

Table 17.2: Homelessness per thousand households, Wales, by area type

	Rural	Semi-rural	Valleys	Urban
2005	7.3	5.7	6.7	7.3

Source: Milbourne et al (2006)

There are, however, critical problems with reliance on these data. It is not only claimed that the figures understate the level of homelessness in rural areas, but also that they result in an emphasis on addressing homelessness in cities when policy solutions are needed within rural areas, from which many homeless people who end up in cities originate (see Cloke et al, 2002; Robinson, 2004).

However, beneath these headline figures, another trend is apparent. Since the 1990s, an increasing proportion of all homeless households have been located in rural areas. The first studies of homelessness in England to disaggregate rural and urban areas in the 1980s and early 1990s highlighted that homelessness rates in rural areas had not only increased (Newton, 1991), but had done so at faster rates than in urban areas (Greve and Currie, 1990; Lambert et al, 1992). This trend also continued into the first decade of the 21st century (Monk et al, 2006; Milbourne and Cloke, 2006). Milbourne and Cloke (2006) pointed out that 18.3 per cent of all homelessness in England in 2002/03 was in rural areas, compared with 14.4 per cent in 1996 and 11.8 per cent of all homelessness cases in 1992. A similar trend was highlighted in a joint statement by the National Housing Federation and the Campaign to Protect Rural England (2008), who noted that the proportion of homeless rural households in the English homelessness figures had more than doubled in the five years prior to 2007, from 16 to 37 per cent of the total. Milbourne et al (2006) highlighted that homelessness in rural areas of Wales had increased by 309 per cent between 1978 and 2005, compared with an increase of 129 per cent in urban areas.

Devolution has led to a widening divergence in homelessness policies between Scotland, England and Wales. It is important to recognise these differing policy contexts when interpreting trends in homelessness. In Scotland, homelessness figures have not fallen to the same extent as in England and Wales; a trend that has been ascribed to the strengthening of the legislative safety net in Scotland for homeless households (this point is discussed later in the chapter). There has been a particularly strong focus on the prevention of homelessness in England through the use of the housing options approach. It is this approach that has been highlighted as the reason for the 21st-century falls in statutory homelessness that have been seen in rural and urban areas alike (Wilcox, 2008). However, as noted by Wilcox (2008), other commentators have been more circumspect about the reasons for this decline. Pawson (2007) argued that the fall in numbers is also a feature of stricter interpretations by local authorities of their duties under the legislation, such that the problem is being redefined, rather than solved. He suggested that a trend towards a denial of state responsibility for their housing difficulties poses a problem for households in both urban and rural areas.

Homelessness and rough-sleeping

As well as the implications of policy and its implementation, there are other ways in which official statistics undercount the extent of homelessness in rural areas. Although a small proportion of all homeless people are rough-sleepers, it is this aspect of homelessness that tends to grab the headlines. Nonetheless, methods of estimating rough-sleeping have come in for particular criticism. The recognised method of evaluating levels of rough-sleepers by national governments is to undertake a headcount of rough-sleepers on a particular night. Such a headcount method is likely to miss a proportion of people sleeping rough in rural areas. The dispersed nature of rough-sleeping is one factor: Evans (1999) identified that people had slept rough in places such as garages, sheds and outhouses, churchyards, barns, parks, fields and woods. Rough-sleepers thus tend to be hidden away, making quantification difficult. In Wales, the challenge of identifying rough-sleepers in rural areas has also been highlighted in national research (Bevan, 2000). Studies at the local level in Wales have highlighted not only the particular nature of rough-sleeping, but also the hidden numbers of people who sleep rough in the countryside (Blythe, 2006). The relevance of the headcount method in rural England continues to be challenged (see for example, Shelter, 2008).

Unfortunately, alternative methods of counting rough-sleepers in the countryside have also got caught up in the way that policy success is measured and defined at national level in England. The lack of attention to, and acceptance of, rural homelessness in the past led to undercounting, which was subsequently challenged. Robinson and Reeve (2002) identified much higher levels of rough-sleeping in North Lincolnshire than official counts suggested. Their (and other authors') methods for identifying rural rough-sleeping had uncomfortable implications for national-level policy discourses about how governments had tackled this aspect of homelessness, and therefore received a very cool reception from policy-makers – with alternative counts not accepted into official statistics. Robinson (2004) argued that the need to show success through a reduction in the level of homelessness as measured by the number of rough-sleepers was a dominant factor in determining the success of policy. This work by Robinson highlights not only that extra-urban levels of rough-sleeping are higher than previously thought, but also that the resistance of government to any evidence challenging the dominance of its discourse over rough-sleeping is also greater than in urban areas. It could be suggested that the potential for raising the profile of rural homelessness areas suffered as a consequence of the poor evidence base prior to the introduction of policies towards rough-sleepers as well as a failure at national levels to adopt context-specific methods for measuring rough-sleeping outwith, as well as within, urban environments.

Hidden homelessness and insecure living

Rough-sleeping represents only one facet of a wider experience of homelessness in the countryside, and research has highlighted its hidden nature: reflecting on the range of insecure housing options that people tend to occupy, as well as the paucity of specialist provision in rural localities (Jones, 1999; Milbourne and Cloke, 2006). Care must be taken in ascribing an 'aspatial', all-encompassing rural dimension to the experience of homelessness in the countryside. Research has emphasised that the incidence and nature of homelessness varies considerably from area to area (Cloke et al, 2002). Nevertheless, research that has adopted a case study approach has identified context-specific characteristics of the experience. A particular feature appears to the number of homeless people staying with friends or family. Robinson and Coward (2003) found that about two thirds (65 per cent) of all homeless people in the rural district of Craven, North Yorkshire had only ever stayed with friends and relatives since becoming homeless (compared with 13 per cent in London and 4 per cent in Sheffield).

People in the countryside may be living in circumstances that are not necessarily described in terms of homelessness, but are so insecure and short term in nature that they can rapidly spiral into a homeless situation. The presence of different types of insecure living arrangements will depend on the nature of the locality and its housing markets. For example, tourist areas with higher than average proportions of holiday cottages tend to see higher levels of people in winter lets. A feature of many remote areas of Scotland is also the number of people living in caravans and mobile homes not intended for residential occupation.

Robinson and Coward (2003) reflected upon rural homelessness being invisible in statistics: only half of the homeless people in Craven who had stayed with a friend or relative had approached the local authority as homeless. Fewer than one in four had been recognised as homeless by the local authority and thus appeared in the official homeless statistics.

Attitudes and representations

Attitudes towards rural homelessness, amongst homeless people themselves and the wider population, as well as practitioners and policy-makers, play a crucial role in the problem being 'hidden'. Why should this be the case? A central argument is the non-coupling of 'rural' and 'homelessness' (Cloke et al, 2000a; Robinson, 2004). In this respect, homelessness forms part of a wider body of research that has examined the way that different groups of people stand apart from, or are embraced by, representations of the countryside (see Cloke et al, 2000a).

Perhaps the most significant contribution of this approach is its examination of the power relations that exist between different groups in rural areas. Cloke et al (2000b) argued that the rural idyll translated into practices by dominant groups within local policy-making to try to deny the existence of homelessness within rural communities and thus the need to devote resources to its alleviation. Resistance is also apparent amongst bodies that claim to represent the countryside. Parish councils have come in for some criticism, because of the denial by some that problems exist and that any response is necessary. It is important, however, to acknowledge a variation in response: some parish councils have been instrumental in attempts to deliver solutions to housing and homelessness problems within their communities. The type of resistance to new affordable housing schemes noted in Chapter 14 also extends to hostility towards schemes that attempt to tackle homelessness within smaller settlements. Oldman (2002) reported particular antipathy towards attempts to set up services for homeless young people in rural communities. Such attitudes were reflected in the views of young homeless people in a study by Evans (1999): whilst older homeless people found rural communities to be friendly and helpful, younger homeless people were more likely to feel isolated and socially rejected.

It is attitudes towards young homeless people that encapsulate how the rural idyll is used to problematise particular groups and seek to push them away from smaller settlements. Resistance to rural homelessness thus comes back to a form of NIMBYism. Ageism focused on young people also continues to bedevil attempts to find solutions to housing and homelessness problems. It is not only that the existence of young homeless people in villages remains heavily contested, controversy also surrounds the case for locating solutions in rural as well as in urban areas. In spite of 'housing for young people' being a clarion call for local needs surveys right through to national reviews, a counter-claim articulated within many communities seems to be that young homeless people do not belong in the countryside, and that specialist services to address their housing and support needs are not welcome.

Cloke et al (2000a, 2000c) identified fundamental reasons why this point should not come as a surprise. Socio-cultural barriers towards recognising rural homelessness by rural-dwellers leads them to deny or downplay this issue. These authors drew upon a range of studies that have highlighted the processes of social change within rural areas and the increasing dominance of middle-class groups. Shucksmith (1990b) argued that the maintenance of the rural idyll could be understood in relation to domestic property classes, and was rooted just as much in production- as in consumption-oriented motives, which were fundamentally concerned with protecting house values. The privileging of representations of the countryside – of a rural idyll – helped in the maintenance not just of house prices but also of particular lifestyles.

Housing supply

A crucial backdrop here is a structural one: a housing supply in rural areas that works for these latter middle-class groups, but which fails people in a range of insecure living arrangements and personal circumstances that render them at risk of homelessness. A host of studies across Britain that have focused upon rural homelessness have drawn attention to the lack of affordable housing as an important driver in the inability of homeless households to satisfy their housing needs within rural areas (Strachan et al, 2000; Cloke et al, 2002; Streich et al, 2002; Milbourne et al, 2006, Briheim-Crookall, 2007). Indeed, whilst overall homelessness rates have been falling, one reason for the increasing pressure evident in Britain's rural areas noted by the National Housing Federation and Campaign to Protect Rural England (2008) appears to be the erosion of the stock of social rented accommodation through the right to buy, with an inadequate rate of replacement new-build.

Further, there are emerging tensions in rural localities in Scotland in relation to the supply of social rented housing, on the one hand, and homelessness policies – namely the intention to widen the safety-net role of local authorities – on the other. This country has taken a very different approach to homelessness in the last few years compared with Wales or England, and has set itself the highly ambitious target that virtually all homeless people in Scotland will be entitled to rehousing by 2012 (Wilcox et al, 2010). The 2003 Homelessness (Scotland) Act (amending the 1987 Housing (Scotland) Act) provides for the ending of the priority need distinction, meaning that councils will have a duty to find permanent housing for *all* persons assessed as unintentionally homeless. It is expected that this change will take place gradually, with the expansion, and then abolition, of priority need status in 2012. Discussions in Scotland have highlighted the potential impact of these changes for rural areas. Based on assumptions provided by local authorities, the projected need of homeless households in either obtaining or requiring permanent accommodation for the mainly rural councils roughly doubles on all projections, from about 3,000 social lets per year to around 6,000 by 2011/12 (Scottish Executive, 2005b). Although projections of homelessness are contested (Bramley et al, 2006), indications show that rural housing providers are going to experience a huge increase in pressure on their resources to accommodate these policy changes. Contributions to the Scottish Parliament's inquiry into rural housing highlighted the tensions in the roles that social renting will increasingly be expected to play in rural areas in response to the ambition of eradicating homelessness in Scotland (see Scottish Parliament Rural Affairs and Environment Committee, 2009). This Committee was keen to stress that the problem lies not with the legislation itself, but with an insufficient supply of social rented accommodation in rural areas to cope with the anticipated changes. Intense pressure on rural social rented stocks (with respect to tackling homelessness) is also apparent elsewhere in Britain. Research in the West Midlands by Land Use Consultants and CCHPR (2005) highlighted that all re-lets in the social rented stock went to homeless households in some rural districts in this region. The conclusions from the research in the West Midlands thus square with the view in Scotland that the supply of social rented housing is barely up to the task of meeting the needs of households in severe housing need, let alone other groups.

More than a housing issue

Research has also been careful to point out that homelessness is more than a housing issue (Cloke et al, 2002). How homelessness links with social exclusion has been recognised in policy (DTLR, 2002) and is consistent with evidence such as that presented by Robinson and Coward (2003). They identified a range of personal issues and challenges for people experiencing homelessness in the rural district of Craven. One third of respondents reported a mental health problem; one quarter reported a problem with drug dependency; over one third had been on probation; almost one in five had spent time in prison or a Young Offenders' Institution; and more than a fifth had spent time in local authority care. Thus, because tackling homelessness requires a range of approaches around prevention, support and access to specialist provision, not just overall housing supply, it also opens up debates about the nature of poverty, vulnerability and exclusion in the countryside. All these features threaten the veracity of idealised views of how the countryside should look. Furthermore, an acceptance of rural homelessness opens up the potential for responses that would assist people at risk of homelessness in maintaining their own lifestyle, not only in terms of the supply of general needs affordable housing, but also specialist accommodation and support options that are appropriate to service delivery within rural contexts.

Developing responses

Since the seminal research conducted by Paul Cloke et al in the mid- to late 1990s (2000a, 2000b, 2000c, 2001a, 2002), it has been possible to see a shift in the responses of agencies and policy-makers. Milbourne et al (2006) noted the engagement of statutory agencies and voluntary bodies with the specific notion of rural homelessness in their research on this issue in Wales. Interestingly, the key location of resistance to rural homelessness identified in this latter study continued to be within rural communities themselves. Tackling homelessness in the countryside has often had to start from the premise that mindsets need to change before getting to the point where addressing needs can be discussed in a meaningful way. Resources have thus had to be invested not only in gaining an acceptance that rural homelessness exists, but also that services within those communities may be the appropriate response. In this respect, part of the problem is down to a lack of awareness, and there is some evidence to suggest that raising the profile of homelessness in the countryside can achieve positive results in facilitating the development of locally based services. Indeed, one scheme reported that it was worth persisting in working with communities to turn around attitudes towards homeless people, which could result in the development of practical local solutions within these communities (Macklin, 1995). To take the example of Northumberland, there is the suggestion that a significant shift has taken place in the way that rural homelessness in the county is perceived, and that the debate has moved on from whether or not there is a youth homelessness problem in rural Northumberland to an assessment of the level of the problem and the causal factors (Burns, 2005). An important finding was that increases in reported levels of rural homelessness were probably not due to any real increase but to improvements in the recording of homelessness. Such developments appear to take on a momentum of their own, with young people who experience homelessness in this part of England apparently more likely to register the fact and have more opportunities to access accommodation and support.

In spite of the controversy surrounding homelessness, distinctive and tailored approaches to tackling this challenge are emerging. Many of these local responses have been drawn together and highlighted in a series of 'best practice' reviews that have sought to raise the profile of rural homelessness (Streich et al, 2002; McNaughton, 2005; Breiheim-Crookall, 2007). These responses highlight the role that communities themselves can play in helping to provide solutions to this issue.[1] The Shelter Single Homeless Person Support Service, based in Dumfries and Galloway, also provides an example of the kinds of role that volunteers in rural areas can engage in. These roles may include practical work such as helping people to move into new accommodation and settle into their new area, as well as undertaking jobs such as DIY, painting and decorating. Other roles include befriending and offering moral support, which may include help with shopping, paying the rent and bills, and visiting health services (Bevan and Rugg, 2006). Cloke et al (2002) highlight the role of voluntary sector activity in rural areas as a future direction for positive responses. Such responses tap into the tradition within rural communities for self-help and voluntarism, which perhaps represents working 'with the grain' in rural locations (see Chapter 18). At the same time, Cloke et al (2007) have noted the important role that local authorities continue to play in enabling and directing responses in the voluntary sector, as well as the limitations of this kind of approach.

A further way that specialist services can develop in rural areas that work with the grain of rural contexts is in relation to the use of 'homeless at home' services. Recognising that many homeless people in rural areas have to resort to staying with family or friends, these services work to help people to sustain these arrangements until such time as alternative and appropriate accommodation becomes available. Indeed, as noted by practitioners working in remote rural areas of the Highlands (Bevan and Rugg, 2006), such services are crucial in enabling homeless people to remain in their own communities. The dearth of alternative housing options for people is such that if arrangements to stay with family or friends fail, for whatever reason, the chances of finding alternative accommodation nearby are virtually non-existent.

However, it is important to note that attitudes within geographical communities at local level are not just fragmented but very fluid and ever-changing, and these can develop in both positive and negative directions. Positively, there has been a flourishing of activities aimed at tackling insecure housing that can lead to homelessness in some parts of rural Scotland such as on Gigha and Iona (also see examples in Chapter 18). A perusal of the Rural Housing Service website[2] spotlights a range of other examples of community-led solutions. At the same time, anecdotal evidence points towards a hardening of attitudes in parts of mainland Scotland towards affordable housing and a rise in NIMBYism within some rural communities, making the work of rural housing enablers harder. The hypothesis that the levels of resistance that are seen south of the border to the kind of solutions that would assist homeless households may be growing in rural Scotland certainly requires investigation.

The future

Any analysis of dominant cultural representations or versions of what constitutes rural Britain must address a basic question: who benefits from the outcomes? People with severe housing and support difficulties shatter representations of the countryside that have been carefully cultivated by dominant groups. A body of research shows that rather than accept the presence of rural homeless people, considerable effort has been expended on denying their existence or pushing for responses in urban locations. There are signs that this discourse is fragmenting. One way that voluntary and statutory activity has achieved help for the rural homeless has been through raising the profile of their situation, an approach that has helped to identify needs, lobby for resources and encouraged the development of local, community-based solutions. The process suggests a reformulation of the way that rural homelessness may become accepted and contested *between* residents in rural settlements. However, overlying these fragmented local contexts remains the bigger picture of reconfiguring the supply of affordable housing to tackle the limited options available to households on low incomes.

Notes

[1] Streich et al (2002) highlight the LINKS volunteer scheme in Northumberland, which recruits, trains and offers ongoing support to a team of 'community befrienders' who support young people in their own accommodation. Another aspect of community involvement relates to the potential role of broader communities in helping homeless people, or people at risk of homelessness, to develop positive social networks (Stenhouse, 2005).

[2] www.ruralhousingscotland.org

Part IV
Answering the rural housing question

EIGHTEEN

Strategic and community initiatives in Britain's countrysides

That the need for affordable housing in rural areas is recognised is not in doubt, but policy instruments for achieving an accelerated supply of new homes have been overshadowed by a broader and pervasive philosophy of 'protecting the countryside' in response to a long-standing 'resource' perspective of rural areas, given new impetus by claims that protection delivers sustainability, and accentuated by post-war counter-urbanisation. Migration into rural areas has placed huge pressure on the rural housing stock, but it has also transformed perceptions of what rural areas are for, and for whom. Consumption interests have come to dominate many areas, resisting significant development and limiting responses to housing stress to those that might be classed as 'tactical interventions'. Whilst the development of solutions to meet housing needs in rural areas are characterised by remarkable innovation and initiative, these are not matched by the types of changes to mainstream policies that would allow such innovation to flourish. In the last few years, there have been signals from government in England that a more fundamental shift might be on the horizon, perhaps even a widespread relaxation of planning restriction in response to the 2008 Taylor Review. Certainly, there appears to be greater urgency in the drive to deliver affordable housing, and rural areas have shared at least some of this urgency. In Scotland, debates in the Scottish Parliament have reflected upon the findings of its Rural Affairs and Environment Committee Report (Scottish Parliament Rural Affairs and Environment Committee Report, 2009): that there needs to be a step change in planning cultures to address the shortfall in housing supply. But in both of these countries (and in Wales) there are grave doubts as to whether anything will really change. Planning authorities have long been the guardians of the status quo, prioritising the interests of a well-housed majority, and seldom risking the wrath of NIMBY interests. If national policies are to influence local outcomes, they must engage more proactively with local and community groups. A culture change may well be incubated in London, Edinburgh and Cardiff, but it is in rural areas where it needs to take root.

The need to incentivise development and win the argument, at a local level, for new homes is outlined by Whitehead (2009: 29) in relation to general supply:

> incentives are needed to make the system more pro development where this supports the national and local economy and provides for more sustainable communities. The planning system cannot play that role at the moment. The current government [in England] has fundamentally

chosen a top-down approach, with increasing use of publicly owned land and an increasing role for the Homes and Communities Agency agreeing large scale development on a site-by-site basis. This cannot win hearts and minds in local communities and it is likely to prove too costly to government over the next few years.

Whitehead points to a fundamentally flawed development strategy, and the need to nurture and grow acceptance of development from the bottom up. Such a view dovetails with the notion of a 'third way', which is dominated neither by the private sector nor by the heavy hand of the state. Incentives for big developments by a mix of private enterprise and social providers have taken the form of additional grant support, directed to those authorities who plan for and deliver more homes. In England, the 'planning delivery grant' has been transformed into a 'housing and planning delivery grant' (Gallent, 2008b) for this purpose. But encouraging authorities to really push for development is one thing: really winning hearts and minds at a neighbourhood or community level is something else. Whitehead (2009: 30) argues that 'central government cannot do it all – people must see that they or their children or others they care about will benefit from building more, better designed and more sustainable housing'. Governments across England, Wales and Scotland show some signs of edging in this direction. There is a view that communities themselves should reach the critical decision over whether to build more homes. An idea currently on the table is that there should be a bigger role for community land trusts (DCLG, 2007c; Conservative Party, 2009), both in urban and in rural areas. If well-designed and resourced, such trusts may over time develop the *potential* to influence local housing outcomes: through empowerment, hearts and minds may be won round, and agreement on the sort of development that communities really need may be reached. But this potential will only become a capacity to act if wider planning processes fall into line with shifting community aspiration. Land trusts have a long history in Scotland, and there is also the experience of locally grown voluntary housing providers to draw upon: their development aspirations have often been thwarted by national policy, becoming mired in a planning process that is unsympathetic to local objectives, despite a rhetoric of support. Likewise, adequate resources are not always forthcoming and the development objectives of some local groups can still conflict with the conservatism of others. The main thrust of this chapter is to set community initiative in Britain's countrysides in the context of national policy, focusing on the value of local actions now and in the future.

A failure of strategy?

Post-1999, there was some divergence in strategic frameworks in England, Wales and Scotland, resulting from devolution and different takes on the appropriate level of responsibility that should be handed to local authorities. However, policy-makers in all three countries have kept faith with the plan-led system. Planning policy structures are top-down, and it is generally agreed that the detail of local action should flow logically from agreed national policies, duly adapted to the peculiarities of local circumstance. It follows that if these policies are 'right', addressing for example the housing needs of rural areas, then local development frameworks will emerge that begin to convincingly answer the rural housing question. However, the move from national strategy to local implementation is never this straightforward. The quality of information varies greatly at the local level, as does the political will to focus on a particular issue, or prioritise one interest above another. Authorities also have a degree of discretion in the way they interpret law and duty, and therefore develop policy. Hence, there is often an 'implementation gap' between what someone in government thinks is needed, and what is actually delivered. Planning in Britain has important 'bottom-up' qualities: adaptation to the particularity of local circumstance (to 'distinctiveness', in current parlance) might mean or be interpreted as a watered-down commitment to national policy objectives. Idealised representations of a neat relationship between national policy and local planning do not tell the full story: adaptation, innovation and 'muddling through' (see Chapter 10) are key aspects of the implementation process and of local action.

Muddling through

As we have seen in previous chapters, the history of planning for affordable housing in small rural communities is replete with reasons why housing for people on low incomes should be directed to larger settlements. Since the early 1990s, sustainability has been a key part of the rationale for concentrated development. Despite rhetoric that favours putting social concerns on an equal footing with environmental sustainability, the emphasis in planning policy is still firmly placed on the latter. Commentators have criticised this approach for failing to address the needs of low-income groups in smaller rural locations, and have highlighted the impact that this failure has continued to have upon residential differentiation and the social make-up of rural areas. In some instances, residents displaced to market towns for their own good (see Chapter 13) and for reasons of sustainability subsequently witness the inequity of 'executive homes' being built by private enterprise in their former village for a limited market of affluent commuters and retirees.

One of the particular difficulties that rural communities face in areas of northern England, close to the large conurbations, is that the need for affordable housing becomes subsumed within regional policies for place-making within low-demand urban housing markets. In an attempt to engineer positive market change in low-demand urban areas, tight limits have been set on housing targets in adjacent rural areas. The intention is to curb the ability of households to migrate from urban areas, whist promoting attractive alternatives within urban neighbourhoods that have been the focus of renewal efforts. Harrogate District is an example of one authority that has seen limits placed on housing targets in this way. East Riding is another. The upshot of this kind of approach is that there are consequently fewer opportunities for delivering affordable housing within market developments. The only housing development permitted in villages tends to be small-scale and high-end. This will not threaten nearby urban renewal, and nor will it address *in situ* rural need.

This example illustrates the way in which the needs of low-income households in rural communities have, in some instances, been hostage to the fortunes of regional policies that remain focused on tackling urban issues. It is right that the attention of regional policy should be concentrated on areas where the scale and depth of deprivation and environmental blight is at its greatest. However, the need for affordable housing in rural areas needs to be uncoupled from these policies.

That planning has been failing to meet housing needs in many rural communities in England and Wales has been tacitly accepted by these countries' use of the exceptions policies examined in Chapter 12. These allow affordable housing development in and on the edges of villages where no other development would normally be permitted. Proponents, particularly practitioners, tend to argue that exception sites are the only means of bringing forward affordable housing in many rural communities. However, much research has shown that, as a mechanism, too little housing is being developed through this route (Gallent, 1998, 2009a; JRF, 2008; Taylor, 2008; DCLG, 2009b). And frankly, why should it be otherwise? The exceptions approach is a product of the ingenuity of practitioners operating in rural areas and is perhaps the most successful of the plethora of innovative solutions for bypassing the myriad difficulties facing affordable housing development in the countryside. Exception sites offer a valuable tool for overcoming the critical impediment of planning and have been most successful where they have the weight of community opinion behind them. The exceptions approach is viewed by some in Scotland with a degree of envy, and there have been suggestions that this approach should be added to the armoury of existing mechanisms employed to deliver low-cost housing (Tribal HCH, 2006). Others see the approach as symptomatic of all that is wrong with the current planning culture and with the policies embedded in that culture. In the context of a dominant environmental planning agenda in Britain's countrysides, the delivery of housing is the product of mere opportunism. Whilst there is a place for opportunism, it should not be the essential basis for meeting the needs of rural communities. But are exceptions a product of the failure to engineer a comprehensive answer to the rural housing question, built on the sufficient release of land for new development, or are they an inevitable consequence of the policy process? Perhaps more importantly, is this the type of approach that will win hearts and minds in rural areas, potentially delivering the scale and type of development that communities need, if such 'innovations' can be routinised, incentivised and rolled out at a more consistent volume? Is there nothing inherently wrong with 'muddling through'?

Local solutions and national frameworks

A key mantra of post-1997 rural policy has been integration delivered through holistic planning and government. This emerged as a key theme in the series of rural White Papers published in 2000, and was a driving force behind the Haskins' Review of Rural Delivery in England (Haskins, 2003) and government's consequent Modernising Rural Delivery (MRD) agenda. Greater coordination through more confident local planning, given impetus by clearer strategic thinking, was to be the means of achieving this integration across different policy agendas and sectoral interests. The implication was that there would be less muddling through – and less reliance on 'incrementalism' – and more direction and strategy at the local level. Clear evidence-based policies would be brought to bear on local problems and there would, presumably, be more systematic treatment of outstanding challenges. There is a danger, however, that heightened faith in normative planning will be accompanied by the relegation of local innovation behind big new initiatives and flagship policies that fail to understand or address the difficulties of housing delivery and rural development in some areas.

For many years, studies of rural planning and action have drawn attention to a traditional reliance on voluntarism and self-help in Britain's countrysides, which, by its very nature, is incremental and responds often in a piecemeal way to arising challenges (see, for example, Moseley, 1999, 2000). Voluntarism has often filled the vacuum left by private enterprise unwilling to invest in weak rural markets, and public intervention unable to provide more comprehensive service coverage in many rural areas. It has become a key policy objective to tap into this voluntarism, nurturing and supporting it as appropriate. However, reliance on voluntary action and community initiative is risk-laden. It means that outcomes on the ground – a much-needed community shop or local bus, or a low-cost housing scheme – are dependent on the strength of local social capital. There need to be people on the ground who will take responsibility, instigate these schemes, working with other agents (including councils, landowners and rural enablers) to see them through to completion.

If community initiative is to be a vehicle for rural housing delivery in those locations untouched by public or private investments, there need to be strategies in place that will support these initiatives: providing technical assistance and resources, and relaxing the planning constraints that so often stand in the way of success. Criticisms of exceptions schemes, noted earlier and in Chapter 12, need to be seen in the context of structural shortcomings. In this case, the initiative, and the incrementalism (responding to local housing needs as they arise and at an appropriate scale), is good, but the level of support that national policy and planning provides may be inadequate. Given that communities are often so instrumental in solving their own needs, might it not be right for planning to make special provisions for community need and initiative within plan-making and development control, perhaps by substituting exception sites with allocations of land for 'community need' outside the development envelope as that need arises?

Community initiatives

Such a strategy recognises that community action is a complement to, but not a substitute for, well-functioning state and market apparatuses. First, such a strategy would not be suited to – or indeed necessary in – all locations. Interventions by the public sector, or by housing associations or other registered social landlords (RSLs), or private enterprise will be well placed to respond to housing needs in many instances. Second, supportive frameworks are vital, giving confidence to and catalysing community initiatives. It is currently the case that communities are reticent about exceptions schemes: the process of bringing them forward may be time-consuming and complex, and they may yield uncertain benefits. They may be thwarted by vested interests or eventual nominations to homes may reflect the strategic priorities of a landlord rather than the priorities of the community (DEFRA, 2010). A system that made additional, systematic allocations of land for community use on the back of local appraisals and community-led plans might give more confidence to communities.

But it is not only more amenable planning frameworks that are critical to the success of such bottom-up initiatives. There needs to be a 'community' in place that has the capacity to embrace opportunities and invest time in bringing forward local projects. There needs to be an abundance of human capital that can be willingly brought together and that shares common concerns and values. Do these things exist within the restructured countryside?

Changing communities

There is an extensive literature on the meaning and dynamics of 'community', and Panelli (2006) argues that the concept has dominated thinking on rural society. Shared interests or beliefs – what Tönnies (1887) called 'unity of will' – are often placed at its core. There is, however, debate over the extent to which a shared 'world view' is critical for social cohesion, or whether competing values can still come together to form a community in which different ideas coexist. This is of course important in communities restructured by economic and demographic change. Past writing on this subject, however, tends to suggest that groups form distinct cliques based on their shared beliefs, and the formation of such cliques, and different interests, is central to social instability and conflict. Cohen (1985), drawing on fieldwork in rural and island communities in Scotland, saw a community as being bound by a common system of values, norms and moral codes. These create a sense of shared identity. He tried to break away from the Chicago School's treatment of communities as being spatially fixed (see, for example, Redfield, 1960), sometimes introverted, but nevertheless stable by virtue of relative isolation. Cohen was the first of many to criticise this closed view of community and, later on, Panelli (2006: 68) drew specific attention to the failure to recognise the heterogeneous nature of rural communities.

Although Tönnies' work is tremendously useful, he must share some of the blame for painting rural communities as homogeneous and closed, and urban society, in contrast, as heterogeneous and open. It is doubtful whether this has ever been entirely true and the distinction led Pahl (1968) to claim that neither the term rural nor urban is useful in a sociological sense, and Young (1990: 339) to argue that simple conceptions of community repress 'the ontological difference of subjects'. Young added that different forms of social relations can be found in different places, characterising 'city life' as 'the being together of strangers' (Young, 1990: 345). This is possibly a useful descriptor of some rural communities, in which the social networks of newer residents may be very different from those found in Martin's village of the 1960s (Martin, 1962).

Change is a key characteristic of modern rural communities and attention needs to be given to the dynamics of relationships and how these vary from one place to another, creating ostensibly different types of community with different capacities. As Panelli and Welch (2005: 1589) point out, 'community is a social construct to be variously and continuously negotiated', rooted in values overlain by patterns of gender, social class, ethnicity, disability or sexuality (Little and Austin, 1996; Cloke and Little, 1997; Neal and Agyeman, 2006). However, the normative view of rural communities, still heavily influenced by the work of Tönnies, remains remarkably static and few links are made between the complexity of communities and the implications for voluntary initiative (Satsangi, forthcoming, 2011).

National policy-makers have neatly sidestepped all such debates (Satsangi, 2007; see also Taylor, 2002; Rowlands and Card, 2007), refusing to see their relevance to the business at hand. 'Community' is used as shorthand for the populace of a particular locale, bound simply by common residence. In instances where communities are distinguished by their values or beliefs, it has become the convention to assume some sort of meeting of minds, irrespective of people's different backgrounds or circumstances. It is now the accepted norm to attribute 'common vision' to the residents of an urban neighbourhood or a rural community (see, for example, Local Government Association, 2004: 7).

That there may be different preferences and interests, material or ideological, within a spatially defined 'community' is seldom acknowledged in policy discourse. Yet such fractures frame local responses to housing questions, dividing populations along pro- and anti-development lines. This means that community reactions to perceived threats, or to what groups see as a local housing shortage, can be mixed. Sometimes there is consensus, but at other times reactions to issues expose deep-seated divisions within a community. Perhaps one of the strangest spectacles in some villages is the ironic alliance between newcomers and more established residents in the face of second home pressures: existing residents see second homes as an inequity, robbing local people of the chance to own a home of their own. Newcomers oppose them because if properties are lost to the local market, there may be a need to build additional housing for lower-income groups. In this instance, 'living countryside' and 'environmental' representations come together around an apparently common interest. However, it is more usual to witness a vocal minority in a village opposing a new development proposal, with this opposition then presented as a 'community reaction', though in reality it may express division rather than any 'unity of will'.

Communities, volunteers and cooperation

Whilst it may be impossible to talk about communities of shared belief, it may be possible to identify a sense of collective responsibility, at least in some sections of rural society, which gives impetus to voluntary action. Cohen's view of community as a system of values, norms and *moral codes* has a resonance in thinking about rural housing in Britain, for the moral value of volunteering on behalf of your neighbour has a particularly acute, though not exclusive, association with rural locations. Individual and collective voluntary action have a long history in Britain in education, care for the young and the elderly, in small-scale agriculture and manufacture, in the retail sector, in transport, and in housing provision (Harris and Rochester, 2000; Kendall, 2003; Rochester et al, 2009). In rural areas, voluntary provision has commonly preceded state intervention or filled gaps that the state and or private enterprise have been unable to fill.

Perhaps the most tangible and well-known outputs of voluntary action are village halls throughout rural Britain, the community cooperatives of the Highlands and Islands of Scotland (Gordon, 2002) and the now largely charitable works to 'preserve rural traditions' performed by the Scottish Women's Rural Institute (SWRI) and the Women's Institute (WI) of England and Wales. It is no accident that the women's institutes have traditionally been so important in rural areas: voluntary work is much more commonly done by women than by men. This is particularly the case in areas that are still, or were until the 1990s, intensively farmed or those, like the former coalfield regions, that maintained a reliance on heavy industry. Rural women's role in voluntary and charitable organisations is therefore seen as a continuation and extension of their 'caring' or 'nurturing' role in the household, reflecting the strength of established patriarchies (Little, 1997; Little and Morris, 2005).

That volunteering across Britain, and in rural areas more particularly, has a gender bias is one of the key messages from the literature on the characteristics of volunteers and their motivations, which followed a claim in the mid-1980s that little was known about the distribution and dynamics of voluntary organisations (Leat, 1986: 315). Survey data for England also show that volunteers are drawn disproportionately from middle to elderly age groups, from people active in their faith, from majority ethnic communities, from the employed, from groups not at risk of disadvantage or deprivation and from people with no long-term illness (Low et al, 2007). Whilst Scottish data are in line with this, models that attempt to explain the propensity to volunteer according to these socio-demographic characteristics have proven unsatisfactory because they fail to take account of motivations (Hurley et al, 2008), which, the two countries' survey evidence shows, fall into a mix of altruism and self-interest, with individuals stating a quite general 'desire to help the community' or more specifically to help people experiencing a situation, problem or condition that has been experienced by the volunteer him or herself, or by a friend or family member. Volunteers have also attested to the self-development benefits of having volunteered. It remains the case, however, that a measure of the true economic contribution of volunteering – be this the value of outputs as a percentage of GDP or as the amount of staff costs saved, for example – remains contested rather than conclusively established. However, it is clear that particular types of people volunteer in rural areas, taking the lead on a range of initiatives including those intended to provide new housing.[1]

Rural development and rural housing

Housing associations

The voluntary housing sector comprising housing associations, trusts and cooperatives[2] has been a feature of Britain's rural landscapes since the middle of the 19th century. Housing associations are now commonly placed with local authorities as 'social housing organisations', though their roots are in the types of voluntary action described earlier. Originating in philanthropy and benign paternalism (Cope, 1999; Malpass, 2000), the movement would have stayed small-scale without the arrival of significant public support systems from the mid-1960s. Capital subsidy has allowed rents to be set at well below market-clearing levels, though dependence on public support, alongside increasing levels of public sector influence over investments, means that for some commentators the housing association movement is now more public than voluntary.

However, associations and trusts are still run by committees of unpaid volunteers, and many remain extremely small-scale and firmly rooted in particular communities or districts. Evidence from England and Scotland suggests that the types of people becoming committee members match the characteristics of those who get involved in other voluntary initiatives. In Scotland, there is also greater involvement of lower-income groups in housing association projects (Cairncross and Pearl, 2003; Pawson et al, 2005), suggesting either a degree of self-help or a desire to help others facing similar problems.

Arguably, associations in Scotland remain a more authentic form of voluntary action in response to community challenges than in England and Wales. They are key to addressing the shortfall in social rented housing noted in Chapter 14, and many have resisted the pressure, to which so many have succumbed south of the border, to grow and play a more 'strategic' housing role. Staying small and resisting the urge to grow are two critical characteristics of Scottish rural housing associations, as is their particular focus on remoter towns and villages. They have been providing more homes, proportionally, in remote small towns than in more accessible towns or in 'second-tier' urban areas. Table 18.1 breaks down the figures for social renting (see also Table 14.4[3] and discussion).

Table 18.1: Social renting in Scotland, 2007

	Total social rented %	Councils %	Voluntary %	Units
Large urban areas	27	15	12	4,547
Other urban areas	26	20	6	3,964
Accessible small towns	23	19	4	1,167
Remote small towns	26	17	9	769
Accessible rural	13	10	3	1,622
Remote rural	13	10	3	1,337

Note: Percentages are of total stock in area type.
Source: Scottish Household Survey Annual Report, 2007, Table 3.14.

This development spread and focus reflects not only capital funding decisions, but also the pattern of voluntary sector initiative in Scotland (Satsangi, 2006). Rural associations tend to have fewer homes and have operational interests in smaller settlements. Nearly 40 per cent of rural associations manage fewer than 500 units, and more than a third of *all* associations in Scotland are similarly sized.[4] In England and Wales, there have been numerous mergers of associations since the 1988 Housing Act tried to reduce the sector's reliance on public funding and encourage a greater element of commercial borrowing. Bigger associations were able to borrow more against their asset bases, hence the mergers. The Regulatory and Statistical Returns for housing associations in England for 2008 show that 90 per cent of all housing association stock was owned by 18 per cent of associations (Tenant Services Authority, 2008: 2): there is a clear concentration of homes in the hands of a few large organisations. However, whilst mergers in England have created some extremely large associations (54 out of 1,578 HAs/RSLs own more than 10,000 units), nearly 60 per cent of all housing associations own less than 250 homes: there are 430 associations with between one and 25 units.[5] It is not clear, however, how many of these are rural associations or how many are actively developing their stocks at the current time. Many of these smaller associations are merely management bodies, looking after historic homes such as almshouses. Development capacity (or rather the capacity to make big strategic contributions to the stock of social housing in England or Scotland) remains in the hands of the big players. It is claimed that large associations are more efficient vehicles for the delivery of new housing (Scotland is a late convert to this thinking: see Scottish Government, 2007), though evidence to support this claim has been thin on the ground (see Satsangi et al, 2005; Gibb and O'Sullivan, 2008). Whilst larger housing stocks have a lower per capita management cost, and future development will undoubtedly benefit from economies of scale, it is doubtful whether the ongoing structural changes in the voluntary sector – which mimic those that have occurred in private house-building (see Chapter 11) – are good for rural areas if programmes here are relegated behind more strategic interventions in cities or in larger towns.

It is within this context of a rescaling of housing association activity that a new wave of community action has been born, seeking now not only to fill the established gaps in public and private housing provision, but also the emerging gaps in housing association development strategies.

Community land ownership and development

Housing associations provide one framework for voluntary action. In policy towards Britain's rural land and housing in the early years of the 21st century, there has been a reawakening of interest in the possibilities offered by direct community land ownership. This form of tenure dates to the Chartist movement of the late 18th and early 19th centuries. What was, for a long time, the community owner of the largest land area – the Stornoway Trust on the island of Lewis – came about as the result of the private owner donating 26,300 hectares to the island's residents in 1923. In the 1980s, the much-publicised purchase of Assynt, a crofting estate in the north west of Scotland, produced another significant community owner, and this was soon followed by other smaller-scale community buyouts. In Chapter 2 we saw that one of the legacies of Scotland's Highland clearances was the centrality of the 'land question' to the country's national identity. Its Parliament, reborn in 1999, took political action on that question by enacting landmark legislation during its first session.

The land reform legislation (in reality three Acts of the new Parliament: the 2000 Abolition of Feudal Tenure (Scotland) Act, the 2003 Title Conditions (Scotland) Act and the 2003 Land Reform (Scotland) Act) was perhaps an inevitable compromise between private land-owning interests and their allies, and those arguing for significant transfers of land from private into public or local community ownership. Nevertheless, it distinguished Scotland from all other countries in the EU or OECD by encouraging the break-up of private monopolies. It facilitated (territorially defined) 'community' purchases of land and, in the seven crofting counties, compelled private owners to part with their landholdings. Highlands and Islands Enterprise[6] has, at the time of writing, a dedicated team that assists community purchase. In the early years, it could also make funds available for this purpose. The *community focus* of the legislation (it was neither about nationalisation nor privatisation) alongside its fusion of *top-down support* for community action and empowerment of communities broadened its appeal, making it acceptable to a spectrum of interest groups (Bryden and Geisler, 2007). Clearly, once the land is in community ownership it can be put to a range of uses, subject to good planning.

A variant model on the community land trusts has also emerged through The Highlands Small Communities Housing Trust and the Dumfries and Galloway Small Communities Housing Trust. These have both benefited from public funding and the transfer of public land. Both of these trusts were established to purchase land and then bank it, not for the purpose of benefiting from the future inflation of land values, but so they can then sell that land to housing associations for affordable housing or individuals for grant-aided self-build housing development (the RHOG, see Chapter 17).

To date, there is little evidence on the performance of the community land trusts, and none on their costs and benefits in comparison to the existing rural alternatives of private monopoly, state or voluntary sector (i.e. housing association) ownership.[7] The evidence (see Satsangi, 2007, 2009) suggests tangible benefits in housing and economic development, in local democracy, and in aspiration and outlook, with communities of optimism replacing communities in decline. Community ownership on the Isle of Gigha, for example, enabled the building of 18 affordable rent and LCHO houses that would not have been possible under previous ownership arrangements. The evidence also suggests, however, that decisions and views are not always shared unanimously and that there can be tensions between different perspectives (see also Brown, 2007). As noted earlier, 'community' needs to be understood as a dynamic process of negotiation and contestation of values and norms. People do not always want the same thing, or understand problems and solutions in the same way. The delivery of local projects can sometimes be fraught with conflict. It is also the case that the legal framework in Scotland is now very different from that which remains in England and Wales, where there is little impetus or appetite for land reform. Here, the key difficulty (after building community support, which is a significant challenge in itself) is the acquisition of land: this will derive either from highly unpredictable patterns of philanthropic gifting, the transfer of land from public ownership (which is rarely an option in rural areas) or community subscription and purchase, which is still likely to rely on the goodwill of a landowner, selling land to the community at less than market value. This is not to say that community land trusts do not have a role to play in the other countries of Britain, but simply that they endure a less hospitable climate. Communities will need greater support if they are to unlock the potential of this mechanism.

Communities: in the lead ... or on a lead?

Many authors have noted that moves to voluntarism and to 'community' are important signifiers of the changing governmentality of Britain (Stoker, 1998; Taylor, 2002). For some (e.g. O'Connor et al, 1999; Clarke et al, 2000; Clarke, 2007; Cloke et al, 2007), such moves are part of the global neo-liberal project of encouraging a smaller state and expanding market provision. Much of the discourse surrounding Britain's 1979 to 1997 Conservative administrations was supportive of shifting responsibility for welfare provision from the public to the private sector. Government needed to acknowledge, however, that privatisation could only be extended into many welfare and public services with great difficulty. The 1980 Housing Act and the Tenants' Rights Etc (Scotland) Act of the same year achieved notable privatisation success through the right to buy. But, whilst the Housing Act and the Housing (Scotland) Act of 1988 set the aspiration of private or quasi-private landlords owning and managing swathes of housing previously under municipal ownership, the operant reality was that the large-scale voluntary transfer of council housing stocks could only be made politically acceptable to tenants if the new landlords were regulated, non-profit providers (Taylor, 2003). As noted in previous chapters, government also promoted voluntary sector provision at the expense of council housing, and the expansion of voluntary provision became an acceptable solution under the Conservatives, albeit second best to the primary goal of privatisation. At the same time, surviving public sector functions were to become more efficient and more businesslike, guided by 'new public management' principles. Under Thatcher, Britain entered an age of performance measurement by cost-centres. The degree to which this enhanced efficiency is widely disputed, though the fundamental changes brought to service delivery are undeniable. At the same time, a much broader range of consumers and communities became part of the machinery of local governance: ordinary citizens suddenly had a role to play in health care trusts, on school boards and in regeneration partnerships. Involvement, participation and empowerment became central to the functioning of these bodies, helping engender a sense of local loyalty and possibly greater acceptance of policies and outcomes. The growth of tenant participation in housing management became perhaps the most visible expression of this change in the housing sector, though many organisations saw tenants and residents as having a more fundamental role to play in shaping their future development. Modern community land trusts can be read as a logical advancement on these trends, providing communities not only with a chance to get involved, but also to take more complete responsibility for outcomes. As Bryden and Geisler (2007) observe, participation devoid of clear rights and responsibilities can end up as mere tokenism.

Under subsequent UK Labour governments, particularly those headed by Tony Blair, the neo-liberal rhetoric was replaced by a 'third way': of a modernisation of government, central and local, of empowering citizens and of reinvigorating democracy (Newman, 2001). Blair introduced a new politics of pragmatism, doing 'what works' even if this meant a continuation of Conservative policies and programmes and the abandonment of long-held Labour principles.[8] However, the rhetoric of *individualism*, a key tenet of Thatcherism, was substituted by a communitarian discourse that placed the individual in social context. 'Community' became the new branding for government policy. Within a year of coming to office, *Planning for Communities of the Future* (ODPM, 1998) was heralding a 'new era' of community development in England (ODPM, 1998: 6) and very soon 'sustainable communities' were being lauded as both a key policy goal and as a device in themselves (with their 'shared vision') for delivering against development ambitions.

Engagement with these communities became increasingly integral to the statutory planning process, with the aim being to renew and re-legitimise long-standing approaches to public involvement in planning decisions. England's major urban renewal programme became the Rooseveltian 'New Deal for Communities'. In Scotland, community planning was intended to bring providers of all services, including local planning, together in fora with the public, to give people the chance to influence land-use decisions and the forces that shaped them. But the reality became one of public agencies locked into a complex process of communication, with reduced room for the involvement of ordinary citizens (Robertson, 2001). A parallel can be drawn here with the introduction and expansion of local strategic partnerships in England (see Morphet, 2008), which although adequately representing the 'community' of local stakeholders, may not always connect with individual lay communities (Gallent and Robinson, 2010).

These undercurrents of change find expression in the voluntary service provision that is now well established in many rural areas. Government in England has recently made efforts to promote community land trusts (DCLG, 2007c), though only on a trial basis. These will need to operate within a context that is very different from that found in Scotland, as noted earlier. They are also being promoted through central government initiatives, with the DCLG taking the lead in identifying locations where a land trust might have a useful contribution to make: hence, these will not 'grow' from communities or a local dynamic, but will be thrust upon an area in which the right conditions are judged to exist (i.e. a group prepared to form the trust and a resource of land or buildings that can be readily transferred into community ownership). Arguably, Scotland's experience of land trusts is more authentic and England's likely experience will raise inevitable questions surrounding agenda-setting, ownership and power.[9]

But if community action is to be given a bigger role in solving future rural housing shortages, attention will inevitably refocus on the uneven geography of community response. This has already happened in relation to the services provided to homeless people in England (Cloke et al, 2007) and can be seen in patterns of third sector housing provision in Scotland (Satsangi, 2006). Great hopes are already being pinned on the future role of community land ownership and what this might mean for rural areas and the ability of communities to meet their own housing needs. Experience in Scotland, however, suggests that without considerably more support – technical and financial – such activities will remain the exception rather than the norm.

Whilst there has been a clear trend towards empowering communities as part of a broader project to renew local and national democracy, there is only so much that local groups can achieve without a mix of public and private assistance. The third way should not perhaps be seen as a discrete mode of delivery, but rather one that builds on community responsibility, nurtures it and provides it with the means to achieve its own ends. The planning system has a critical role to play in rural areas in creating the conditions in which communities have the confidence and the opportunities to initiate local projects. This might mean releasing land specifically for community use. Businesses will also play a role in supporting local housing development that serves their interests as local employers. Such a partnership – between communities, planning and business – could fire a return to the common-sense approach to rural development that existed a hundred years ago (see Chapter 1), but only if the different interests that combine within modern rural communities can reach consensus and avoid the resistance to change that defeats so many local housing projects.

Notes

[1] Similarly, the same groups may initiate community-led planning initiatives that aim to oppose development of various types, including housing development, viewed as inappropriate or potentially harmful.

[2] Strictly speaking, housing cooperatives are not, in general, true cooperatives, as they do not seek development capital from their members. They are, however, owned by their members and exist to provide services for members rather than distribute profits to shareholders (they are mutual organisations). This last characteristic is shared with housing associations and trusts. It is also shared with all forms of charity, the advantages of this status explaining why so many associations maintain their charitable status.

[3] Although the percentages are rounded differently.

[4] Sourced from the Annual Performance and Statistical Returns to the Scottish Housing Regulator, 2007/08.

[5] These figures are from the Regulatory and Statistical Returns from RSLs in England, 31 March 2009.

[6] A non-departmental public body with a broad local economic and community development remit.

[7] Nor has there been any systematic assessment of the impact of land reform regulations though some commentary attests a weakness (Wightman, 2007)

[8] Famously, Labour's National Executive Committee pledged in 1979 to repeal the right to buy once a Labour government was returned to power.

[9] Other initiatives in England, however, are truer expressions of community-led action. These may take the form of land trusts, or the similar activities undertaken by Community Development Trusts (Giddens et al, 2008), most notably in Cumbria and Northumberland (see Cumbria Rural Housing Trust, 2008).

NINETEEN

England, Scotland and Wales in context

How does the situation in England, Scotland and Wales compare with that found in other countries? In particular, how do different governments address their own rural housing questions; what are the prevailing attitudes to rural resources and rural development; and are approaches found elsewhere rationalised by a broad developmental or environmental perspective of 'the countryside'? Throughout this book, we have implied that collectively (but not withstanding local differences) England, Scotland and Wales provide a unique or at least an 'extreme' case, with planning restriction creating a hostile environment for development generally and residential development more specifically. This, we have suggested, has been a bitter pill for some communities to swallow, denying some households access to homes, inhibiting the future development of rural communities and economies, and leading government to press continually for innovative circumventions of its own restrictions.

But is the rural planning and housing context in our case studies really so unique? Other developed countries have experienced rapid urban growth during the last hundred or so years; land-take for human use has increased and the boundaries of human habitation have expanded. Other countries have, invariably, created their own planning systems, establishing policy frameworks on the back of political processes that reflect prevailing social attitudes and cultural preferences. It seems almost inevitable that other countries face broadly comparable challenges, and that their populations share a concern with the use of land resources and the impact of change on open, green space and on natural and semi-natural environments. Surely, all countries have a concern to conserve something of their past and set restrictions on the sprawl of cities or the general spread of development over their open, more sparsely populated areas. These assertions are all broadly true: all countries share these concerns to a greater or lesser degree, but the critical difference between nations and between policy and planning frameworks is in the point of balance between an acceptance of development and the need to conserve, unchanged, areas of relative openness beyond cities and other built-up spaces.

Understanding the relative experiences of different countries is a hugely complex task with basic questions of understanding and perspective at its heart: what do different cultures understand by the word countryside? How is it made? And how will it be maintained in the future, if it is to remain recognisable as countryside?

In some countries, a predominant view seems to be that the landscape of the countryside is not 'made' by people's activity; or, rather, it does not *continue* to be made at the current time by the 'gentle processes' of change that made it during centuries past. It is seen as a landscape of physical attributes, requiring *maintenance* rather than making, and this can be achieved chiefly by placing restrictions on direct human influence: by rigid preservation.

An alternate view is that all landscapes are products of human contrivance, of a struggle to domesticate space, and that this struggle is an inevitable and necessary part of the evolution of place. A landscape devoid of people, of communities, has no human reference and therefore ceases to be a landscape in any meaningful sense of the word. This is the community view, which accepts that landscapes are not changeless or timeless but are continually *remade* by people's actions: that to some extent the countryside is a resource for people to bend to their own needs. Planning systems express these underlying views.

In the remainder of this chapter, we place the countries of Britain in a wider review of European experiences, attitudes and responses and, in doing so, try to understand how the underlying rationale of rural planning in Britain's countrysides (what assumptions guide its course) compares to that found elsewhere. Can the environmental rationale of planning here be seen as inevitable if countries elsewhere have been touched by similar experiences but arrived at different responses? Following a necessarily brief pan-European review, we compare the British nations more explicitly with the Republic of Ireland. Ireland's legal and planning systems share their more distant historic roots with those of Britain. Britain and the Irish Republic were once joined – not, however, in an equal partnership, but by centuries of imperial rule from England – and their populations might be expected to share similar views towards the function of rural land, grounded in both common law and tradition. The fact that there is clear sky between planning in the countries of Britain and in Ireland, with the systems arguably driven by opposite rationalities (with freedoms over the use of rural land in Ireland reflecting the broader freedoms that were won through the overthrow of British rule), not only suggests an interesting comparison, but also the possibility of the two countries learning critical lessons from one another.

Cohesion, division and consensus across rural Europe

At the beginning of the 2000s, research funded by the Scottish Executive, and published as a collection of European rural housing profiles, sought to draw clear distinctions between the 'policy regimes' underpinning responses to rural housing 'pressures' across Europe (Gallent et al, 2003). In its analytical stage, this work tried to understand the 'cultural conditions and values that underpin rural housing politics and policies' in a cross-section of countries (Gallent and Allen, 2003: 211). This understanding was expected to flow from answers to a series of basic questions concerning the social transformation of respective rural areas (perhaps as a result of counter-urbanisation: introducing new values that lead, and also express, a restructuring of rural economies), the political relationship and distinction between 'town and country', and how this central relationship is mediated by issues of consumption and production (whether rural areas retain their endogenous economic life, or whether this life is now secondary to the exogenous forces of consumption). In other words, how has 'power' in the countryside changed, and what agendas – environmental or developmental – are promoted by those who now find themselves in the driving seat: perhaps an ex-urban middle class or a more traditional working population?

The authors explain that in arriving at a classification of European rural 'policy regimes', their focus is on the link between culture, experience and regulatory outcome (Gallent and Allen, 2003: 211). An analysis of 10 profiles (with separate profiles for England, Scotland and Wales) leads to the conclusion that the regimes framing rural policy and planning, across Europe, sit between two extremes:

> At one extreme political debate has resulted in a system of tight regulation. At the other, far more *laissez-faire* approaches have either consciously been developed, or have been allowed to develop under the auspices of weak state direction. Between these two extremes … some countries have engaged in a political debate that has resulted in a factional split between groups who desire a gravitational shift towards a more fixed position where either the market or informality are assigned primacy. (Gallent and Allen, 2003: 211)

A case for the existence of three cultures and three consequent regimes is posited. One might imagine that 'tight regulation' is driven by a desire to protect and conserve the countryside, and is synonymous with an environmental rationale for planning (Murdoch and Abram, 2002) built on a clichéd representation of the countryside as a place of quiet enjoyment (Woods, 2005b: 210). It would then follow that the *laissez-faire* approach is essentially about giving communities free rein to use rural land as they see fit. Between these extremes, the 'factional split' would generate a tension between different rationalities, pushing and pulling in opposing directions, perhaps over time (with the environmental and developmental rationales underpinning the planning system advancing or retreating with shifts in political power) and certainly across space, with some areas being more conservative than others. The assumption would then be that the countries of Britain, as extreme cases, would sit at the far end of this spectrum: obviously enduring, or enjoying – depending on one's point of view – stricter regulation.

But this was not the interpretation of the study's authors. The 'regulatory regimes' did not necessarily favour conservation over development, but sought to regulate change across their national territories in a more even-handed way because of a weak cultural and political distinction between urban and rural areas. This weakness led, for example, to strong intervention for the sake of community well-being, with policies applied in urban neighbourhoods also being applied in the countryside. If countries developed strong environmental policies, then these were extended across the national territory: territorial *cohesion* (see Faludi, 2005) generated a concern for linked environmental systems, not a policy for rural areas that was separate – at a strategic level – from that developed for urban areas. It was suggested that regulatory regimes arise where the 'omniscient state is deemed to act in the best interests of society and therefore individuals, irrespective of where or in what type of community they reside'[1] (Gallent and Allen, 2003: 220).

Four out of the 10 countries examined were slotted into this category: Norway, Sweden, The Netherlands and France. In three of these cases, strong policy intervention was designed to conserve not the characteristics of the landscape, but the character of communities as a core component of overall countryside character. At a cultural level, Norway was held up as a society predicated on weak urbanisation, which meant that its population made little distinction between rural and urban areas, or indeed between rural and urban society. However, a decline in agricultural production had disrupted the traditional equilibrium between production and recreational consumption. The building of 'extra homes' (essentially second homes) by people who do not farm but work in factory or office jobs in areas of more concentrated population is not seen as an intrusion into the countryside, but as a crucial plank of the rural economy – as a traditional rural activity, standing shoulder-to-shoulder with farming. But it was felt that a skewing of economic activities in favour of recreation would threaten the established balance within communities, changing their physical appearance and also threatening the retention of permanent populations. For this reason, Norway has developed policies to support agricultural communities without limiting opportunities for recreation. Economic and housing interventions try to ensure year-round occupancy of homes, limiting the power of private interests in housing markets, and promoting the wider needs of communities. Primary legislation has been enacted that limits the transformation of farms into 'recreational' homes, and this move (alongside similar moves in Sweden and Denmark) has been held up in Britain as the type of 'restriction' that its national governments should be considering (for a critique, see Satsangi and Crawford, 2009). However, the purpose is not to curtail the countryside's economic transformation, but simply to maintain an essential feature of the Norwegian landscape: the traditional mix of consumption and production uses.

The extreme opposition of this regulatory regime (which is underpinned by common purpose, and built on a political cooperative or socialist tradition) is the *laissez-faire* approach. *Laissez-faire* policy regimes emerge from private 'atomistic' cultures and are 'hollow' (Rhodes, 1997), conceding power more readily to the market. The market, in the sense used here, is an aggregation of transactions between local actors, and it is these actors who become the recipients of this power. These might also be described as weaker regulatory regimes (Gallent and Allen, 2003: 221), characterised by 'informalities in political and policy' processes, where the agents of change are not the public sector, but private actors motivated by profit or by personal, family or community responsibility. Such regimes build on local networks, tend to be resistant to central control and are accepted by the state because they appear self-regulating and result in broadly acceptable (that is, culturally tolerable) local outcomes. But in practice, conceding power to local actors means that communities are put in the driving seat and that outcomes do not always meet the expectations, or the high standards, of policy-makers.

Three of the 10 reviewed countries seemed to fit into this category: Spain, Italy and the Republic of Ireland. Because Ireland is examined in greater detail below, Italy can be used here to highlight the essential characteristics of weak regulation. History is of course important. The Italian state, with its capital in Rome, did not form until 1871. Before then Italy's major cities managed their own affairs. The country comprised an 'intricately complex network of highly urban cultures' (Angotti, 1977: 3), with the countryside viewed as being on the distant edge of political concern. For this reason, isolated rural communities – especially in the south of the country – became accustomed to managing their own affairs. This remains especially true in the southernmost regions, including Sicily, Calabria and Campania, where 'informal' but highly organised networks continue to play a big part in the political process and in development outcomes. Drawing on a review by Padovani and Vettoretto (2003), the Italian cultural condition was ascribed to the atomistic group, with the 'family rather than the state as the agent of welfare ... a culture of resisting regulation [and] a culture of innovation, including new forms of economic activity and social praxis' (Gallent and Allen, 2003: 212). This rather grand description and generalisation of Italy's underlying culture translates into a 'flouting of planning regulation in some parts of the country [and] a reliance on family-centred networks for housing and support' (Gallent and Allen, 2003: 212). Italy is in fact famous for tolerating and ultimately condoning illegal development. After the Second World War, rural migrants from the south headed north in huge numbers, often settling in and informally expanding city suburbs, with families and neighbours clubbing together to extend properties or build new ones for the next generation. This way of meeting need had been imported from the countryside of the south. Little regard was given to the *Legge Urbanistica* (planning law) or to local building regulations. But in the 1980s, government in Rome conceded that this was simply the Italian way, introducing the *Condono Edilizio* (an amnesty for illegal buildings: see Fera and Gianatempo, 1985), accepting that everything built illegally in the past now had legal status (for the payment of a fee).

'Traditional reliance on the family as an agent of social welfare' (Gallent and Allen, 2003: 218) produced a policy tolerance to illegal development[2] that contrasts markedly with the full force of laws brought to bear on illegal occupation of rural space in the countries of Britain.[3] But underpinning this tolerance was a very different view towards land rights and development; with communities occupying centre stage, and land seen as a resource for the development of those communities, supporting the future needs of local families. The pattern of development in rural Italy is, in some respects, very similar to that found in Spain and Ireland (see later): it is characterised by the development of single houses on private plots dotted over the landscape, suggesting that environmental concerns bow to the greater weight of developmental considerations.

One might imagine that the third category defined by the authors would occupy a simple midpoint, mixing – in equal measure – characteristics of these regulatory and *laissez-faire* policy regimes. However, the first two categories are defined as much by *consensus* as by the retention of power centrally or its release to local groups: there is consensus around the need for more authoritarian control or around private choice. The third category is in fact defined by the 'existence of a continuous tension, and sometimes overt conflict, between town and country' (Gallent and Allen, 2003: 215) and between 'the centre' and 'the local'. There is *no clear consensus* around the need for a regulatory approach over a more *laissez-faire* one, or vice versa. This has generated a standard British perspective on rural issues, in which conflict (of values, representations and rationales) is used as the central point of reference in understanding the dynamics of communities or the politics of the environment. Housing conflict is critically important:

> Conflicts are sometimes expressed in terms of housing market distortions, issues of housing access and questions over affordability. The rural culture may be viewed as being predominantly 'productionist', whilst the encroaching urban culture is largely one of consumption underpinned by greater market power. Resultant inequalities between 'newcomers' and local populations have driven a wide ranging debate over the role of the state and the nature of policy intervention. Some observers argue that less regulation is the logical response to stronger market pressure, and seek to adopt a more 'atomistic' approach. Others contend that only stronger regulation and market intervention will meet both local need and the need to protect the rural environment. Hence, they would see greater wisdom in a more regulatory approach, akin to that which has developed under ... more coherent cultural conditions. (Gallent and Allen, 2003: 216)

England, Scotland and Wales – the remaining three of the 10 countries profiled – can all be put in this category, but that is not to say that their prevailing cultural conditions are identical. The authors noted that whilst England might occupy an absolute midpoint, Scotland – with its greater confidence in public intervention and historical wariness of private power (owing to a negative experience of landlordism) – draws nearer to the regulatory regime built on greater territorial cohesion. Wales, on the other hand – with its culture rooted in community and a traditional reliance on voluntary and private action – seems drawn towards the atomistic cultures of southern Europe and Ireland. But the central tendency in all three is towards policy instability built on a divisive rural–urban culture.

England, for example, has long been the home of partisan power: a bipartite political system that emphasises and advances competing interests, setting clear policy directions but that has hitherto rejected consensus as a basis of decision-making. The 'first-past-the-post' system supports strong government but also absolutist ideological positions: power swings from left to right, from the state to the market, and arguably from town to country. There are discernible rural interests that are separate from distinctly urban ones; and there has been a clear policy emphasis placed on keeping these interests apart. Physically, this has been to some extent achievable, but culturally, the boundary between town and country has become blurred during the latter half of the 20th century; ideas and values have clashed, and the countryside has become a hotbed of conflict.

Housing conflicts in the countryside have resulted from market distortions, accentuated by planning restrictions. Broader conflicts – of which these housing conflicts are a part – are arguably generated by the friction resultant on 'social configuration as the countryside moves away from cohesive communities based on production to fragmented ones based on different forms of consumption' (Gallent and Allen, 2003: 213). Unlike the situation in Norway, there is no belief in the power of regulation to deliver a satisfactory balance (it either over-restricts or it arrives at development solutions that are centrally orchestrated); and this has generated, in some quarters, a desire for power to be conceded to local groups who might therefore be able to address their own needs more effectively. The counter-view is that 'atomisation' of this kind will simply import sporadic development to the English countryside.

The debate is cyclical: a developmental rationale could be better served by weaker regulation, so the solution lies in devolved control and local decision-making. But this level of empowerment (to self-regulate) would threaten strategic coherency and the big agendas – environmental and economic – that governments promote, so the solution really lies in stronger regulation grounded in a full-system view (seeing the environment as important everywhere; giving communities equal opportunities to flourish irrespective of location; disbanding the CPRE and building a lobby with a more holistic outlook). However, despite the conflicts that are apparent and persistent in England, Scotland and Wales, the pendulum has swung in favour of an environmental agenda and rationale. Whilst this may sound like good news for Britain as a whole, the discussions contained in earlier chapters of this book suggest that selective groups in the countryside find their livelihoods and their futures undermined by the predominance of an environmental planning rationale. The practical question at the forefront of their minds is this: what is rural land for if it is not for the communities that live and work in the countryside? Digging deeper, the underlying question, therefore, is not how we can accommodate a more environmental rationale for planning, but a more developmental one. In this context, the Republic of Ireland, with its similar planning history – but its very different position on the continuum of planning regimes – stands out as a potential source of inspiration.

British and Irish experiences

Since breaking away from Britain, Irish political discourse and planning policy has come to reflect a very different attitude to land and property rights and, perhaps more crucially, to the function of rural areas. The politics of the countryside is driven, in part, by an overt rejection of 'British attitudes' bound with emancipation from the experience of colonial landlordism in which rich owners from Britain had treated Ireland as a playground (a place of recreational consumption) or as a source of personal profit. It has also been driven by historically high levels of out-migration from rural communities, creating a political vacuum and a 'liberal planning system in rural Ireland' (Scott, forthcoming) with land rights – and the right to develop land – being one of the key freedoms won during the Irish War of Independence.

Ireland is often characterised as a predominantly rural nation (McDonagh, 2001), with its fight against British rule being rooted in the countryside. The rural communities of the west won their freedom, and their right to the land, from the British colonial administration based in Dublin. From this experience has grown a strong preference for local choice, with local actors deciding what is best for their communities and the rural landscape. The environmental rationale that drives planning decisions in the countries of Britain is often viewed as entirely inappropriate in Ireland and is continually contested, even in the north (Scott and Murray, 2009).

From a British perspective (one that reads by reference to conflicting positions and consequent frictions), a 'working countryside' view has prevailed. Communities have greater freedom to shape the environment to their needs; and local landowners have a right to profit from their landholdings, which has resulted in a proliferation of single-dwelling developments (or 'one-off houses') across the Irish countryside (Scott and Murray, 2009) and to what is sometimes referred to, ironically, as 'Bungalow Bliss' (after a 1971 publication of the same name: see Fitzsimons, 1971; Gkartzios and Redmond, 2008: 56). Many commentators have decried the environmental cost of this attitude towards rural areas and the development free-for-all that has ensued (Scott, 2006). But such criticisms are frequently shrugged off, being attributed to a British-influenced way of thinking (Scott, forthcoming).

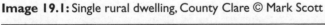

Image 19.1: Single rural dwelling, County Clare © Mark Scott

Scott (2006 and forthcoming) and Scott and Murray (2009) have been instrumental in unpacking the Irish condition and the politics of development in the country's rural areas. As in Britain, land-use planning in Ireland is 'largely the responsibility of local government' (Scott and Murray, 2009: 763), but central policy has been strongly influenced by political lobbying by rural stakeholders who have been successful in ensuring that planning guidelines 'provide a presumption in favour of accommodating new housing development in rural areas' (Scott and Murray, 2009: 764). The ambition of Ireland's rural lobby stands in marked contrast to that found in Britain: its goals could not be more different. Good rural planning, in Ireland, is presented as that which extends the constitutional right of individuals to build, without let or hindrance, on private land; runs with the grain of a traditionally dispersed Irish settlement pattern; and prevents communities suffering the blight of depopulation (Gkartzios and Redmond, 2008: 58).

Image 19.2: Single rural dwelling, County Clare: typical of larger rural house design common in the 2000s. Approximately 70 per cent of rural dwellings are 'one-off' dwellings in the open countryside © Mark Scott

A study by Scott (forthcoming) of local elected members sheds considerable light on prevailing attitudes and on the rationale driving planning decisions. He argues that 'an analysis of councillor perspectives on planning, housing and rurality gives us insights into how the "politics" of the rural is constructed' (Scott, forthcoming). These politics have changed over time. Historically, attitudes to rural development were shaped by the experience of out-migration, which meant little demand for change and limited concern for the incremental effects of planning decisions. In the 1990s, however, there was an unprecedented boom in house-building:[4] a close to 200 per cent increase between 1994 and 2004, with as much as 40 per cent of this increase in rural areas and in the form of one-off houses (Scott, forthcoming). As in England, the challenge of housing growth triggered a new enthusiasm for regulatory reform, which arrived in the form of a Planning and Development Act in 2000 and a National Spatial Strategy (NSS) in 2002. These ushered in a new era of potentially tighter control over rural development, bringing a 'logic of concentration ... widely perceived as anti-rural' (Scott, forthcoming).

In the early 2000s, a heated debate accompanied the publication of the Irish government's major reform proposals. These proposals – including the NSS – seemed to seek greater balance between, first, concentrated, 'sustainable' development that prioritised landscape protection and, second, preservation of the tradition of dispersed rural settlement. It is indicative of the prevailing Irish attitude that the 'pro-rural stakeholders' were able to steer eventual guidelines towards a presumption in favour of housing development. Planning Guidelines for Sustainable Rural Housing published for consultation in 2004 and, quoted by Scott (2009), stipulate that:

> people who are part of and contribute to the rural community will get planning permission in all rural areas, including those areas under urban-based pressures, subject to the normal rules in relation to good site planning [and that] anyone wishing to build a house in rural areas suffering persistent and substantial population decline will be accommodated, subject to good site planning. (DoEHLG, 2004: 1–2)

Scott underscores this strong pro-development position by quoting the Minister for the Environment in July 2005:

> The sons and daughters of farmers, men and women who were born and were reared in the countryside, people who live in the countryside and work in the countryside – whatever their following in life – have the same right to have a home of their own and a home in their own place as anybody else.... All too often planning is seen as a way of preventing people building and living in their own place. (Quoted in Scott, forthcoming; see also Norris and Redmond, 2005: 355–62)

This position seems unequivocal: the rights of the individual far outweigh the regulatory power of planning, which acts only to undermine these rights. Indeed, it can presumably be wielded or influenced by those who seek to deny basic freedoms, as is the case in many parts of Britain when planning is supposedly hijacked by NIMBY interests. The contrast with the inherent trust in planning (or, rather, trust in the need for planning to restrict, but dismay when it appears too lax) in Britain – which is arguably strongest in England – could not be clearer. Yet the working assumption set out by the Minister for the Environment in 2005 does vie against other rationales. Scott deploys the same framework for understanding the politics of rural development as UK-based researchers. Following the tradition of Murdoch and Abram (2002) and Woods (2005b), he describes 'narratives' that underpin ethics, and which, in turn, drive decision-making. This thinking follows closely the idea that representations of rural space drive rationales and shape planning decisions. The two narratives in Ireland are the same as those found in Britain: a heritage/resource representation that compels decision makers to conserve rural space versus a cultural/community representation that is expressed through *laissez-faire* planning and one-off houses.

Seen in these terms, the difference between Ireland and the countries of Britain primarily hinges on which narrative is stronger: who has the upper hand. As we saw in Chapters 2 and 3, the idea of the countryside as a monument, as a relic even, has a pervasive and persistent impact on the nature of planning for rural areas in parts of Britain. The idea has of course been moderated, but it still shapes attitudes to rural change, and it has been championed by numerous lobby groups, notably the CPRE and its equivalents in Scotland and Wales (see Chapters 3 and 4). These have become key players in rural planning debates in Britain's countrysides. In contrast, a key player in Ireland has been the Irish Rural Dwellers' Association (IRDA): a 'multi-scalar' organisation campaigning on behalf of a 'broad coalition' of *pro-development* interests (Scott, forthcoming). IRDA – formed in 2002 – captures a very different perspective of rural areas and has been instrumental in ensuring that planning policies on rural housing 'are responsive to the dispersed patterns of settlement in Ireland' (DoEHLG, 2004: 1). Its influence derives from grass-root and broad institutional support. Arguably, IRDA in Ireland has become more powerful than the CPRE in England – gaining a tangible foothold in the process of policy design – but both express prevailing preferences in their respective countries, and underlying representations of rural space: as a working landscape in need of people versus a heritage landscape in need of preservation.

Returning to Scott's study of local elected members (as a proxy for Irish attitudes towards rural development) it is useful to reflect on some of the author's key findings. The survey, conducted in 2007, sought to collect views from all rural county councillors. It focused on community life, the landscape and key rural challenges. Respondents shared three central concerns: restrictions on rural housing, the inadequacy of infrastructure and population decline. Delving deeper, Scott found that councillors were concerned about a lack of housing for young people. Only 2 per cent of respondents saw one-off housing as problematic. The inevitable conclusion was that the 'majority of councillors construct a narrative of the rural as a social/community space rather than as an environmental resource to protect and conserve' (Scott, forthcoming).

This conclusion was reinforced by subsequent questioning: the vast majority of respondents wanted government to make community concerns a policy priority; far fewer prioritised protection of the landscape. However, protection was a bigger priority in the Greater Dublin Area, with Scott suggesting that 'this difference may … reflect local voters' concerns … suggesting that local interests in the Greater Dublin Area may become more resistant to further change' (Scott, forthcoming).The possibility that Dublin is exporting an environmental rationality to its hinterland (and perhaps beyond) is both interesting and potentially worrying. NIMBYism could be fanning out from the capital. As families counter-urbanise, they carry with them a distinctly different set of values, built upon a different understanding of the countryside.This might suggest that the Irish condition is set to change in the decades ahead, and might converge with the British disposition towards environmental protection – and a heritage perspective – in rural areas.

But the current pro-development stance is strong. Councillors generally agree that one-off housing in the countryside provides a good quality of life, and this benefit overrides its externalities. Whilst acknowledging the idyllic qualities of the Irish landscape, few believe that one-off houses will in any way compromise the integrity of the landscape. Indeed, housing is part of the rural idyll: it is an idyll to be lived and experienced, not frozen in aspic.

However, there is growing concern over the influence of central policy-makers and other 'outsiders' who attempt to apply urban values to the planning of the countryside. Contrary to the analysis of Gallent et al (2003) quoted above, Scott is able to show that many local groups in the countryside regard planning policy as too restrictive.They perceive planning officers to have little understanding of the rural way of life: as outsiders who 'fail to empathise' (Scott, forthcoming) and as 'British-influenced' by virtue of their training. An environmental narrative is extending outwards from urban areas: it is not only new residents who introduce it, but also planning professionals whose understanding of the countryside is shaped by a foreign influence.

Lessons from Ireland?

The obvious question to conclude on is whether Ireland's attitude towards rural housing is underpinned by a deep-seated cultural difference, when contrasted with the countries of Britain, or whether it simply lags behind in the evolution of ideas. If we accept that the latter is true then we seem to be suggesting that Irish attitudes are fundamentally flawed, that one-off housing is damaging the landscape, and that Ireland should learn lessons from Britain. But the imposition of British attitudes and practices remains fiercely contested. In Northern Ireland, Republicans and Unionists have united around the belief that rural policy must be closer to that found in the Republic than in the rest of Britain (Friends of the Earth, 2008). The consensus is that Britain, and particularly England, has got it wrong: that the pendulum has swung too far in favour of environmental protection and that planning, wielded by those not primarily driven by community or social concerns, but by vested private interest, is no longer a means of serving the long-term needs of rural communities.

In many respects, attitudes in Ireland find their closest parallel in Britain in the Scottish Highlands, where settlement morphology is far more scattered and there is arguably less deference to an explicit environmental rationale and greater concern for the survival of local communities (though the former is implicitly served by much lower population densities). As in parts of the Republic, the emphasis is often on self-build, planning that accommodates community need and how house-building in general can contribute to supporting fragile communities, encouraging people to stay or encouraging an inflow of 'new blood'. However, like the alternative perspective rolling out from Dublin, there is also anecdotal evidence of increasing resistance to development and a growth of NIMBYism in the Highlands, cutting across a culture that tended to accept the incremental growth of rural communities and the tradition of community support for affordable housing development. Such local traditions and differences have tended to lessen talk of a uniformly 'British' brand of rural settlement planning, and the general differences between England, Scotland and Wales were highlighted earlier in this chapter. But arguably, there is a creeping infiltration of policies that take a more 'purified' view of rural space, giving less credence to pragmatic, local solutions to satisfying community needs, and a commensurate hardening of attitudes in local planning authorities against the flexibility that had been the hallmark of Highland practice. The pendulum in Scotland may be sharing the trajectory of its counterpart in England.

The Irish position with regards to rural settlement planning, expressed in 2005 by the Minister for the Environment, might seem hard-line; but the British position, seen through Irish eyes, is no less retrenched in ideology and an anachronistic understanding of rural economies and communities. The Irish have been having their own debate on the future of the countryside for the past decade: so far, this has confirmed Ireland's pro-development tendency. The countries of Britain have been having the same debate since the onset of mass counter-urbanisation in the 1960s. Review after review has questioned the balance between environmental and social priority, but little has changed since 1947. Rural areas have been transformed by a rebalancing of their economies, away from farming and towards consumption in various guises. But this transformation has not triggered any fundamental shift in planning policy. It is difficult to see Irish planning completely converging with the British situation, despite a potential fanning out of environmental sensibility from Dublin. It is far more likely that a new accommodation will be reached – albeit in the context of Ireland's more dispersed rural settlement pattern – that *might* present interesting lessons for Britain. At the very least, it will be fascinating to see, over time, what balance can be struck between people and preservation, and whether Ireland – north and south – is able to meet the accelerating demand for homes in the countryside in a sustainable way. Talk of 'lessons' might be a little presumptuous, though mutual observation is likely to prove useful.

Notes

[1] There are of course echoes here of the 'third way' (Giddens, 1998) and the message is reminiscent of those contained in the 2004 Rural Strategy (DEFRA, 2004) with its emphasis on 'social justice for all' (DEFRA, 2004: 5) and tackling spatial social exclusion.
[2] Though in some instances, illegal building in southern Italy took the form of systematic speculation overseen by organised criminal groups including the Ndrangheta or the Mafia

(Quattrone, 2000: 7), with local authorities often being party, or turning a blind eye, to such criminal activities.

[3] A recent example of an attempt to 'purify' rural space from such illegality, and one which has been well-publicised, is that of 60 caravans sited without planning permission at the Lunga Estate, on Craignish peninsula in Argyll. A local landowner had allowed people who were working in the local area to erect temporary dwellings on his land. In 2005, the local authority began issuing enforcement notices against caravan owners, initiating a process that has been likened to a modern-day 'highland clearance' (English, 2005).

[4] This growth was built on the usual drivers: demographic growth fuelled by in-migration, rising disposable incomes, and a fall in mortgage interest rates (Fahey and Duffy, 2007).

TWENTY

The rural housing question: towards an answer

We began this book by posing a series of questions about the supply of housing in Britain's countrysides, its quality, its location, its connection with the state of rural economies and rural society, and whether patterns of supply deliver social equity as well as sustainability. We asked also about some of the key pressures on housing resources, emanating from patterns of retirement, second home purchasing and from general migration to and from different rural areas. And finally, we alluded to more fundamental questions that bind all other concerns together: how representations of the countryside find expression in attitudes towards development and in planning's treatment of different rural areas: essentially, what are society's expectations of rural land: who can use it and for what purpose? The opening chapter began a process of defining what exactly we mean by the 'rural housing question': is it a simple question to which there is a simple answer, or is it a set of interlinked questions that each need addressing separately? It would be much too easy at this stage to conclude that attitudes towards Britain's countrysides must change, that government must take a firmer lead in 'winning hearts and minds' and delivering solutions to rural challenges that put community needs on a equal footing with the undisputed importance of maintaining environmental and landscape quality. Whilst this is true, it does not really move the debate forward. Advancing a convincing answer to the rural housing question seems as far off now as it did in the time of Savage (1919). Almost a hundred years have passed since he documented the inadequacies of rural housing provision in the first decades of the 20th century. Whilst the 'barbaric' conditions he witnessed have undoubtedly improved, significant sections of rural society today are either inadequately housed, homeless or displaced up the urban hierarchy.

The planning system and local planning practice are not helpless in the face of such issues, but make rational choices that often appear quite heartless. Strict limits are placed on the amount of housing directed to villages and emphasis is put on the concentration of development in larger centres. This makes a lot of sense: services are easier to provide, councils are able to facilitate development by private enterprise and new jobs can be co-located with new homes. The volume of development in the wider countryside is contained – though 'containment' is now presented as part of a 'sustainability' package – and all the theories, statistics and appraisals confirm that this is the right thing to do. However, in the face of this normative response, concerns over the state of Britain's countrysides have not subsided. Village services and small schools face the constant threat of closure; rural poverty is a persistent problem; rural economies are weakened by labour shortages; and at a time when governments are promoting 'social balance and mix' as being central to their communities agendas, the countryside is becoming increasingly polarised in this respect. Until the 1940s, the lowland English village, for example, was perhaps a model of social diversity: today it is often the preserve of a very limited range of socio-economic and demographic groups – the affluent retired, commuting households and, in some instances, absentee owners. This picture, suggesting the displacement of 'reluctant leavers', is not present everywhere. Different nations, regions, counties and districts have their own rural housing questions. But these questions are often bound together around issues of representation, planning and land. What is the countryside for? Whose countryside are we planning for? And what rights should communities have over the land they are living and working on?

In this book, we have covered a range of topics and policy areas in some detail, and we have also shown that issues play out differently in different places. The experiences of rural areas and of communities are determined by patterns of migration and economic change, by the strength of those communities and by the innovations of policy that often deliver ingenious solutions to local housing problems. Planning sometimes has a heart, supporting local initiative and doing the best it can to help create thriving rural communities. But is it sufficiently consistent? At various points, we have discussed the nature of policy-making and argued that comprehensive solutions often bow to local innovation. National frameworks must be adapted to local circumstances, and this means that actions at a local level are often incremental, responding to challenges as they arise. This has been characterised as a process of 'muddling through', and given the diversity of rural circumstances, in different parts of Britain's countrysides, there is nothing inherently wrong with such an approach. It would be madness to argue that all villages must grow: that there should be a minimum level of growth (10 or 20 per cent) over the next decade or so. Communities face different contexts and challenges with housing need being bound up with economic change and opportunity. This often means that the appropriate level for dealing with housing, service and economic needs is at the community level rather than through national edict. But it is often the case that communities cannot be treated as 'third parties' or 'consultees' in the planning processes that shape their environments. There is a case for more direct responsibility and control. They already have a significant role to play in low-cost housing schemes delivered on exception sites, with the evidence for such developments often coming through community or parish councils. But the exceptions system is uncertain and cumbersome and should be replaced with a more consistent means of supporting community initiative. We alluded to this in Chapter 18: a stronger decision-taking role for communities within a framework of responsibility, supported by a planning system that delivers land for community use, and by national policy that encourages local businesses to invest in community housing projects. This would be an attempt to reconstruct the link between community development, housing and economic change that was once part of the natural process of village life.

That is not to say that the clock can be turned back or that Britain's countrysides have not experienced fundamental and sometimes revolutionary change over the past 50 to 100 years. Rural Britain has been subject to economic shift, from an agricultural to a service industry base. It has experienced successive bouts of selective depopulation and repopulation. Its social composition, as noted earlier, has been transformed so that now it is possible to claim that the countryside is more elderly than it once was, but generally better off. Over this period, there has also been unremitting interest in the transformation of rural areas. This interest has come from policy-makers, from academics, from local authorities and from communities themselves. It presents two contrasting pictures of the countryside in the 21st century: one is of a 'grey and pleasant land' populated by the retired or near-retired who have become the new custodians of the country's national heritage. The other is of a countryside struggling to come to terms with new economic realities and receiving limited help from an unsympathetic planning system. The countryside is not only the subject of newspaper reporting or academic consideration: it is also a lived reality. Both of these pictures tell part of a real story. For some rural residents, the countryside is an authentic idyll and the realisation of an ambition to decamp to a more pleasant environment. But for others, life is harder. The buses are infrequent, the shops are closing and buying a home is becoming an increasingly distant dream. Personal experiences are of course determined by relative wealth and opportunity: this is true for any place, from the inner city to the remotest countryside. In cities, physical interventions aiming to correct inequalities are arguably easier, though success is not assured. In Britain's countrysides, the smaller affluent villages within commuter belts or other sought-after locations are becoming islands of wealth, drifting away from neighbouring towns, some of which have become islands of increasing poverty.

We have tried, however, to unpack this generalisation in a number of thematic chapters, exploring the demographic, market and planning factors that have conspired to produce local outcomes. We have looked also at interventions in 'normal' market processes, and the variable results these deliver. The roles that different forms of housing play in rural areas have been examined too; and we have held homelessness to be the clearest expression of market and policy failure in Britain's countrysides, though often this is hidden and disputed. But in the last two chapters, there has been some focus on remedial action. This has addressed three key areas: local action, carried forward by communities of volunteers; broad strategy and support for that local action; and a reappraisal of the values and assumptions that underpin rural land policy.

We have already made some quite detailed observations concerning current planning and policy frameworks, though we have avoided prescribing very specific actions or alterations to existing policy and practice. There have been a number of reviews over recent years, each offering its own list of recommendations to government in London, Edinburgh and Cardiff. These reviews have become more sophisticated and reflect today's much deeper understanding and concern for the challenges faced by rural areas. It would be impossible to arrive at anything more comprehensive than has already been put before the politicians. A book of this nature, built around a personal re-evaluation of the evidence, must accept more modest ambitions. But it is worth re-reflecting on our three areas of remedial action, as these seem to go to the heart of the rural housing question.

Local action

Communities are diverse entities and rarely share a common vision. They are dynamic rather than static, but are nonetheless able to reach decisions on what they need to thrive, whether this is more or less housing. Resistance to development may not be in a community's collective interest, but this is for the community to work out. If communities are given real responsibility to take development decisions, it is likely that this will cause a reappraisal of current attitudes. Those groups looking for additional assistance will no longer refer to a local authority or some other distant body, but will ask what the community itself is doing to address local needs. There will likely be a renegotiation at the level of the community or parish council. One result could be increased conflict. But another could be greater cohesion, a more balanced outlook and decisions that reflect collective rather than minority – or even just majority – interests. The experience of the past is that rural communities reject those changes that are imposed upon them, but there is no evidence that they will not bring about the changes that they themselves deem necessary. There are already a number of models of local action to be drawn upon, but the most popular at the present time is the community land trust. Residents want to participate in things that make a real difference, but not necessarily in processes that do not deliver clear results. There is regular resistance to decisions and priorities that are imposed on rural communities, but land trusts offer a route to genuinely devolved decision-making. How land is acquired remains a key question, though monies could be diverted from other forms of housing delivery, or secured though planning obligations or infrastructure levies for this purpose. Housing that people can access is *the* critical infrastructure for rural communities.

Supporting local action

There needs to be a framework in which all of this can happen. Although the planning system writ large has not always shown due regard for the needs of smaller communities in rural areas, local planning practice has frequently been willing to innovate solutions to local housing supply issues. In many instances, there has been a positive partnership between landowners, planning authorities and community groups. Planning has actively sought ways of overcoming land costs to deliver affordable homes in ways that are now considered rather conventional – including exceptions – but which are in fact rather ingenious and demonstrate a clear willingness to work with rural communities. But in some cases, communities are doubtful over how much their efforts will yield in terms of housing for local people. They are worried about the involvement of an HA/RSL, fearing perhaps that the allocation priorities of this 'outside' body will not correspond with their own. They want the type of direct control outlined earlier, and if they are to achieve this and have greater confidence in the system, they need to receive more consistent plan-led support. Therefore, we will risk a little more prescription here and say that land should be allocated within planning frameworks for community use, available for purchase by land trusts, but not available to private enterprise for commercial gain. The types of projects admissible on such land should be clearly specified and might include a range of uses serving against community requirement, with a strong presumption in favour of self-directed housing for people whom the community deems to be in priority need. The allocation of land for community use could be viewed as part of a community infrastructure strategy, with monies from community infrastructure levy receipts[1] or planning obligations, and indeed from national housing agencies, directed to projects on this land. Such a system may not be immediately popular with local authorities, and it may not be seen as the most efficient distribution from the cost-centres, but it may well overcome some of the resistance to development that has been a hallmark of past rural planning.

Values, assumptions and land policy

These measures will begin to address the assumptions that surround the use of land in Britain's countrysides. Re-evaluating power and responsibility and the role of 'the state' in rural development may challenge the assumption that decisions, made behind closed doors, are imposed on rural areas. The palpable sense of powerlessness in the face of centralised planning and big business interests is partly responsible for the resistance to development, and the apparent 'parochialism', that defeats what many commentators claim are eminently sensible planning proposals. To some extent, parochialism may be as much part of the cure as part of the disease. However, the way the countryside is conceived in many parts of Britain remains a critical problem. Government has made significant attempts to sell the idea of living and working rural areas that need their fair share of investment and development. A number of White Papers in recent years have been rightly hailed as landmark documents, spelling out the sorts of investment in services and housing that are needed to ensure rural communities thrive. Of course, these White Papers have often set aspirations for market towns that are very different from those for villages. But the fact remains that some attempt has been made to articulate a vision for Britain's countrysides in which development and change has a place. And yet, rural Britain remains a popular destination for rural retirees, commuters, lifestyle downshifters and second home buyers. A home or retreat in the countryside remains an aspiration of many Britons. And this is not a countryside despoiled by shoddy housing development, but something serene and exclusive, invoking a childhood memory of the Cotswolds, the Grampians or Snowdonia, or even of a foreign countryside that we expect to rediscover somewhere in Britain. We have a deep cultural attachment to that memory that we will not relinquish easily. But unless we understand the needs of rural communities and the many forms that acceptable development can take, we will probably wait another hundred years before answering the rural housing question.

Note
[1] In England and Wales only.

Defining rurality

This appendix provides an overview of what we mean by rural areas in Britain. The basis of our argument in this book has been the paucity of development of housing that is inclusive of all sections of the population, and which can help facilitate the economic potential of rural localities. The thrust of this argument is that housing development for lower-income groups has been stymied in the smallest settlements of the three nations that constitute Britain, but how do we define which communities we are talking about?

Reviews of definitions emphasise the variety of ways in which rurality can be classified (WAG, 2008c). In part, this variety reflects the purposes such definitions are intended to serve. There are two elements in defining rural areas for this book. The first element reflects the fact that a central argument has been the way that social representations of rural areas impact upon the housing opportunities of households. The way that the idea of 'rural' is conceived by various groups translates into contested versions of how the countryside can and should look (see for example, Halfacree, 1993, and also the discussion in Chapter 2). Lowe and Ward (2007) have argued that the balance of different interests in various localities helps to shape the nature of housing markets within these localities, in addition to decision-making within local, regional and national governments. It is the notion of rural idylls that provides an important theme for the book and helps to frame the different housing opportunities for households on low incomes across the various countrysides of Britain.

The second element concerns the need to provide a functional definition, which fixes individual settlements within a hierarchy of rural or urban categories. This approach is essential in providing a geographical reference for our arguments, and a way of locating the smallest communities across Britain's countrysides. The following sections set out the basis of rural and urban definitions that have been developed for policy-makers within England, Scotland and Wales, which provide the basis for our understanding of rural settlements for this book.

A definition of rural settlements

England

Notwithstanding the inevitable arbitrariness in deciding whether settlements count as rural or urban, recent official definitions developed for the national governments have aimed to provide a consistent approach to defining rural localities. In 2004 a definition of urban and rural areas was published covering England. This Office for National Statistics (ONS) definition incorporated the earlier distinction between urban and rural settlements, where the cut-off between the two has traditionally been 10,000 households. The new ONS definition was based upon population density and focused on two dimensions.

The first dimension was a consideration of the morphology – the physical form – of settlements. All settlements above 10,000 population were classified as urban. Settlements below 10,000 (including isolated dwellings) were categorised by *settlement type* in three ways (see Table A.1).

The second dimension comprised the wider geographic *context* in which settlements are situated, with a focus on sparsity. The rationale for providing an assessment of context was to encapsulate the wider accessibility of a settlement, and the sparsity of population within a broad area. The measure was intended to be indicative of the potential costs of overcoming distance to supply settlements with various public and private services. Settlements under 10,000 population, including isolated dwellings, were classified as either 'Less sparse' or 'Sparse' (Table A.1).

The categorisation of rural settlements was derived from a grid covering about 35 million cells, each of about 1 hectare. Residential addresses within each cell were identified and an average density was calculated for each cell, also taking into account varying radii around the cells. The resulting categorisation was then related to Census Output Areas. The two categorisations, by *settlement type* and *context*, thus allow Output Areas to be classified in the following ways:

Table A.1: Categorisation of rural Output Areas

Settlement type	Context
Town and fringe	Less sparse
Village	Less sparse
Hamlets and isolated dwellings	Less sparse
Town and fringe	Sparse
Village	Sparse
Hamlets and isolated dwellings	Sparse

Source: CRC (2007c)

A summary of the approaches used to generate the definition was produced by the Commission for Rural Communities (CRC, 2007c). A detailed account of the methods, as well as maps of the ONS classification for England, is available from National Statistics: www.statistics.gov.uk/geography/urban_rural.asp (accessed 20 February 2010); and also from DEFRA: http://www.defra.gov.uk/evidence/statistics/rural/rural-definition.htm

One aspect of the ONS definition was that it cannot be applied at local authority district and unitary levels. An alternative classification was therefore necessary to categorise local authorities in England, based on the number or proportion of their population living in urban centres or in rural settlements and large market towns. The definition classifies local authorities in the following ways:

- **Major Urban**: districts with either 100,000 people *or* 50 per cent of their population in urban areas with a population of more than 750,000.
- **Large Urban**: districts with either 50,000 people *or* 25 per cent of their population in one of 17 urban areas with a population between 250,000 and 750,000.
- **Other Urban**: districts with fewer than 40,000 people *or* less than 25 per cent of their population in rural settlements.
- **Significant Rural**: districts with at least 40,000 people *or* at least 25 per cent of their population in rural settlements.
- **Rural-50**: districts with at least 50 per cent but less than 80 per cent of their population in rural settlements (including urban areas with between 10,000 and 30,000 population that are of rural functional importance).
- **Rural-80**: districts with at least 80 per cent of their population in rural settlements (including urban areas with between 10,000 and 30,000 population that are of rural functional importance).

Further details of the local authority classification can be found at: www.defra.gov.uk/evidence/statistics/rural/rural-definition.htm (accessed 20 February 2010). (For information on the methods used, see also: www.defra.gov.uk/evidence/statistics/rural/documents/rural–defn/laclassifications-techguide0409.pdf)

Wales

The Welsh Assembly Government (WAG, 2008a: 1) noted that there is no universally accepted definition of rural Wales. The ONS definition developed for England, as highlighted earlier, also covers Wales. A critical assessment of how the ONS definition was received by practitioners and agencies suggested substantial 'buy-in' to the approach adopted (Webster et al, 2006). Inevitably, however, there was some criticism of the ability of the ONS classification to reflect the subtleties and nuances that pertain in all areas, especially in relation to the classification of a number of market towns and localities fringing urban centres. It was perhaps with this kind of issue in mind that an approach taken in Wales was to refine the ONS classification through a process of consultation with local authorities. Alongside the ONS classification, therefore, this consultation process led to an alternative definition in Wales, as a basis for possible funding decisions: the Rural Development Plan for Wales 2007–13 Classification. This classification incorporates statistical and non-statistical data to classify rural and urban areas (see WAG, 2006b).

A classification of local authorities was adopted in Wales that was also distinct from the approach in England. The Welsh Assembly Government used a measure of population density, whereby if a local authority has a density of less than 150 residents per square kilometre (a definition specified by the OECD), then it is classified as rural. Based on the population density of the 22 unitary authorities, nine fall below this threshold (WAG, 2008a):

- **Rural authorities** (Isle of Anglesey; Gwynedd; Conwy; Denbighshire; Powys; Ceredigion; Pembrokeshire; Carmarthenshire; and Monmouthshire).
- **Valleys authorities** – these authorities are categorised as populated areas confined by a unique physical environment (Rhondda, Cynon, Taff; Merthyr Tydfil; Caerphilly; Blaenau Gwent; and Torfaen).
- **Urban authorities** – the three most heavily populated authorities in Wales (Swansea; Cardiff; and Newport).
- **'Other' authorities** – authorities with a mix of rural and urban characteristics (Neath Port Talbot; Bridgend; Flintshire; Wrexham; and Vale of Glamorgan) (WAG, 2008c).

Scotland

In contrast with the ONS definition in England and Wales, an alternative approach was adopted in Scotland. As the Scottish Government noted in relation to Scotland on the one hand, and England and Wales on the other, 'different urban rural definitions are required as the nature of rurality is different in each country' (Scottish Government, 2008e: 10). The detailed definition was first developed in 2000, and was based on two criteria. The first is population as defined by the General Register Office for Scotland (GROS). The second is a measure of accessibility, based on drive times, to differentiate between accessible and remote areas of the country. Since 2000, the definition has been updated and refined, and a detailed account of the methods used can be found in Appendix A of the Urban Rural Classification, 2007–08 (Scottish Government, 2008f). The emphasis on accessibility and remoteness, rather than sparsity, captures well the Scottish context of the isolation of many communities. For example, it is not only the physical separation of people on the islands, but also the potential for isolation based on transport arrangements. Notably, people on Jura live with 'double isolation' due to the need for two ferries to reach the mainland, via Islay.

A sixfold classification has been produced to identify urban, rural and remote areas within Scotland. The Scottish Government takes its core definition of rurality as settlements of 3,000 people or less. The sixfold classification can be reduced to this core definition, with categories 5 and 6 counting as rural, and categories 1 to 4 encompassing the rest of Scotland (a map of the sixfold classification can be found in Scottish Government, 2008f: 32).

The Scottish Government definition for Scotland also profiles local authorities in relation to the proportion of their populations living within the sixfold classification of urban, rural and remote areas, as well as the eightfold classification distinguishing remote and very remote areas (see Scottish Government, 2008f: 13–14).

Table A.2: Scottish government urban/rural sixfold classification

1 Large Urban Areas	Settlements of over 125,000 people.
2 Other Urban Areas	Settlements of 10,000 to 125,000 people.
3 Accessible Small Towns	Settlements of between 3,000 and 10,000 people and within 30 minutes' drive of a settlement of 10,000 or more.
4 Remote Small Towns	Settlements of between 3,000 and 10,000 people and with a drive time of over 30 minutes to a settlement of 10,000 or more.
5 Accessible Rural	Settlements of less than 3,000 people and within 30 minutes' drive of a settlement of 10,000 or more.
6 Remote Rural	Settlements of less than 3,000 people and with a drive time of over 30 minutes to a settlement of 10,000 or more.

Source: Scottish Government (2008f) © Crown copyright

References

Abbott, R. (2005) *Social Housing Allocations and Family Networks*, Young Foundation Working Paper No.1, Young Foundation: London.

Abercrombie, P. (1926) *The Preservation of Rural England*, Hodder and Stoughton: London.

Accent Scotland and Mauthner, N. (2006) *Service Priority, Accessibility and Quality in Rural Scotland*, The Scottish Executive: Edinburgh.

ACRE (Action for Communities in Rural England) (1988) *Who Can Afford to Live in the Countryside? Access to Housing Land*, ACRE: Cirencester.

Adams, D. and Watkins, C. (2002) *Greenfields, Brownfields and Housing Development*, Blackwell: Oxford.

Affordable Rural Housing Commission (2006) *Final Report*, DEFRA: London.

Allanson, P. and Whitby, M. (1996) 'Prologue: Rural policy and the British countryside', in Allanson, P. and Whitby, M. (eds) *The Rural Economy and the British Countryside*, Earthscan: London, pp 1–16.

Angotti, T. (1977) *Housing in Italy: Urban Development and Political Change*, Praeger: New York.

Armstrong, W.A. (1993) 'The countryside', in Thompson, F.M.L (ed) *The Cambridge Social History of Britain, 1750–1950 (Volume 1: Regions and Communities)*, Cambridge University Press: Cambridge, pp 87–154.

Arnold, D. (2009) 'Whatever happened to eco-towns?', in *Architects' Journal*, 25 June 2009, pp 10–13.

Asthana, S., Gibson, A., Moon, G. and Brigham, P. (2003) 'Allocating resources for health and social care: The significance of rurality', in *Health and Social Care in the Community*, 11, 6, pp 486–93.

Auchincloss, M. (2008) 'Keys to the door', in *Planning*, 3 October 2008.

Audit Commission (2007) *Crossing Borders: Responding to the Local Challenges of Migrant Workers*, Audit Commission: London.

Balchin, P. (1995) *Housing Policy: An Introduction*, Routledge: London.

Ball, M. (1983) *Housing Policy and Economic Power: The Political Economy of Owner-Occupation*, Methuen: London.

Ball, M. (1999) 'Chasing a snail: innovation and housebuilding firms' strategies', in *Housing Studies*, 14, 1, pp 9–22.

Ball, M. (2006) *Markets and Institutions in Real Estate and Construction*, Blackwell: Oxford.

Ball, M., Harloe, M. and Martens, M. (1988) *Housing and Social Change in Europe and the USA*, Routledge: London.

Ball, M., Lizieri, C. and MacGregor, B.D. (1998) *The Economics of Commercial Property Markets*, Routledge: London.

Barlow, J. (1999) 'From craft production to mass customisation: Innovation requirements for the UK house-building industry', in *Housing Studies*, 14, 1, pp 23–42.

Barlow, J., Jackson, R. and Meikle, J. (2001) *Homes to DIY for: The UK's Self-build Housing Market in the Twenty-first Century*, YPS: York.

Barrett, S., Stewart, M. and Underwood, J. (1978) *The Land Market and the Development Process*, Occasional Paper 2, School for Advanced Urban Studies: Bristol.

Beer, A., Delfabbro, P., Natalier, K., Oakley, S. and Verity, F. (2003) *Developing Models of Good Practice in Meeting the Needs of Homeless Young People in Rural Areas: A Position Paper*, Australian Housing and Urban Research Institute: Melbourne.

Bell, D. (1997) 'Anti-idyll: Rural horror', in Cloke, P. and Little, J. (eds) *Contested Countryside Cultures: Otherness, Marginalisation and Rurality*, Routledge: London, pp 94–108.

Best, R. and Shucksmith, M. (2006) *Homes for Rural Communities: Report of the Joseph Rowntree Foundation Rural Housing Policy Forum*, Joseph Rowntree Foundation: York.

Bevan, M. and Rhodes, D. (2005) *The Impact of Second and Holiday Homes in Rural Scotland*, Communities Scotland: Edinburgh.

Bevan, M. and Rugg, J. (2006) *Providing Homelessness Support Services in Rural Areas: Exploring Models for Providing more Effective Local Support*, Communities Scotland: Edinburgh.

Bevan, M. and Sanderling, L. (1996) *Private Renting in Rural Areas*, Centre for Housing Policy: York.

Bevan, M., Cameron, S., Coombes, M., Merridew, T. and Raybould, S. (2001) *The Role of Social Housing in Rural Areas*, Chartered Institute of Housing: Coventry.

Bevan, M., Croucher, K., Fletcher, P., Rhodes, D. and Riseborough, M. (2006) *The Housing and Support Needs of Older People in Rural Areas* (CRC 26), The Countryside Agency: London.

Bevan, P. (2000) *Rough Sleeping in Wales*, National Assembly for Wales: Cardiff.

Birchall, J. (ed) (1992) *Housing Policy in the 1990s*, Routledge: London.

Blenkinship, J. (2004) *Housing: An Effective Way to Sustain our Rural Communities: Part I: The Effects of Affordable Housing on Rural Communities*, Cumbria Rural Housing Trust: Penrith.

Blenkinship, J. and Gibbons, J. (2004) *Housing Markets: Preparing for Change*, Impact Housing Association: Workington.

Blythe, H. (2006) *The Stigma of Rural Homelessness in Wales*, Wallich Clifford: Cardiff

Bosworth, G. (2006) *Counterurbanisation and Job Creation: Entrepreneurial In-migration and Rural Economic Development*, Centre for Rural Economy, University of Newcastle: Newcastle upon Tyne.

Bowie, F. and Davies, O. (eds) (1992) *Discovering Welshness*, Gomer Press: Dyfedd.

Bowler, I. and Lewis, G. (1987) 'The decline of private rental housing in rural areas: A case study of villages in Northamptonshire', in Lockhart, D.G. and Ilbery, B. (eds) *The Future of the British Rural Landscape*, GeoBooks: Norwich, pp 115–36.

Boyle, P. and Halfacree, K. (eds) (1998) *Migration into Rural Areas: Theories and Issues*, Wiley: Chichester.

Bramley, G. (1993a) 'Land-use planning and the housing market in Britain: The impact on house-building and house prices', in *Environment and Planning A: Environment and Planning*, 25, pp 1025–51.

Bramley, G. (1993b) 'The impact of land-use planning and tax subsidies on the supply and price of housing in Britain', in *Urban Studies*, 30, 1, pp 5–30.

Bramley, G. (1996) 'Impact of land-use planning on the supply and price of housing in Britain: Reply to comment by Alan W. Evans', in *Urban Studies*, 33, 9, pp 1733–7.

Bramley, G. (1998) 'Measuring planning: Indicators of planning restraint and its impact on housing land supply', in *Environment and Planning B: Planning and Design*, 25, pp 31–57.

Bramley, G. (1999) 'Housing market adjustment and land supply constraints', *Environment and Planning A: Environment and Planning*, 31, pp 1169–88.

Bramley, G. and Watkins, D. (2009) 'Affordability and supply: The rural dimension', in *Planning Practice and Research*, 24, 2, pp 185–210.

Bramley, G., Bartlett, W. and Lambert, C. (1995) *Planning, the Market and Private Housebuilding*, UCL Press: London.

Bramley, G., Hague, C., Kirk, K., Prior, A., Raemaekers, J. and Smith, H. with Robinson, A. and Bushnell, R. (2004) *Review of Green Belt Policy in Scotland*, Scottish Executive: Edinburgh.

Bramley, G., Watkins, D. and Karley, N.K. (2006) *Local Housing Need and Affordability Model for Scotland, 2005 Update*, Communities Scotland: Edinburgh.

Bramley, G., Morgan, J. and Littlewood, M. (2007) *Initial Evaluation of the Open Market HomeStake Pilot*, Communities Scotland: Edinburgh.

Briheim-Crookall, L. (2007) *Supporting Homelessness Agencies to Deliver Services in Rural Areas*, Homeless Link: London.

Brown, K.M. (2007) 'Reconciling moral and legal collective entitlement: Implications for community-based land reform', in *Land Use Policy*, 24, pp 633–43.

Bryden, J. and Geisler, C.C. (2007) 'Community-based land reform: Lessons from Scotland', in *Land Use Policy*, 24, pp 24–34.

Bryden, J. and Hart, K. (2001) *Dynamics of Rural Areas: The International Comparison*, Arkleton Centre for Rural Development Research: Aberdeen.

Buller, H. and Hoggart, K. (1994) *International Counterurbanisation: British Migrants in Rural France*, Avebury: Aldershot.

Buller, H., Morris, C. and Wright, E. (2003) *The Demography of Rural Areas: A Literature Review*, DEFRA: London.

Bunce, M. (2003) 'Reproducing rural idylls', in Cloke, P. (ed) *Country Visions*, Pearson Education Ltd: Harlow, pp 14–30.

Burchardt, J. (2007) 'Agricultural history, rural history, or countryside history?' in *The Historical Journal*, 50, 2, pp 465–81.

Burgess, J. (1987) 'Landscapes in the living room: Television and landscape research', in *Landscape Research*, 12, pp 1–7.

Burholt, V. (2006) '"Adref": Theoretical contexts of attachment to place for mature and older people in rural North Wales', in *Environment and Planning A*, 38, pp 1095–114.

Burns, M. (2005) *Youth Homelessness in Rural Northumberland: An Analysis of Levels, Causes and Trends*, Community Foundation: Tyne and Wear.

CABE (Commission for Architecture and the Built Environment (2009) *Space in New Homes: What Residents Think*, CABE: London.

Cabinet Office (1999) *Rural Economies*, Cabinet Office, Performance and Innovation Unit: London.

Cadman, D. and Austin-Crowe, L. (1991) *Property Development*, Spon Press: London.

Cairncross, L. and Pearl, M. (2003) *Taking the Lead: Report of a Survey of Housing Association Board Members*, Housing Corporation: London.

Cairncross, L., Downing, L., Chadwick, A., Satsangi, M., Morgan, J. and Wager, F. (2006) *The Use of Existing Housing Stock in Rural Areas*, Commission for Rural Communities: Cheltenham.

Cambridge City Council (2009) Memorandum submitted by Cambridge City Council (LH58) to the Commons Select Committee Inquiry into the Local Housing Allowance, House of Commons: London.

Cameron, S. and Shucksmith, M. (2007) 'Market towns, housing and social inclusion', in Powe, N., Hart, T. and Shaw, T. (eds) *Market Towns: Roles, Challenges and Prospects*, Routledge: London, pp 81–92.

Capstick, M. (1987) *Housing Dilemmas in the Lake District*, Centre for North-West Regional Studies: Lancaster.

Carmona, M. (2001) *Housing Design Quality: Through Policy, Guidance and Review*, Routledge: London.

Carmona, M., Carmona, S. and Gallent, N. (2003) *Delivering New Homes: Processes, Planners and Providers*, Routledge: London.

Carter, H. and Williams, S. (1978) 'Aggregate studies of language and culture change in Wales', in Williams, G. (ed) *Social and Cultural Change in Contemporary Wales*, Routledge: London, pp 143–65.

Central Housing Advisory Committee (1937) *Rural Housing*, HM Stationery Office: London.

Central Housing Advisory Committee (1944) *Rural Housing – Third Report of the Rural Housing Sub-committee of the Central Housing Advisory Committee*, HM Stationery Office: London.

Centre for Cities (2008) *The Credit Crunch and Implications for the UK Housing Market*, Centre for Cities: London.

Centrepoint (2009) Memorandum Submitted by Centrepoint (LH 75) to the Commons Select Committee Inquiry into the Local Housing Allowance, House of Commons: London.

Champion, A.G. (2000) 'Flight from the Cities?' in Bate, R., Best, R. and Holmans, A. (eds) *On the Move: The Housing Consequences of Migration*, York Publishing Services: York, pp 10–19.

Champion, A.G. (2007) *Reviewing Rural Futures: Population Projections and Migration Across the Urban–Rural System*, Rural Evidence Research Centre: Birkbeck, University of London, www.rerc.ac.uk/findings/documents_demography/Proj_Ests_ReportsA_F.pdf (accessed 26 February 2010).

Champion, A.G. and Shepherd, J. (2006) 'Demographic change in rural England', in Lowe, P. and Speakman, L. (eds) *The Ageing Countryside: The Growing Older Population of Rural England*, Age Concern: London.

Champion, A.G. (2009) 'Urban-rural differences in commuting in England: a challenge to the rural sustainability agenda?', in *Planning Practice & Research*, 24, 2, pp 161–82.

Chaney, P. and Sherwood, K. (2000) 'The resale o.f right to buy dwellings: A case study of migration and social change in rural England', in *Journal of Rural Studies*, 16, pp 79–94.

Chappell, L., Latorre, M., Rutter, J. and Shah, J. (2009) *Migration and Rural Economies: Assessing and Addressing Risks*, Economics of Migration Working Paper No 6, Institute for Public Policy Research: London.

Chartered Institute of Housing (2009) *News: Young People Move Away From Homeownership*, www.cih.org/news/view.php?id=1070, accessed 28 June 2008.

Cheshire, P. and Sheppard, S. (1995) 'On the price of land and the value of amenities', in *Economics*, 62, pp 247–67.

CIH (Chartered Institute of Housing) Scotland (2009) *Arrested Development: The Challenges Facing RSLs in Building Affordable Housing*, CIH Scotland: Edinburgh.

Clarke, J. (2007) 'Subordinating the social? Neo-liberalism and the remaking of welfare capitalism', in *Cultural Studies*, 21, 6, pp 974–87.

Clarke, J., Gewirtz, S. and McLaughlin, E. (eds) (2000) *New Managerialism, New Welfare?* Sage: London.

Cloke, P. (1979) *Key Settlements in Rural Areas*, Methuen: London.

Cloke, P. (2003) *Country Visions*, Pearson/Prentice Hall: Harlow.

Cloke, P. (2004) 'Rurality and racialised others: Out of place in the countryside?' in Chakraborti, N. and Garland, J. (eds) *Rural Racism*, Willan Publishing: Uffculme, pp 17–35.

Cloke, P. and Goodwin, M. (1992) 'The changing function and position of rural areas in Europe', in Huigen, P., Paul, L. and Volkers, K. (eds) *The Changing Function and Position of Rural Areas in Europe*, Netherlands Geographical Studies No 153, University of Utrecht: Utrecht, pp 19–36.

Cloke, P. and Little, J. (eds) (1997) *Contested Countryside Cultures: Otherness, Marginalisation and Rurality*, Routledge: London.

Cloke, P., Phillips, M. and Thrift, N. (1995) 'The new middle classes and the social constructs of rural living', in Butler, T. and Savage, M. (eds) *Social Change and the Middle Classes*, UCL Press: London, pp 220–38.

Cloke, P., Goodwin, M. and Milbourne, P. (eds) (1997) *Rural Wales: Community and Marginalisation*, University of Wales Press, Cardiff.

Cloke, P., Milbourne, P. and Widdowfield, R. (2000a) 'Homelessness and rurality: "Out-of-place" in purified space?' in *Environment and Planning D: Society and Space*, 18, pp 715–35.

Cloke, P., Milbourne, P. and Widdowfield, R. (2000b) 'Partnerships and policy networks in rural local governance: Homelessness in Taunton', in *Public Administration*, 78, pp 111–33.

Cloke, P., Milbourne, P. and Widdowfield, R. (2000c) 'The hidden and emerging spaces of rural homelessness', in *Environment and Planning A: Environment and Planning*, 32, pp 77–90.

Cloke, P., Milbourne, P. and Widdowfield, R. (2001a) 'The local spaces of welfare provision: Responding to homelessness in rural England', in *Political Geography*, 20, pp 493–512.

Cloke, P., Milbourne, P. and Widdowfield, R. (2001b) 'The geographies of homelessness in rural England' in *Regional Studies*, 35, 1, pp 23-37.

Cloke, P., Milbourne, P. and Widdowfield, R. (2002) *Rural Homelessness: Issues, Experiences and Policy Responses*, The Policy Press: Bristol.

Cloke, P., Johnsen, S. and May, J. (2007) 'Ethical citizenship? Volunteers and the ethics of providing services for homeless people', in *Geoforum*, 38, pp 1089–101.

Clough, R., Leamy, M., Miller, V. and Bright, L. (2004) *Housing Decisions in Later Life*, Palgrave: Basingstoke.

Cohen, A.P. (1985) *The Symbolic Construction of Community*, Routledge: London

Cole, I. (2007) 'What future for social housing in England?' in *People, Place and Policy Online*, 1, 1, pp 3–13.

Commission on Integration and Cohesion (2007) *Our Shared Future*, Commission on Integration and Cohesion: Wetherby.

Communities Scotland (2005) *The Impact of Second and Holiday Homes on Rural Communities in Scotland (Précis No 70)*, Communities Scotland: Edinburgh.

Conservative Party (2009) *Strong Foundations: Building Homes and Communities* (Green Paper), The Conservative Party: London.

Coombes, M. (2009) 'English rural housing market policy: Some inconvenient truths?', in *Planning Practice and Research*, 24, 2, pp 211–31.

Cooper, Y. (2007) 'New eco-towns could help tackle climate change', DCLG Press Release, 7 March 2007, DCLG: London.

Cope, H.F. (1999) *Housing Associations: Policy and Practice*, Macmillan: Basingstoke.

Cornwall Community Land Trust (2009) *Cornwall Community Land Trust Project: Final Report*, Cornwall Rural Housing Association: Bodmin.

Council of Mortgage Lenders (2009) 'Press release: First quarter figures suggest 75,000 repossessions this year now looks pessimistic, says CML', CML: London

Countryside Agency (2003) *Sustaining Rural Communities*, Countryside Agency: Cheltenham.

Countryside Commission (1991) *Fit for the Future: Report of the National Parks Review Panel (Edwards Report)*, Countryside Commission: Cheltenham.

CPRE (Campaign to Protect Rural England) (1998) *Urban Exodus*, CPRE: London.

Craigforth Research and Consultancy (2006) *Dumfries and Galloway Affordable Housing Study*, Dumfries and Galloway Council: Dumfries.

CRC (Commission for Rural Communities) (2006) *State of the Countryside 2006*, CRC: Cheltenham.

CRC (2007a) *State of the Countryside 2007*, CRC: Cheltenham.

CRC (2007b) *A8 Migrant Workers in Rural Areas: Briefing Paper*, CRC: Cheltenham

CRC (2007c) *Defining Rural England*, CRC: Cheltenham.

CRC (2008a) *State of the Countryside 2008*, CRC: Cheltenham.

CRC (2008b) *State of the Countryside Update: Rural Analysis of the Index of Multiple Deprivation 2007*, CRC: Cheltenham.

Crook, A.D.H. and Hughes, J. (2003) *Disrepair in the Private Rented Sector in Scotland: A Review of Policy Options in Reserved Areas*, Communities Scotland: Edinburgh.

Crook, A.D.H, Monk, S., Rowley, S. and Whitehead, C.M.E. (2006) 'Planning gain and the supply of new affordable housing in England: Understanding the numbers', in *Town Planning Review*, 77, 3, pp 353–73.

Cruikshank, G. (1832) *Scraps and Sketches*, published by the artist, Myddleton Terrace: Pentonville.

Cullingworth, J.B. (1962) *New Towns for Old: The Problem of Urban Renewal*, The Fabian Society: London.

Cullingworth, J.B. and Nadin, V. (2002) *Town and Country Planning in the UK*, Routledge: London.

Cullingworth, J.B. and Nadin, V. (2010) *Town and Country Planning in the UK, Fifteenth Edition*, Routledge: London.

Cumbria Rural Housing Trust (2004) *Housing: An Effective Way to Sustain our Rural Communities (Part I: The Effects of Affordable Housing on Rural Communities)*, Cumbria Rural Housing Trust and Jacqueline Blenkinship: Penrith.

Cumbria Rural Housing Trust (2008) *Cumbria Community Land Trust Handbook*, Cumbria Rural Housing Trust: Penrith.

Cymdeithas Yr Iaith Cymraeg (1971) *Tai Haf*, Welsh Language Society: Aberystwyth.

DART (Dartington Amenity Research Trust) (1977) *Second Homes in Scotland: a report to Countryside Commission for Scotland, Scottish Tourist Board, Highlands and Island Development Board, Scottish Development Department*, DART: Totnes.

DCLG (Department for Communities and Local Government) (2006a) *Delivering Affordable Housing*, DCLG: London.

DCLG (2006b) *Planning Policy Statement 3: Housing*, DCLG: London.

DCLG (2006c) *Survey of English Housing – Live Tables*, DCLG: London.

DCLG (2007a) *Generalized Land Use Database Statistics for England 2005*, DCLG: London.

DCLG (2007b) *English House Condition Survey 2007: Annual Report*, DCLG: London.

DCLG (2007c) *Homes for the Future: More Affordable, More Sustainable* (Housing Green Paper), DCLG: London.

DCLG (2008a) 'Press release: Ensuring a fair housing market for all', 2 September, DCLG: London.

DCLG (2008b) *Lifetime Homes, Lifetime Neighbourhoods, A National Strategy for Housing in an Ageing Society*, DCLG: London.

DCLG (2009a) *The Government Response to the Taylor Review of Rural Economy and Affordable Housing*, DCLG: London.

DCLG (2009b) *Guidance for Local Authorities on Incentivising Landowners to Bring Forward Additional Land for Rural Affordable Housing on Rural Exception Sites*, DCLG: London.

DCLG (2009c) *Planning Policy Statement 4: Planning for Sustainable Economic Growth*, DCLG: London.

DCLG (2009d) *Eco-towns: Location Decision Statement*, DCLG: London.

DEFRA (Department for Environment, Food and Rural Affairs) (2004) *Rural Strategy 2004*, DEFRA: London.

DEFRA (2008) *The Potential of England's Rural Economy*, DEFRA: London.

DEFRA (2009) *Headline Statement on Supporting Rural Communities*, DEFRA: London.

DEFRA (2010) *Rural Housing: A Report to DEFRA by Colin Buchanan and Partners and UCL*, DEFRA: London.

de Lima, P. (2001) *Needs Not Numbers: An Exploration of Minority Ethnic Groups in Scotland*, Commission for Racial Equality and Community Development Foundation: London.

de Lima, P. (2004) 'John O'Groats to Land's End: Racial equality in rural Britain?' in Chakraborti, N. and Garland, J. (eds) *Rural Racism*, Willan Publishing: Uffculme, pp 36–60.

de Lima, P. (2006) '"Let's keep our heads down and maybe the problem will go away": Experiences of rural minority ethnic households in Scotland', in Neal, S. and Agyeman, J. (eds) *The New Countryside? Ethnicity, Nation and Exclusion in Contemporary Rural Britain*, The Policy Press: Bristol, pp 73–98.

de Lima, P., Jentsch, B. and Whelton, R. (2005) *Migrant Workers in the Highlands and Islands*, Highlands and Islands Enterprise: Inverness.

DETR (Department for the Environment, Transport and the Regions) (2001) *Planning Policy Guidance Note 7: The Countryside – Environmental Quality and Social and Economic Development*, TSO: London.

Diacon, D., Pattison, B., Vine, J. and Yafai, S. (2008) *Home from Home. Addressing the Issues of Migrant Workers' Accommodation*, Building and Social Housing Foundation: London.

Dickens, P., Duncan, S., Goodwin, M. and Gray, F. (1985) *Housing, States and Localities*, Methuen: London.

DoE (Department of the Environment) (1981) *Proposed Modifications to the Cumbria and Lake District Joint Structure Plan*, DoE: London.

DoE (1985) *Development in the Countryside and Green Belts, Circular 24/85*, HMSO: London.

DoE (1989) *Planning Policy Guidance Note 3: Housing (Redraft)*, HMSO: London.

DoE (1993) *The effectiveness of Green Belts*, HMSO: London.

DoEHLG (Department of the Environment, Heritage and Local Government) (2004) *Sustainable Rural Housing: Consultation Draft of Guidelines for Planning Authorities*, DoEHLG: Dublin.

Douglas Birt Consulting (2004) *Grant-free Models for Housing Essential Workers*, Douglas Birt Consulting: London.

DTLR (Department for Transport, Local Government and the Regions) (2002) *More Than a Roof – A Report into Tackling Homelessness*, DTLR: London.

Dunn, M., Rawson, M. and Rogers A. (1981) *Rural Housing: Competition and Choice*, Allen and Unwin: London.

Echenique, M., Barton, H., Marshall, S., Mitchell, G., Nelson, J. and Thorpe, N. (2009) *Sustainability of Land-use and Transport in Outer Neighbourhoods*, http://www.suburbansolutions.ac.uk/DocumentManager/secure0/SOLUTIONSFinalDraftReportonStrategicScaleResearch.pdf, accessed on 17 July 2009.

ECOTEC (2008) *The Provision of New Affordable Housing in Larger Rural Settlements*, ECOTEC: London.

Ehrentraut, A. (1996) 'Globalization and the representation of rurality: Alpine open-air museums in advanced industrial societies', in *Sociologia Ruralis*, 36, 1, pp 4–26.

English, S. (2005) 'Highland clearance threatens 60 homes on estate', *The Times*, 14 November.

Evandrou, M. and Falkingham, J. (2000) 'Looking back to look forwards: Lessons from the four birth cohorts for ageing in the 21st century', *Population Trends*, 99, pp 27–36.

Evans, A.W. (1991) '"Rabbit hutches on postage stamps": Planning, development and political economy', in *Urban Studies*, 28, 6, pp 853–70.

Evans, A.W. (1996) 'The impact of land-use planning and tax subsidies on the supply and price of housing in Britain: A comment', in *Urban Studies*, 33, 3, pp 581–5.

Evans, A. (1999) *'They Think I Don't Exist': The Hidden Nature of Rural Homelessness*, Crisis: London.

Evans, A.W. and Hartwich, O.M. (2005) *Unaffordable Housing: Fables and Myths*, Policy Exchange: London.

Evans, A.W. and Hartwich, O.M. (2006) *Better Homes, Greener Cities*, Policy Exchange: London.

Evans, A.W. and Hartwich, O.M. (2007) *The Best Laid Plans: How Planning Prevents Economic Growth*, Policy Exchange: London.

Fahey, T. and Duffy, D. (2007) 'The housing boom', in Fahey, T., Russell, H. and Whelan, C.T. (eds) *Best of Times? The Social Impact of the Celtic Tiger*, Institute of Public Administration: Dublin, pp 123–38.

Faludi, A. (2005) 'Territorial cohesion: An unidentified political objective', in *Town Planning Review*, 76, 1, pp 1–13.

Fera, G. and Gianatempo, N. (1985) *L'Autocostruzione Spontanea nel Mezzogiorno (Spontaneous Self-build in Southern Italy)*, Franco Angeli: Milano.

Fielding, A. (1982) 'Counterurbanisation in Western Europe', in *Progress in Planning*, 17, pp 1–52.

Findlay, A., Short, D. and Stockdale, A (1999) *Migration Impacts in Rural England*, Countryside Agency: Wetherby.

Fitzpatrick, S. and Pawson, H. (2007) 'Welfare safety net or tenure of choice? The dilemma facing social housing policy in England', in *Housing Studies*, 22, 2, pp 163–82.

Fitzpatrick, S., Quilgars, D. and Pleace, N. (2009) *Homelessness in the UK: Problems and Solutions*, Chartered Institute of Housing: Coventry.

Fitzsimons, J. (1971) *Bungalow Bliss: Twenty Designs for which Plans, Specifications and Forms of Contract are Available at Very Low Cost*, 1st edn, Kells Art Studios: Kells, County Meath.

Flint, A. and Currie, H. (2009) *Bringing Private Sector Empty Houses Back into Use, Volume 4,* Scottish Government: Edinburgh.

Ford, J., Quilgars, D. and Burrows, R. with Pleace, N. (1997) *Young People and Housing*, Rural Research Report No. 31, The Rural Development Commission: Salisbury.

Forrest, R. and Murie, A. (1992) *Housing change in a rural area: an analysis of dwelling histories*. Working Paper 101, School for Advanced Urban Studies: Bristol

Foucault, M. (1991) 'Governmentality' (translated by Braidotti, R. and Gordon, C.), in Burchell, G., Gordon, C. and Miller, P. (eds) *The Foucault Effect: Studies in Governmentality*, University of Chicago Press: Chicago, pp 87–104.

Fox, S. and Gullen, R. (2006) *The Extent, Size and Characteristics of the Migrant Worker Workforce in the Vale of Evesham*, Wychavon District Council: Pershore.

Frey, H. (2000) 'Not green belts but green wedges: The precarious relationship between city and country', in *Urban Design International*, 5, 1, pp 13-25.

Friends of the Earth (2008) 'Political dealing on rural planning policy', in *Northern Ireland Newsletter*, 17, autumn 2008.

Gallent, N. (1997) 'Planning for affordable rural housing in England and Wales', in *Housing Studies*, 12, 1, pp 127–37.

Gallent, N. (1998) 'Local housing agencies in rural Wales', in *Housing Studies*, 13, 1, pp 59-81.

Gallent, N. (2000) 'Planning and affordable housing: From old values to New Labour', in *Town Planning Review*, 71, 2, pp 123–47.

Gallent, N. (2005) 'Regional housing figures in England: Policy, politics and ownership', in *Housing Studies*, 20, 6, pp 973–88.

Gallent, N. (2007) 'Second homes, community and a hierarchy of dwelling', in *Area*, 39, 1, pp 97–106.

Gallent, N. (2008a) 'Rural housing – reaching the parts that other policies cannot reach', in *Town and Country Planning*, March 2008, pp 122–5.

Gallent, N. (2008b) 'Strategic–local tensions and the spatial planning approach in England', in *Planning Theory & Practice*, 9, 3, pp 307–23.

Gallent, N. (2009a) 'Affordable housing in "village England": Towards a more systematic approach', in *Planning Practice and Research*, 24, 2, pp 263–83.

Gallent, N. (2009b) 'The future of housing and homes', in *Land Use Policy*, 26S, pp 93–102.

Gallent, N. and Allen, C. (2003) 'Housing pressure and policy in Europe: A power regime perspective', in Gallent, N., Shucksmith, M. and Tewdwr-Jones, M. (eds) *Housing in the European Countryside: Rural Pressure and Policy in Western Europe*, Routledge: London, pp 208–25.

Gallent, N. and Bell, P. (2000) 'Planning exceptions in rural England – past, present and future', in *Planning Practice and Research*, 15, 4, pp 375–84.

Gallent, N. and Robinson, S. (2010) *The Politics of Scale: Network Capacity in Community Planning: Final Report to the ESRC*, Economic and Social Research Council: Swindon.

Gallent, N. and Tewdwr-Jones, M. (2007) *Decent Homes for All? Planning's Evolving Role in Housing Provision*, Routledge: London.

Gallent, N., Mace, A. and Tewdwr-Jones, M. (2002a) 'Delivering affordable housing through planning: Explaining variable policy usage across rural England and Wales', in *Planning Practice and Research*, 17, 4, pp 465–83.

Gallent, N., Tewdwr-Jones, M. and Mace, A. (2002b) *Second Homes in Rural Areas in England*, Countryside Agency: Cheltenham.

Gallent, N., Mace, A. and Tewdwr-Jones, M. (2003) 'Dispelling a myth? Second homes in rural Wales', in *Area*, 35, 3, pp 271–84.

Gallent, N., Mace, A. and Tewdwr-Jones, M. (2005) *Second Homes: European Perspectives and UK Policies*, Ashgate: Aldershot.

Gallent, N., Juntti, M., Kidd, S. and Shaw, D. (2008) *Introduction to Rural Planning*, Routledge: London.

Gallent, N., Madeddu, M. and Mace, A. (2010) *Internal Housing Space Standards in Italy and England: Unpacking the 'Conditions' of Regulation*, RICS Education Trust: London.

Garland, J. and Chakraborti N. (2006) '"Race", space and place: Examining identity and cultures of exclusion in rural England', in *Ethnicities*, 6, 2, pp 159–77.

Gauldie, E. (1974) *Cruel Habitations: A History of Working Class Housing 1780–1918*, Allen and Unwin: London.

Gaze, C., Ross, K., Nolan, E., Novakovic, O. and Cartwright, P. (2007) *Modern Methods of Construction (MMC) in Housing: Drivers and Barriers to Their Use*, BRE Information Paper 3/07 Part 1, Building Research Establishment: Bracknell.

Gibb, K.D.B. (1999) 'Regional differentiation and the Scottish private house-building sector', in *Housing Studies*, 14, 1, pp 43–56.

Gibb, K.D.B. and O'Sullivan, A.J. (2008) *Explaining the Relative Development Costs of Social Housing in Scotland*, Scottish Federation of Housing Associations: Edinburgh.

Giddens, A. (1998) *The Third Way: The Renewal of Social Democracy*, Polity Press: London.

Giddens, B., Paterson, E. and Dunn, M. (2008) *Affordable Housing and Community Land Trusts in North East England*, School of the Built Environment, Northumbria University: Newcastle.

Gilroy, R., Brooks, L. and Shaw, T. (2007) 'Ready or not: The ageing of the market towns' population', in Powe, N., Hart, T. and Shaw, T. (eds) *Market Towns: Roles, Challenges and Prospects*, Routledge: London, pp 69–80.

Gkartzios, M. and Redmond, D. (2008) 'Occupancy conditions in rural housing: Republic of Ireland', in Satsangi, M. and Crawford, J. (eds) *An Investigation of Housing Occupancy Conditions in Rural Housing*, Scottish Government: Edinburgh, pp 49–79.

Glass, R. (1964) *London: Aspects of Change*, MacGibbon and Kee: London.

Golland, A. and Blake, R. (2004) *Housing Development: Theory, Process and Practice*, Routledge: London.

Goodchild, R. and Munton, R. (1985) *Development and the Landowner: An Analysis of the British Experience*, George Allen and Unwin: London.

Goodwin, M. (1998) 'The governance of rural areas: Some emerging research issues and agendas', in *Journal of Rural Studies*, 14, pp 5–12.

Gordon, M. (2002) 'The contribution of the community co-operatives of the Highlands and Islands of Scotland to the development of the social economy', in *Regions*, 242, 1, pp 12–13.

GOSW (Government Office for the South West) (2009) *Cornwall and the Isles of Scilly Brief*, GOSW: Bristol.

Gregory, R.C. (1989) 'Political rationality or "incrementalism"?' in *Policy and Politics*, 17, 2, pp 139–54.

Greve, J. and Currie, E. (1990) *Homelessness in Britain*, Joseph Rowntree Memorial Trust: York.

Halfacree, K.H. (1993) 'Locality and social representation: Space, discourse and alternative definitions of the rural', in *Journal of Rural Studies*, 9, 1, pp 23–37.

Halfacree, K.H. (1998) 'Neo-tribes, migration and the post-productivist countryside', in Boyle, P. and Halfacree, K. (eds) (1998) *Migration into Rural Areas: Theories and Issues*, Wiley: Chichester, pp 200–14.

Hall Aitken (2007) *Outer Hebrides Migration Study: Final Report*, Comhairle nan Eilean Siar, Western Isles Enterprise and Communities: Lewis.

Hall, P. (1975) *Urban and Regional Planning*, Penguin: Harmondsworth.

Hall, P., Gracey, H., Drewett, R. and Thomas, R. (1973) *The Containment of Urban England: Volume 1: Urban and Metropolitan Growth Processes or Megalopolis Denied*, George Allen and Unwin: London.

Hancock, J. (2002) 'The private rented sector in rural areas', in Lowe, S. and Hughes, D. (eds) *The Private Rented Sector in a New Century*, The Policy Press: Bristol, pp 65–78.

Hardill, I. (2006) '"A place in the countryside" – migration and the construction of rural living', in Lowe, P. and Speakman, L. (eds) *The Ageing Countryside. The Growing Older Population of Rural England*, Age Concern England: London, pp 51–68.

Harding, E. (2007) *Towards Lifetime Neighbourhoods: Designing Sustainable Communities for All: A Discussion Paper*, DCLG: London.

Harris, M. and Rochester, C. (2000) *Voluntary Organisations and Social Policy in Britain: Perspectives on Change and Choice*, Palgrave: Basingstoke.

Harvey, J. (1996) *Urban Land Economics*, Macmillan: Basingstoke.

Haskins, C. (2003) *Rural Delivery Review*, DEFRA: London.

Hetherington, P. (2008) 'Danger of the doldrums', in *The Guardian* (Society, News and Features Section), 9 July, p 1.

Hickman, P. and Robinson, D. (2006) 'Transforming social housing: Taking stock of new complexities', in *Housing Studies*, 21, 2, pp 157–70.

Hills, J. (2007) *Ends and Means: The Future Roles of Social Housing in England*, CASE Report 34, London School of Economics: London.

HM Government (1987) *Housing: The Government's Proposals* (White Paper), HMSO: London.

HM Treasury (2004) *Delivering Stability: Securing Our Future Housing Needs* (the Barker Review of Housing Supply), HM Treasury: London.

Hodge, I. and Monk, S. (2004) 'The economic diversity of rural England: Stylised fallacies and uncertain evidence', in *Journal of Rural Studies*, 20, pp 263–72.

Hoggart, K. (ed) (2005) *The City's Hinterland: Dynamism and Divergence in Europe's Peri-Urban Territories*, Ashgate: Aldershot.

Hoggart, K. and Henderson, S. (2005) 'Excluding exceptions: Housing non-affordability and the oppression of environmental sustainability?' in *Journal of Rural Studies*, 21, pp 181–96.

Hogwood, B.W. and Gunn, L.A. (1984) *Policy Analysis for the Real World*, Oxford University Press: Oxford.

Holmans, A. with Whitehead, C.M.E. (2008) *New and Higher Projections of Future Population in England*, Town and Country Planning Tomorrow Series Paper 10, TCPA: London.

Hope, S., Murray, L. and Martin, C. (2004) *In-migration to the Highlands and Islands*, NFO Social Research: Edinburgh.

House of Commons Committee of Public Accounts (2007) *A Foot on the Ladder: Low Cost Home Ownership Assistance, Nineteenth Report of Session 2006/07*, The Stationery Office: London.

House of Commons Council Housing Group (2009) *Council Housing: Time to Invest (Paper 6)*, House of Commons Council Housing Group: London.

Housing Corporation (1992) *F2-03/92 Shared Ownership in Rural Areas. Housing Association Repurchase Scheme and Restricted Stair-Casing*, Housing Corporation: London.

Housing Corporation (1990) *F2-34/90 Shared Ownership in Rural Areas: Housing Association Repurchase Scheme*, London: Housing Corporation.

Houston, D., Barr, K. and Dean, J. (2002) *Research on the Private Rented Sector in Scotland*, Scottish Executive: Edinburgh.

Howard, E. (1898) *To-morrow: A Peaceful Path to Real Reform*, Swan Sonnenschein & Co Ltd: London.

Huebener, T. (1940) *'La Douce France': An Introduction to France and its People* (English translation), Holt and Company: New York.

Hughes, C. (2006) 'Do village design statements make a difference?', in *Town and Country Planning*, 27, pp 119–21.

Hughes, R. and Hartwell, S. (2006) *Homelessness in Rural Wales*, Research Report Number 9, Wales Rural Observatory: Cardiff.

Huigen, P., Paul, L. and Volkers, K. (1992) 'The changing function and position of rural areas in Europe: A post-modern challenge', in Huigen, P., Paul, L. and Volkers, K. (eds) *The Changing Function and Position of Rural Areas in Europe*, Netherlands Geographical Studies No 153, University of Utrecht: Utrecht, pp 169–80.

Hunter, J. (1976) *The Making of the Crofting Community*, John Donald: Edinburgh.

Hunter, J. (1994) *A Dance Called America: the Scottish Highlands, the United States and Canada*, Mainstream: Edinburgh.

Hunter, J. (1999) *Last of the Free: A Millennial History of the Highlands and Islands of Scotland*, Mainstream: Edinburgh.

Hurley, N., Wilson, L. and Christie, I. (2008) *Scottish Household Survey Analytical Topic Report: Volunteering*, Scottish Government: Edinburgh.

Hutton, R.H. (1991) 'Local needs policy initiatives in rural areas: Missing the target', in *Journal of Planning and Environment Law*, April, pp 303–11.

Imrie, R. (2004) The role of the building regulations in achieving housing quality', in *Environment and Planning B: Planning and Design*, 31, 3, pp 419-437.

Integration Lincolnshire (2007) *Migrant Workers' Housing Needs*, Integration Lincolnshire: Sleaford.

Jackson, A. (2001) *An Evaluation of the 'HomeBuy' Scheme in England*, Joseph Rowntree Foundation: York.

Jacobs, C.A.J. (1972) *Second Homes in Denbighshire*, Tourism and Recreation Report No. 3, County of Denbigh: Ruthin.

Jamieson, L. and Groves, L. (2008) *Drivers of Youth Out-migration from Rural Scotland: Key Issues and Annotated Bibliography*, Scottish Government: Edinburgh.

Jarvie, G. and Jackson, L. (1998) 'Deer forests, sporting estates and the aristocracy', in *The Sports Historian*, 18, 1, 24–54.

Jedrej, C. and Nuttall, M. (1996) *White Settlers: The Impact of Rural Repopulation in Scotland*, Harwood Academic Press: Luxembourg.

Jenkins, S. (2008) 'Eco towns are the greatest try-on in the history of property speculation', in *The Guardian*, 4 April.

Jentsch, B., de Lima, P. and MacDonald, B. (2007) 'Migrant workers in rural Scotland: "Going to the middle of nowhere"', in *International Journal on Multicultural Societies*, 9, 1, pp 35–53.

Jones, A. (1999) 'No cardboard boxes, so no problem? Young people and housing in rural areas', in Rugg, J. (ed) *Young People, Housing and Social Policy*, Routledge: London, pp 145–58.

Jones, M. (2007) *A Review of LCHO in Wales*, Presentation to the Affordable Housing Solutions in Wales Conference, Llandrindod Wells, 16 April 2007.

JRF. (2008) *Rural Housing in Wales*, JRF: York.

Karn, V. and Sheridan, L. (1994) *New Homes in the 1990s: Study of Design, Space and Amenity in Housing Association and Private Sector Production*, Manchester University Press: Manchester.

Karn, V. (1995) 'Housing standards', in Smith, M. (ed) *Housing – Today and Tomorrow*, 2nd Supplement to the Guide to Housing (3rd edn), Housing Centre Trust: London, pp 104–19.

Keeble, D. and Tyler, P. (1995) 'Enterprising behaviour and the urban–rural shift', in *Urban Studies*, 32, 6, pp 975–97.

Kemp, P.A. (2004) *Private Renting in Transition*, Chartered Institute of Housing: Coventry.

Kemp, P.A. and Keoghan, M. (2001) Movement into and out of the private rented sector in England, *Housing Studies*, 16, 1, pp 21-37.

Kendall, J. (2003) *The Voluntary Sector: Comparative Perspectives in the UK*, Routledge: London.

Kofman, E., Lukes, S., D'Angelo, A. and Montagna, N. (2009) *The Equality Implications of Being a Migrant in Britain*, Equality and Human Rights Commission: Manchester.

Lambert, C., Jeffers, S., Burton, P. and Bramley, G. (1992) *Homelessness in Rural Areas*, Rural Development Commission: Salisbury.

Land Use Consultants and CCHPR (Cambridge Centre for Housing and Planning Research) (2005) *West Midlands Rural Housing Research*, Land Use Consultants: Bristol.

Lantra (2007) *A Study of the Business Needs of those Employing Migrant Workers in the Land-based Sector in England*, DEFRA: London.

Lavis, J. (2007) *An Evaluation of the North Yorkshire Rural Housing Enabler Programme*, Yorkshire Rural Community Council: York.

Law, C.M. (1967) 'The growth of urban population in England and Wales, 1801–1911', in *Transactions of the Institute of British Geographers*, 41, pp 125–43.

LDSPB (Lake District Special Planning Board) (1977) *Draft National Park Plan*, LDSPB: Carlisle.

LDSPB (1980) *Cumbria and Lake District Joint Structure Plan, Written Statement*, LDSPB, Kendal/Cumbria County Council: Carlisle.

Leat, D. (1986) 'Privatisation and voluntarisation', in *Quarterly Journal of Social Affairs*, 2, 3, pp 285–320.

Leishman, C., Aspinall, P., Munro, M. and Warren, F. (2004) *Preferences, Quality and Choice in New-build Housing*, Joseph Rowntree Foundation: York.

Le Mesurier, N. (2003) *The Hidden Store – Older People's Contributions to Rural Communities*, Age Concern: London.

Lindblom, C.E. (1959) 'The science of "muddling through"', in *Public Administration Review*, 19, pp 79–88.

Linneker, B. and Shepherd, J. (2005) *Rural England: Demographic Change and Projections 1991–2028: A Source Document*, Birkbeck College, University of London: London.

Lipsky, M. (1980) *Street-level Bureaucracy: Dilemmas of the Individual in Public Services*, Russell Sage Foundation: New York.

Little, J. (1997) 'Constructions of rural women's voluntary work', in *Gender, Place and Culture*, 4, 2, pp 197–209.

Little, J. (2002) *Gender and Rural Geography: Identity, Sexuality and Power in the Countryside*, Pearson International: Harlow.

Little, J. and Austin, P. (1996) 'Women and the rural idyll', in *Journal of Rural Studies*, 12, 2, pp 101–11.

Little, J. and Morris, C. (eds) (2005) *Critical Studies in Rural Gender Issues*, Ashgate: Aldershot.

Llewelyn, E. (1986) 'What is Adfer?' in Hume, I. and Pryce, W.T.R. (eds) *The Welsh and their Country*, Gomer Press: Llandysul, pp 244–52.

Local Government Association (2004) *Community Cohesion: An Action Guide*, LGA: London.

Long, I. (2005) 'Fiscal conservatism versus local paternalism: Divergent experiences of public housing decline in rural areas of England during the 1980s', in *Journal of Rural Studies*, 21, pp 111–29.

Low, N., Butt, S., Ellis Paine, A. and Davis Smith, J. (2007) *Helping Out: A National Survey of Volunteering and Charitable Giving*, The Cabinet Office: London.

Lowe, P. (1989) 'The rural idyll defended: From preservation to conservation', in Mingay, G.E. (ed) *The Rural Idyll*, Routledge: London, pp 113–31.

Lowe, P. and Speakman, L. (2006) 'The greying countryside', in Lowe, P. and Speakman, L. (eds) *The Ageing Countryside: The Growing Older Population of Rural England*, Age Concern: London.

Lowe, P. and Ward, N. (2007) *Rural Futures: A Socio-geographical Approach to Scenarios Analysis*, Position Paper for Regions and Regionalism in Europe and Beyond, Institute for Advanced Studies, Lancaster University: Lancaster.

Lukes, S. (1974) *Power: A Radical View*, Macmillan: Basingstoke.

MacGregor, B.D. (1976) 'Village life: Facts and myths', in *Town and Country Planning*, 44, 11, pp 524–7.

MacGregor, B.D. (1993) *Land Tenure in Scotland*, the John McEwen Memorial Lecture, Rural Forum: Perth.

MacKinnon, D. (2002) 'Rural governance and local involvement: Assessing state–community relations in the Scottish Highlands', in *Journal of Rural Studies*, 18, pp 307–24.

Macklin, J. (1995) 'Housing advice response to homelessness and housing problems – what housing advice can achieve', in Ransley, S. (ed) *Developing Effective Responses to Rural Homelessness. The Report on Shelter's Rural Housing Aid Conference*, Shelter: London.

MacLean, S. (1943) *Dàin do Eimhir agus Dàin Eile*, William MacLellan: Glasgow.

Maclennan, D. (2007) *Better Futures for Social Housing in England*, Joseph Rowntree Foundation: York.

Macpherson, J. (1765) *The Works of Ossian, the Son of Fingal: in two volumes, translated from the Gaelic language*, T. Becket and P.A. Dehondt: Edinburgh.

Malpass, P. (2000) *Housing Associations and Housing Policy: A Historical Perspective*, Macmillan: Basingstoke.

Malpass, P. (2009) 'The rise (and rise?) of housing associations', in Malpass, P. and Rowlands, R. (eds) *Housing, Markets and Policy*, Routledge: London, pp 101–21.

Malpass, P. and Murie, A. (1987) *Housing Policy and Practice*, 2nd edn, Macmillan: Basingstoke.

Marsden, T., Murdoch, J., Lowe, P., Munton, R. and Flynn, A. (1993) *Constructing the Countryside*, UCL Press: London.

Marsh, A. and Mullins, D. (1998) 'The social exclusion perspective and housing studies: Origins, applications and limitations', in *Housing Studies*, 13, 6, pp 749–59.

Marsh, D. and Rhodes, R. (eds) (1992) *Policy Networks in British Governance*, Oxford University Press: Oxford.

Martin, E.W. (1962) *The Book of the Village*, Phoenix House: London.

Massey, D. (1984) *Spatial Divisions of Labour: Social Structures and the Geography of Production*, Macmillan: Basingstoke.

Massey, D. and Meegan, R. (1982) *The Anatomy of Job Loss: The How, Why and Where of Employment Decline*, Methuen: London.

Mayhew, S. (ed) (2004) *A Dictionary of Geography*, Oxford University Press: Oxford.

McCallum, J.D. (1980) 'Statistical trends of the British conurbations', in Cameron, G.C. (ed) *The Future of the British Conurbations: Policies and Prescriptions for Change*, Longman: London, pp 14–53.

McCrone, D. (2001) *Understanding Scotland: The Sociology of a Nation*, Routledge: London.

McDonagh, J. (2001) *Renegotiating Rural Development in Ireland*, Ashgate: Aldershot.

McGrath, J. (1981) *The Cheviot, the Stag and the Black, Black Oil*, Methuen: London.

McNaughton, C. (2005) *Crossing the Continuum: Understanding Routes out of Homelessness and Examining 'What Works'*, Glasgow Simon Community: Glasgow.

Milbourne, P. (1998) 'Local responses to central state restructuring of social housing provision in rural areas', in *Journal of Rural Studies*, 14, 2, pp 167–84.

Milbourne, P. (2006) 'Rural housing and homelessness', in Cloke, P., Marsden, T. and Mooney, P. (eds) *Handbook of Rural Studies*, Sage: London, pp 427–44.

Milbourne, P. and Cloke, P. (2006) 'Rural homelessness', in Milbourne, P. and Cloke, P. (eds) *International Perspectives on Rural Homelessness*, Routledge: London, pp 79–96.

Milbourne, P., Edwards, W.J., Hughes, R. and Orford, S. (2006) *The Role of the Housing System in Rural Wales*, Welsh Assembly Government: Cardiff.

Millington, A. (1988) *An Introduction to Property Valuation*, 3rd edn, Estates Gazette: London.

Milne, A., Hatzidimitriadou, E. and Wiseman, J. (2007) 'Health and quality of life among older people in rural England: Exploring the impact and efficacy of policy', in *Journal of Social Policy*, 36, 3, pp 477–95.

Milner, J. and Madigan, R. (2004) 'Regulation and innovation: Rethinking inclusive housing design', in *Housing Studies*, 19, pp 727–44.

Ministry of Works and Planning (1942) *Report of the Committee on Land Utilisation in Rural Areas*, HMSO: London.

Moir, J., Rice, D. and Watt, A. (1997) 'Visual amenity and housing in the countryside – Scottish local planning authority approaches', in *Land Use Policy*, 14, 4, pp 325–30.

Molineux, P. and Appleton, N. (2005) *An Introduction to Ageing in Rural Areas and Extra Care Housing*, Housing Learning and Improvement Network: Factsheet No 12, Department of Health: London.

Monbiot, G. (1999) 'Cannibal feast', in *The Guardian*, 2 October.

Monbiot, G. (2006) 'Britain's most selfish people', in *The Guardian*, 23 May 2006.

Monk, S. (2009) 'Understanding the demand for social housing: Some implications for policy', in *International Journal of Housing Markets and Analysis*, 2, 1, pp 21–38.

Monk, S. and Ni Luanaigh, A. (2006) 'Rural housing affordability and sustainable communities', in Midgley, J. (ed) *A New Rural Agenda*, IPPR North: Newcastle upon Tyne, pp 114–35.

Monk, S. and Whitehead, C.M.E. (1996) 'Land supply and housing: A case study', in *Housing Studies*, 11, 3, pp 407–23.

Monk, S. and Whitehead, C.M.E. (1999) 'Evaluating the economic impact of planning controls in the United Kingdom: Some implications for housing', in *Land Economics*, 75, 1, pp 74–93.

Monk, S., Pearce, B.J. and Whitehead, C.M.E (1996) 'Land-use planning, land supply and house prices', in *Environment and Planning A: Environment and Planning*, 28, pp 495–511.

Monk, S., Clarke, A., Fenton, A., Ni Luanaigh, A., Shorten, J., Bridges, M., Daniels, I. and Chitonga, M. (2006) *The Extent and Impacts of Rural Housing Need*, DEFRA: London.

Monmouthshire County Council (2009) *Affordable Housing Delivery Statement 2007–2011*, Monmouthshire County Council: Cwmbran.

Morgan, J. and Satsangi, M. (forthcoming, 2011) 'Reaching the parts other grants don't go? Supporting self-provided housing in rural Scotland', in *Housing Studies*, 26, 4.

Morphet, J. (2008) *Modern Local Government*, Sage: London.

Morris, P. (1932) *Rural Housing*, CPRE: London.

Morris, H. (2009) 'Eco-towns risk becoming a car-dependent "joke"', in *Planning Resource* (on-line), 24 April.

Morris, H. (2010) 'House building to hit lowest levels since 1923', in *Planning Resource* (on-line), 8 February.

Moseley, M. (1999) *Innovation and Rural Development – Inaugural Lecture*, Countryside and Community Research Unit: Cheltenham.

Moseley, M. (2000) 'England's village services in the 1990s: Entrepreneurialism, community involvement and the state', in *Town Planning Review*, 74, 1, pp 415–33.

Mullins, D. and Murie, A. (2006) *Housing Policy in the UK*, Palgrave Macmillan: Basingstoke.

Murdoch, J. and Abram, S. (2002) *Rationalities of Planning: Development versus Environment in Planning for Housing*, Ashgate: Aldershot.

Murdoch, J. and Lowe, P. (2003) 'The preservationist paradox: Modernism, environmentalism and the politics of spatial division', *Transactions of the Institute of British Geographers New Series*, 28, pp 318–32.

Murdoch, J. and Ward, N. (1997) 'Governmentality and territoriality: The statistical manufacture of Britain's "national farm"', in *Political Geography*, 16, pp 307–24.

Murdoch, J., Lowe, P., Ward, N. and Marsden, T. (2003) *The Differentiated Countryside*, Routledge: London.

Murie, A., Pocock, R. and Gulliver, K. (2007) *Hills, Cave and After: Renewing Social Housing*, Human City Institute: Birmingham.

National Self Build Association (2008) *Self Build as a Volume Housing Solution*, National Self Build Association, www.nasba.org.uk , accessed 15 February 2010.

Neal, S. (2002) 'Rural landscapes, representations and racism: Examining multicultural citizenship and policy-making in the English countryside', in *Ethnic and Racial Studies*, 25, 3, pp 442–61.

Neal, S. and Agyeman, J. (eds) (2006) *The New Countryside? Ethnicity, Nation and Exclusion in Contemporary Rural Britain*, The Policy Press: Bristol.

Needleman, L. (1965) *The Economics of Housing*, Staples Press: London.

Newby, H. (1979) *Green and Pleasant Land? Social change in Rural England*, Penguin: Harmondsworth.

Newby, H., Bell, C., Rose, D. and Saunders, P. (1978) *Property, Paternalism and Power: Class and Control in Rural England*, Hutchinson: London.

Newhaven Research (2008) *All Pain, No Gain? Finding the Balance: Delivering Affordable Housing through the Planning System in Scotland*, Chartered Institute of Housing (Scotland): Edinburgh.

Newman, J.E. (2001) *Modernizing Governance: New Labour, Policy and Society*, Sage: London.

Newton, J. (1991) *All in One Place: The British Housing Story 1971–91*, CHAS: London.

NHBC (National Housebuilding Council) (2009) *New Housebuilding Statistics 2008 Quarter 4*, NHBC: Amersham.

NHF (National Housing Federation) (2009) *A Place in the Country? An Inquiry into the North's Rural Housing Challenges*, NHF North: Manchester.

NHF and CPRE (Campaign to Protect Rural England) (2008) *Save Rural England – Build Affordable Homes*, National Housing Federation: London.

Nicol, C. and Hooper, A. (1999) 'Contemporary change and the house-building industry: Concentration and standardisation in production', in *Housing Studies*, 14, 1, pp 57–76.

Niner, P. (2004) 'Accommodating nomadism? An examination of accommodation options for Gypsies and Travellers in England', in *Housing Studies*, 19, pp 141–59.

Norris, M. and Redmond, D. (2005) *Housing Contemporary Ireland: Policy, Society and Shelter*, Institute of Public Administration: Dublin.

Oakeshott, I. (2009) 'Gordon Brown to bulldoze rural housing curbs', in *The Sunday Times* (online), 4 January.

O'Connor, J., Orloff, A. and Shaver, S. (1999) *States, Markets, Families: Gender, Liberalism and Social Policy in Australia, Canada, Great Britain and the United States*, Cambridge University Press: Cambridge.

ODPM (Office of the Deputy Prime Minister) (1998) *Planning for Communities of the Future*, ODPM: London.

ODPM (2004) *Planning Policy Statement 7: Sustainable Development in Rural Areas*, The Stationery Office: London.

ODPM, DoH (Department of Health) and the Housing Corporation (2003) *Preparing Older People's Strategies: Linking Housing to Health, Social Care and Other Local Strategies*, ODPM: London.

Oldfield King Planning Ltd (1997) *Housing Plus in Rural Areas*, Housing Corporation: London.

Oldman, C. (2002) *Support and Housing in the Countryside: Innovation and Choice*, The Countryside Agency: Wetherby.

Orr, D. (2009) 'Is council housing the answer to our problems?', in *The Independent*, 5 March.

Owen, S. (1999) 'Village design statements: Some aspects of the evolution of a planning tool in the UK', in *Town Planning Review*, 70, 1, pp 41–59.

Owen, S. (2002a) 'From Village Design Statements to Parish Plans: Some pointers towards community decision making in the planning system in England', in *Planning Practice and Research*, 17, 1, pp 81–9.

Owen, S. (2002b) 'Locality and community: Towards a vehicle for community-based decision making in rural localities in England', in *Town Planning Review* 73, 1, pp 41–61.

Oxley, M., Brown, T., Lishman, R. and Turkington, R. (2008) *Rapid Evidence Assessment of the Research Literature on the Purchase and Use of Second Homes*, National Housing and Planning Advice Unit: Fareham.

Padovani, L. and Vettoretto, L. (2003) 'Italy', in Gallent, N., Shucksmith, M. and Tewdwr-Jones, M. (eds) (2003) *Housing in the European Countryside: Rural Pressure and Policy in Western Europe*, Routledge: London, pp 91–115.

Pahl, R.E. (1964) 'The two class village', in *New Society*, 27 February.

Pahl, R.E. (1965) *Urbs in Rure: The Metropolitan Fringe in Hertfordshire*, Geographical Papers No 2, London School of Economics and Political Science: London.

Pahl, R.E. (1968) 'The rural–urban continuum', in Pahl, R.E. (ed) *Readings in Urban Sociology*, Pergamon Press: Oxford, pp 263–97.

Pahl, R.E. (1975) *Whose City? And Further Essays on Urban Society*, Penguin: Harmondsworth.

Panelli, R. (2006) 'Rural society', in Cloke, P., Marsden, T. and Mooney, P (eds) *Handbook of Rural Studies*, Sage: London, pp 63–90.

Panelli, R. and Welch, W. (2005) 'Why community? Reading difference and singularity with community', in *Environment and Planning A: Environment and Planning*, 37, pp 1589–611.

Parsons, D. (1980) *Rural Gentrification: The Influence of Rural Settlement Planning Policies*, Department of Geography Research Papers No 3, University of Sussex: Brighton.

Pati, A. (2008) 'Gangmasters break house rules', in *The Guardian*, 28 March.

Pavis, S., Platt, S. and Hubbard, G. (2000) *Young People in Rural Scotland: Pathways to Social Inclusion and Exclusion*, YPS: York.

Pawson, H. (2007) 'Local authority homelessness prevention in England: Empowering consumers or denying rights?' in *Housing Studies*, 22, 6, pp 867–83.

Pawson, H. and Kintrea, K. (2002) 'Part of the problem or part of the solution? Social housing allocation policies and social exclusion in Britain', in *Journal of Social Policy*, 31, 4, pp 643–67.

Pawson, H., Satsangi, M., Munro, M., Cairncross, L., Warren, F. and Lomax, D.M. (2005) *A Framework for Governance of Registered Social Landlords: Baseline Survey of Governing Body Members and Review of Governance*, Communities Scotland: Edinburgh.

PCC (Pembrokeshire County Council) and PCNPA (Pembrokeshire Coast National Park Authority) (2002) *Joint Unitary Development Plan Deposit (2000–2016)*, Pembrokeshire Coast National Park Authority: Haverford West.

Peace, S., Holland, C. and Kellaher, L. (2006) *Growing Older: Environment and Identity in Later Life*, Open University Press: Maidenhead.

Philip, L., Gilbert, A., Mauthner, N. and Phimister, E. (2003) *Scoping Study of Older People in Rural Scotland*, Scottish Executive: Edinburgh.

Phillips, M. (2005) 'Differential productions of rural gentrification: Illustrations from North and South Norfolk', in *Geoforum*, 36, pp 477–94.

Phillips, M., Fish, R. and Agg, J. (2001) 'Putting together ruralities: Towards a symbolic analysis of rurality in the British mass media', in *Journal of Rural Studies*, 17, 1, pp 1–27.

Phillipson, C. (2007) 'The "elected" and the "excluded": Sociological perspectives on the experience of place and community in old age', in *Ageing & Society*, 27, 3, pp 321–42.

Pilkington, C. (2002) *Devolution in Britain Today*, Manchester University Press: Manchester.

Pollard, N., Latorre, M. and Sriskandarajah, D. (2008) *Floodgates or Turnstiles? Post-EU Enlargement Migration to (and from) the UK*, Institute for Public Policy Research: London.

Pressman, J. and Wildavsky, A. (1973) *Implementation*, University of California Press: Berkeley.

Prior, A. (1999) 'Development plans', in Allmendinger, P., Prior, A. and Raemaekers, J. (eds) *Introduction to Planning Practice*, Wiley: London, pp 49–82.

Pyne, C.B. (1973) *Second Homes*, Caernarvonshire County Planning Department: Caernarfon.

Quattrone, G. (2000) 'Territorial planning and urban governance in Mediterranean areas', Paper presented to the 40th Congress of the European Regional Science Association, 29 August to 1 September, Barcelona.

Randall, J.N. (1980) 'Central Clydeside – a case study of one conurbation', in Cameron, G.C. (ed) *The Future of the British Conurbations: Policies and Prescriptions for Change*, Longman: London, pp 101–24.

Redfield, R. (1960; also 1989) *The Little Community and Peasant Society and Culture*, University of Chicago Press: Chicago.

Rhodes, D. (2006) *The Modern Private Rented Sector*, Centre for Housing Policy: York.

Rhodes, R.A.W. (1997) *Understanding Governance: Policy Networks, Governance, Reflexivity and Accountability*, Open University Press: Buckingham.

RHT (Rural Housing Trust) (2008) *What is Shared Ownership?* RHT: London.

RHT (2009) 'Press release: Press statement concerning The Rural Housing Trust and RHT developments', 19 January, RHT: London.

RIBA (Royal Institute of British Architects) (2007) *Better Homes and Neighbourhoods*, RIBA: London.

Richards, E. (2007) *Debating the Highland Clearances*, Edinburgh University Press: Edinburgh.

Richards, F. and Satsangi, M. (2004) 'Importing a policy problem? Affordable housing provision in Britain's national parks', in *Planning Practice and Research*, 19, 3, pp 251–66.

Robertson, D. (2001) 'Community planning: Right sentiments, wrong approach', in *Scottish Affairs*, 34, pp 68–90.

Robertson, V. and Satsangi, M. (2003) *In-migration, Housing, Employment, and the Use of Language: A Literature Review*, School of the Built Environment, Heriot-Watt University: Edinburgh.

Robinson, D. (2004) 'Rough sleeping in rural England: Challenging a problem denied', in *Policy and Politics*, 32, 4, pp 471–86.

Robinson, D. and Coward S. (2003) *Your Place, Not Mine: The Experiences of Homeless People Staying with Family and Friends*, Crisis: London.

Robinson, D. and Reeve, K. (2002) *Homelessness and Rough Sleeping in North Lincolnshire*, Centre for Regional Economic and Social Research, Sheffield Hallam University: Sheffield.

Robinson, D. and Reeve, K. (2006) *Neighbourhood Experiences of New Immigration: Reflections from the Evidence Base*, Joseph Rowntree Foundation: York.

Robinson, V. and Gardner, H. (2006) 'Place matters: Exploring the distinctiveness of racism in rural Wales', in Neal, S. and Agyeman, J. (eds) (2006) *The New Countryside? Ethnicity, Nation and Exclusion in Contemporary Rural Britain*, The Policy Press: Bristol, pp 47–72.

Rochester, C., Paine, A.E. and Howlett, S. with Zimmeck, M. (2009) *Volunteering and Society in the 21st Century*, Palgrave: Basingstoke.

Roger Tym and Partners and Jordan Research (2006) *Calculating Housing Needs in Rural England (CRC28)*, Commission for Rural Communities: Cheltenham.

Rogers, A.W. (1985) 'Local claims on rural housing', in *Town Planning Review*, 56, pp 367–80.

Rolfe, H. and Metcalf, H. (2009) *Recent Migration into Scotland: The Evidence Base*, Scottish Government: Edinburgh.

Rosnes, A.E. (1987) 'Self-built housing', in *Housing, Theory and Society*, 4, 1, pp 55–68.

Rowlands, R. and Card, P. (2007) 'Communities, networks and power: Is there a localisation of decision-making?' in Beider, H. (ed) *Housing, Neighbourhood Renewal and Community Engagement*, Blackwell: Oxford, pp 290–313.

Rowlands, R. and Murie, A. (2008) *Evaluation of Social HomeBuy Pilot Scheme for Affordable Housing*, DCLG: London.

Rugg, J. and Jones, A. (1999) *Getting a Job, Finding a Home: Rural Youth Transitions*, The Policy Press: Bristol.

Rugg, J. and Rhodes, D. (2008) *The Private Rented Sector: Its Contribution and Potential*, Centre for Housing Policy: York.

Rydin, Y. (2003) *Urban and Environmental Planning in the UK*, Palgrave Macmillan: London.

Satsangi, M. (2002) 'Rental housing supply in rural Scotland: The role of private landowners', in Lowe, S. and Hughes, D. (eds) *The Private Rented Sector in a New Century*, The Policy Press: Bristol, pp 79–94.

Satsangi, M. (2006) '"The best laid plans …"? An assessment of housing association provision in rural Scotland', in *Policy & Politics*, 34, 4, pp 731–52.

Satsangi, M. (2007) 'Land tenure change and rural housing in Scotland', in *Scottish Geographical Journal*, 123, 1, pp 33–47.

Satsangi, M. (2008) *Evidence submitted to the Scottish Parliament Rural housing inquiry*, available online at www.scottish.parliament.uk/S3/committees/rae/inquiries/ruralHousing/WrittenEvidence.htm

Satsangi, M. (2009) 'Community land ownership, housing and sustainable rural communities', in *Planning Practice and Research*, 24, 2, pp 251–62.

Satsangi, M. (2011, forthcoming) 'Feminist epistemologies and the social relations of housing provision', in *Housing, Theory and Society*.

Satsangi, M. and Crawford, J. (2009) *An Investigation of Housing Occupancy Conditions in Rural Housing*, Scottish Government: Edinburgh.

Satsangi, M. and Dunmore, K. (2003) 'The planning system and the provision of affordable housing in rural Britain: A comparison of the Scottish and English experience', in *Housing Studies*, 18, 2, pp 201–17.

Satsangi, M., Storey, C., Bramley, G. and Dunmore, K. (2000) *Selling and Developing Land and Building for Renting and Low Cost Home Ownership – the Views of Landowners*, Scottish Homes/Scottish Landowners' Federation: Edinburgh.

Satsangi, M., Higgins, M., Pawson, H., Rosenburg, L., Hague, C., Bramley, G. and Storey, C. (2001) *Factors Affecting Land Supply for Affordable Housing in Rural Scotland*, Scottish Executive: Edinburgh.

Satsangi, M., Bramley, G., Morgan, J., Bowles, G., Wilcox, S. and Karley, N.K. (2005) *Evaluation of Housing Association Grant for Rent in Scotland, 1989–2002*, Scottish Executive: Edinburgh.

Savage, M., Barlow, J., Dickens, P. and Fielding, T. (1992) *Property, Bureaucracy and Culture: Middle Class Formation in Contemporary Britain*, Routledge: London.

Savage, W.G. (1919) *Rural Housing: With a Chapter on the After-war Problem*, T.F. Unwin: London.

SBE (School of the Built Environment), Heriot-Watt University, School of Architecture at Edinburgh University and the School of Architecture at Edinburgh College of Art (2007) *Design at the Heart of Housebuilding*, Scottish Government: Edinburgh.

Scanlon, K. and Whitehead, C.M.E. (2005) *The Profile and Intentions of Buy to Let Investors*, London School of Economics: London.

Scharf, T. and Bartlam, B. (2008) 'Ageing and social exclusion in rural communities', in Keating, N. (ed) *Rural Ageing: A Good Place to Grow Old?* The Policy Press: Bristol, pp 97–108.

Scott, M. (2006) 'Strategic spatial planning and contested ruralities: Insights from the Republic of Ireland', in *European Planning Studies*, 14, 6, pp 811–29.

Scott, M. (forthcoming) 'The "politics of the rural": Local councillors and rural housing', in *Policy & Politics*.

Scott, M. and M. Murray (2009) 'Housing rural communities: Connecting rural dwellings to rural development in Ireland', in *Housing Studies*, 24, 6, pp 755–74.

Scott, W. (2008 [1832]) *Waverley*, Oxford University Press: Oxford.

Scottish Borders Council (2008) *Housing in the Countryside Report*, Scottish Borders Council: Melrose.

Scottish Executive (2005a) *Planning Advice Note 74: Affordable Housing*, Scottish Executive: Edinburgh.

Scottish Executive (2005b) *Ministerial Statement on Abolition of Priority Need by 2012 (Technical Appendix to Ministerial Statement required by section 3 of the Homelessness etc (Scotland) Act 2003)*, Scottish Executive: Edinburgh.

Scottish Executive (2006) *The Futures Project: Trend Analysis Papers*, Scottish Executive: Edinburgh.

Scottish Government (2007) *Scottish Housing Market Review, 2007*, Scottish Government: Edinburgh.

Scottish Government (2008a) *Rural Scotland Key Facts 2008: People and Communities, Services and Lifestyle, Economy and Enterprise*, Scottish Government: Edinburgh.

Scottish Government (2008b) *Scottish Planning Policy 3: Planning for Homes*, Scottish Government: Edinburgh.

Scottish Government (2008c) *Responding to the Changing Economic Climate: Further Action on Housing*, Scottish Government: Edinburgh.

Scottish Government (2008d) *LIFT: New Supply Shared Equity*, Scottish Government: Edinburgh.

Scottish Government (2008e) *Rural Homes for Rent: Model Allocations Policy*, Scottish Government: Edinburgh.

Scottish Government (2008f) *Urban Rural Classification 2007–2008*, Scottish Government: Edinburgh.

Scottish Government (2009a) *Headline Statement on Rural Issues in Scotland*, accessed online at www.scotland.gov.uk/Topics/Rural on 3 July 2009.

Scottish Government (2009b) *Affordable Housing Securing Planning Consent 2008–2009, Tables and Charts*, Scottish Government: Edinburgh.

Scottish Government (2010) *Low-cost Initiative for First Time Buyers: LIFT*, Scottish Government: Edinburgh.

Scottish Homes (1990) *The Rural Housing Challenge: A Consultative Paper*, Scottish Homes: Edinburgh.

Scottish Housing Advisory Committee (1937) *Report on Rural Housing in Scotland*, HM Stationery Office: London.

Scottish Parliament (2001) *The Impact of Changing Employment Patterns in Rural Scotland*, Rural Development Committee, Scottish Parliament: Edinburgh.

Scottish Parliament Rural Affairs and Environment Committee (2009) *Rural Housing, 5th Report 2009 SP Paper 256*, Scottish Parliament: Edinburgh.

Shelter (2008) *Shelter's Response to the Government Discussion Paper – Rough Sleeping 10 years on: From the Streets to Independent Living and Opportunity*, Shelter: London.

Shepherd, T. (1999) 'A brief history of low cost home ownership', in Cowans, J. (ed) *Inclusive Housing: The Role of Low Cost Home Ownership*, JRF: York, pp 35–7.

Shiel, L., Richards, F., Robertson, M. and Innes, C. (2007) *Allocation of Land for Affordable Housing through the Planning System*, Scottish Government: Edinburgh

Shoard, M. (1980) *The Theft of the Countryside*, Temple Smith: London.

Short, J.R. (1982) *Housing in Britain: The Post-War Experience*, Taylor and Francis: London.

Shucksmith, M. (1981) *No Homes for Locals?*, Gower Publishing: Farnborough.

Shucksmith, M. (1990a) 'A theoretical perspective on rural housing: Housing classes in rural Britain', in *Sociologia Ruralis*, 30, 2, pp 210–29.

Shucksmith, M. (1990b) *Housebuilding in Britain's Countryside*, Routledge: London.

Shucksmith, M. (2007a) *The Continuing Challenge of Rural Housing: Evidence from Recent Research*, available online at www.northernruralnetwork.co.uk, accessed September 2009.

Shucksmith, M. (2007b) 'Sustainable development and sustainable rural communities – who gains and who loses?' Paper presented at the Housing Studies Association Annual Conference, York, 11–13 April.

Shucksmith, M. and Conway, E. (2003) 'Scotland', in Gallent, N., Shucksmith, M. and Tewdwr-Jones, M. (eds) *Housing in the European Countryside: Rural Pressure and Policy in Western Europe*, Routledge: London, pp 168–87.

Shucksmith, M. and Philip, L. (2000) *Social Exclusion in Rural Areas: A Literature Review and Conceptual Framework*, Scottish Executive Central Research Unit: Edinburgh.

Shucksmith, M., Watkins, L. and Henderson, M. (1993) 'Attitudes and policies towards residential development in the Scottish countryside', in *Journal of Rural Studies*, 9, 3, pp 243–55.

Shucksmith, M., Henderson, M., Raybould, S., Coombes, M. and Wong, C. (1995) *A Classification of Rural Housing Markets in England*, HMSO: London.

Sillince, J.A.A. (1986) 'Why did Warwickshire Key Settlement Policy change in 1982? An assessment of the political implications of cuts in rural services', in *The Geographical Journal*, 152, 2, pp 176–92.

Simon, H.A. (1947) *Administrative Behaviour*, Macmillan: London.

Simon, H.A. (1960) *The New Science of Management Decision*, Prentice Hall: Englewood Cliffs.

Skott-Myhre, H., Raby, R. and Nikolaou, J. (2008) 'Towards a delivery system of services for rural homeless youth: A literature review and case study', in *Child Youth Care Forum*, 37, pp 87–102.

Sleat Community Trust (2005) *A Community Plan for Sleat*, Isle of Skye, Sleat Community Trust: Sleat.

Smith, D. (2007) 'The changing faces of rural populations: "'(Re)fixing' the gaze" or "eyes wide shut"?' in *Journal of Rural Studies*, 23, pp 275–82.

Smith, D. and Phillips, D. (2001) 'Socio-cultural representations of greentrified Pennine rurality', in *Journal of Rural Studies*, 17, pp 457–69.

Smith, I.C. (1968; also 2001) *Consider the Lilies*, Phoenix: London.

Somerville, C. (2001) *Images of Rural Britain*, New Holland Publishers: London.

Speakman, L. and Lowe, P. (2006) *The Ageing Countryside: The Growing Older Population of Rural England*, Age Concern: London.

Spedding, A. (2007) *Migrant Workers in Rural Areas, Briefing 457*, Arthur Rank Centre: Stoneleigh.

Spedding, A. (2009) *Rural Economies Recession Intelligence, Briefing 749*, Arthur Rank Centre: Stoneleigh.

Spencer, D. (1997) 'Counterurbanisation and rural depopulation revisited: Landowners, planners and the rural development process', in *Journal of Rural Studies*, 13, 1, pp 75–92.

Stanley, J.P. (1974) *Shared Purchase: A New Route to Home-ownership*, Conservative Political Centre: London.

Stanley, K.G., Marsden, T.K. and Milbourne, P. (2005) 'Governance, rurality and nature: Exploring emerging discourses of state forestry in Britain', in *Environment and Planning C: Government and Policy*, 23, pp 679–95.

Stenhouse, L. (2005) *Developing Social Networks: Reducing Homelessness*, Shelter: London.

Stockdale, A. (2006) 'The role of a "retirement transition" in the repopulation of rural areas', in *Population, Space and Place*, 12, pp 1–13.

Stockdale, A., Findlay, A. and Short, D. (2000) 'A repopulation of the countryside: Opportunity or threat', in *Journal of Rural Studies*, 16, pp 243–57.

Stoker, G. (1998) 'Governance as theory: Five propositions', in *International Social Science Journal*, 50, 155, pp 17–28.

Strachan, V. and Donohoe, T. (2009) *Views and Experiences of Tenants in the Private Rented Sector in Scotland, Volume 2*, Scottish Government: Edinburgh.

Strachan, V., Wood, P., Thomson, A., Hope, S. and Playfair, A. (2000) *Homelessness in Rural Scotland*, Scottish Homes: Edinburgh.

Streich, L., Havell, C. and Spafford, J. (2002) *Preventing Homelessness in the Countryside: What Works? A Guide for Local Authorities and the Voluntary Sector Demonstrating Effective Practice*, The Countryside Agency: Wetherby.

Sturzaker, J. (2009) 'Planning and affordable rural housing: The limits to rational policy', Unpublished PhD thesis, University of Newcastle: Newcastle upon Tyne.

Svendsen, G.L.H. (2004) 'The right to development: Construction of a non-agriculturalist discourse of rurality in Denmark', in *Journal of Rural Studies*, 20, pp 79–94.

Taylor, Marilyn (2002) *Public Policy in the Community*, Palgrave: Basingstoke.

Taylor, Mary (2003) 'Voluntary housing transfer in Scotland: A case of policy emergence?' Unpublished PhD thesis, University of Stirling: Stirling.

Taylor, Matthew (2008) *Living, Working Countryside: The Taylor Review of Rural Economy and Affordable Housing*, Department for Communities and Local Government: London.

Tenant Services Authority (2008) *Regulatory and Statistical Return Factsheet 2008*, TSO: London.

Terry, R. (1999) 'Low cost home ownership', in Cowans, J. (ed) *Inclusive Housing: The Role of Low Cost Home Ownership*, JRF: York, pp 25–31.

Tewdwr-Jones, M. (1997) 'Green belts or green wedges for Wales: A flexible approach to planning in the urban periphery', in *Regional Studies*, 31, 1, pp 73–7.

Tewdwr-Jones, M. (2002) *The Planning Polity: Planning, Government and the Policy Process*, Routledge: London.

Tewdwr-Jones, M. and Gallent, N. (2002) *The Socio-economic Impacts of Local and Essential Needs Housing in Pembrokeshire Coast National Park*, UCL Bartlett School of Planning: London.

Thin, A. (2003) *Speech* at the formal opening of the Cairngorms National Park, 1 September, available online at: www.cairngorms.co.uk/news/speech.html, accessed 18 November 2003.

Thomas, C. (1967) 'Enclosure and the rural landscape of Merioneth in the sixteenth century', in *Transactions of the Institute of British Geographers*, 42, pp 153–62.

Tibbetts, G. (2007) 'Rural migrant workers "drive out young"', in *Daily Telegraph*, 17 July.

Tiesdell, S. (2009) 'A Scottish approach to inspirational development', in *Town and Country Planning*, July/August 2009, pp 316–21.

Tönnies, F. (1887) *Gemeinschaft und Gesellschaft*, Fues's Verlag: Leipzig (translated as [1988] *Community and Society*, Library of Congress Publications: Washington, DC).

Torrance, D. (2009) *We in Scotland – Thatcherism in a Cold Climate*, Birlinn Press: Edinburgh.

Towers, W., Grieve, I.C., Hudson, G., Campbell, C.D., Lilly, A., Davidson, D.A., Bacon, J.R., Langan, S.J. and Hopkins, D.W. (2006) *Scotland's Soil Resource: Current State and Threats*, Scottish Executive: Edinburgh.

Tribal HCH (2006) *Allocation of Land for Affordable Housing through the Planning System*, Scottish Executive: Edinburgh.

Tullock, G. (1976) *The Vote Motive*, Institute for Economic Affairs: London.

University of Aberdeen, Department of Agriculture and Forestry and Macaulay Land Use Research Institute (2001) *Agriculture's Contribution to Scottish Society, Economy and Environment*, Scottish Executive: Edinburgh.

WAG (Welsh Assembly Government) (2002a) *Planning Policy Wales*, Welsh Assembly Government: Cardiff.

WAG (2002b) *Review of the Private Rented Sector in Wales*, Welsh Assembly Government: Cardiff.

WAG (2006a) *Technical Advice Note 2: Planning and Affordable Housing*, Welsh Assembly Government: Cardiff.

WAG (2006b) *Rural Development Plan for Wales 2007-2013 Consultation Draft*, Welsh Assembly Government, Cardiff, available online at: wales.gov.uk/docrepos/40382/epc/countryruralpayments/642119/4038291/consrdpw0713_ept1.pdf?lang=en&ts=4 (accessed 26 February 2010).

WAG (2007) *A Review of the HomeBuy Scheme in Wales*, Welsh Assembly Government: Cardiff.

WAG (2008a) *A Statistical Focus on Rural Wales*, Welsh Assembly Government: Cardiff.

WAG (2008b) *Delivering Affordable Housing Using Section 106 Agreements: Practice Guidance*, Welsh Assembly Government: Cardiff.

WAG (2008c) *'Rural Wales' – Definitions and How to Choose Between Them*, Statistical Bulletin, Welsh Assembly Government: Cardiff

WAG (2009) *Headline Statement on Rural Affairs*, available online from wales.gov.uk (accessed on 3 July 2009).

Wales Rural Observatory (2005) *A Survey of Rural Services in Wales*, Wales Rural Observatory: Cardiff.

Wales Rural Observatory (2006) *Scoping Study on Eastern and Central European Migrant Workers in Rural Wales*, Wales Rural Observatory: Cardiff.

Warnes, A. (1992) 'Migration and the life course', in Champion, A. and Fielding, A. (eds) *Migration Processes and Patterns Vol. 1*, Belhaven Press: London, pp 175–82

Warnes, A. and Law, C. (1984) 'The elderly population of Great Britain: Locational trends and policy', in *Transactions of the Institute of British Geographers New Series*, 9, pp 37–59.

Warnes, A. and McInerney, B. (2004) *The English Regions and Population Ageing*, Age Concern England: London.

WCED (World Commission on Environment and Development) (1987) *Our Common Future*, Oxford University Press: Oxford.

Webster, S., Jones, P. and Beedell, J. (2006) *An Evaluation of the Adoption and Application of the Rural and Urban Definition*, Commission for Rural Communities: Cheltenham.

Wellings, F. (2006) *British Housebuilders: History and Analysis*, Blackwell Publishing: London.

Wenger, G.C. (2001) 'Myths and realities of ageing in rural Britain', in *Ageing and Society*, 21, pp 117–30.

White, M. and Allmendinger, P. (2003) 'Land-use planning and the housing market: A comparative review of the UK and the USA', in *Urban Studies*, 40, 5–6, pp 953–72.

Whitehead, C.M.E (2009) 'Land supply and the planning system', in CABE (ed) *Who Should Build Our Homes? Six Experts Challenge the Status Quo*, Commission for Architecture and the Built Environment: London, pp 8–31.

Wightman, A. (1996) *Who Owns Scotland?* Canongate: Edinburgh.

Wightman, A. (2007) *Land Reform (Scotland) Act 2003 (Part 2 The Community Right to Buy): A Two Year Review*, Caledonia Centre for Social Development: Edinburgh.

Wilcox, S. (2007) *Can't Buy, Can Rent: The Affordability of Private Housing in Great Britain – Summary Report*, Hometrack: London.

Wilcox, S. (2008) *UK Housing Review, 2008/2009*, available online at www.ukhousingreview.org.uk, accessed September 2009.

Wilcox, S., Fitzpatrick, S., Stephens, M., Pleace, N., Wallace, A. and Rhodes, D. (2010) *The Impact of Devolution: Housing and Homelessness*, York: Joseph Rowntree Foundation.

Williams, N., Shucksmith, M., Edmond, H. and Gemmell, A. (1998) *Scottish Rural Life Update: A Revised Socio-Economic Profile of Rural Scotland, Rural Affairs and Natural Heritage Research Findings No. 4*, The Scottish Office: Edinburgh.

Wiltshire Fire Service (2009) *Fire Safety*, available online at www.wiltsfire.gov.uk/Fire_Safety/Safety_Advice/fire_safety_caravan.htm, accessed September 2009.

Winter, M. (1996) *Rural Politics: Policies for Agriculture, Forestry and the Environment*, Routledge: London.

Wood, R. and Bain, M. (2001) *The Health and Well-being of Older People in Scotland: Insights from National Data*, Scottish Executive Information and Statistics Division: Edinburgh.

Woods, M. (1998) 'Advocating rurality? The repositioning of rural local government', in *Journal of Rural Studies*, 14, 1, pp 13–26.

Woods, M. (2005a) *Contesting Rurality: Politics in the British Countryside*, Ashgate: Aldershot.

Woods, M. (2005b) *Rural Geography: Processes, Responses and Experiences in Rural Restructuring*, Sage: London.

Woods, M. (ed) (2008) *New Labour's Countryside: Rural Policy in Britain since 1997*, The Policy Press: Bristol.

Woods, M. and Watkin, S. (2008) *Central and Eastern European Migrant Workers in Rural Wales, Report 20*, Wales Rural Observatory: Cardiff.

Woof, T. (2009) *Affordable Housing Presentation*, Upper Eden Community Plan: Kirby Stephen www.uecp.org.uk (accessed April, 2010).

Yarwood, R. (2002) 'Parish councils, partnership and governance: The development of exceptions housing in Malvern Hills District, England', in *Journal of Rural Studies*, 18, 3, pp 275–91.

Young, I.M. (1990) *Justice and the Politics of Difference*, Princeton University Press: Princeton, selection republished in 2003 as 'City life and difference', in Campbell, S. and. Fainstein, S. (eds) *Readings in Planning Theory*, 2nd edn, Blackwell: Oxford, pp 336–55.

Index

Page references for images are in *italics*; those for notes are followed by n